*As yet I am as strong this day as on the day that
Moses sent me; just as my strength was then, so now is
my strength for war, both for going out and for coming in.
Now therefore, give me this mountain.*
—JOSHUA 14:11-12

*The torrent of Kishon swept them away,
that ancient torrent, the torrent of Kishon.
O my soul, march on in strength!*
—JUDGES 5:21

*But even after we had suffered before and were spitefully
treated at Philippi, as you know, we were bold in our
God to speak to you the gospel of God in much conflict.*
—1 THESSALONIANS 2:2

*And the LORD said to Moses, "Why do you cry to Me?
Tell the children of Israel to go forward. But lift up your
rod, and stretch out your hand over the sea and divide it.*
—EXODUS 14:15-16

*O God the Lord, the strength of my salvation,
You have covered my head in the day of battle.*
—PSALM 140:7

Advancing under Fire

by
Rev. Mike Keyes, Sr.

Advancing under Fire
ISBN 978-1-939570-47-5
Copyright © 2014 by Mike Keyes, Sr.
P.O. Box 91916
Tucson, Arizona 85752-1916

Published by Word & Spirit Publishing
P.O. Box 701403
Tulsa, OK 74170

Printed in the United States of America.

CONTENTS

Foreword

When Jesus prophesied about the end-times, which are the times we are living in now, He told us that there would be rampant sin, deception, and compromise everywhere. He told us, in chapters like Matthew 24, that there would be many false prophets, false teachers, and false "Christs" who would rise up *and deceive many!* Not just a few would be deceived He said, but *many!* We are seeing this everywhere we turn, and the level of deception is increasing more and more as the day of our Lord's return draws closer.

Evil is being called good, good is being called evil, and gross sin and perverted lifestyles are no longer just being tolerated, but are now actually being trumpeted and promoted as normal. Preaching about sin, the eternal consequences of rebellion against God and His Word, hell, and other very clear and important topics found throughout the scriptures are being ignored, impugned, or made fun of in many places today. Where is this happening? Out in the world? Of course, but sadly, it is also taking place within the Body of Christ as well.

This book's content was given to me as an extension of the revelation God gave me concerning the book I wrote called *Military Mentality*. I recommend you read that book in conjunction with this one. The revelation God gave me in that book lit a fire in me, to not only understand the warfare we're involved in, but to excel at the waging of it—in my life and in the lives of others of like precious faith and passion.

All over the world, the devil and his forces are working very hard to water down the truth of the gospel, deceiving Christians and unbelievers alike—promoting other false religions, cults, and splinter groups, claiming that their errant and heretical beliefs are as valid and as relevant as Christianity. Any way to God is openly promoted as being legitimate—whether it be Jesus, Buddha, Mohammed, the Pope, or Mother Nature itself. Sin of all kinds is being trumpeted as being perfectly normal for human beings to embrace and practice. It's okay though, because after all, God is a God of love, so He understands us and our rebellion, and will joyfully overlook all of our sins come judgment time, someday—or maybe there won't even *be* a judgment!

Sadly, but predictably, as we draw ever closer to the return of our Lord Jesus, we see that darkness has become darker than ever before. Multitudes of so-called believers are hiding in fear, afraid to take a stand for anything holy and pure, bound in their own unrepentant and unremorseful sins, and totally seduced by these demonic lies, half-truths, and perverted doctrines being circulated on the subject of life, death, Heaven, hell, salvation, and impending eternal judgment.

The lines are being drawn, and things like this, which Christians have tolerated for so long, must no longer be tolerated. Sin is sin, and the wages of sin is *death*. God's righteous standards have never changed, no matter who says otherwise. With this awareness, Christians must be ready to not only stand up for righteousness, holiness, purity, passion, and doctrinal integrity, but to confront and repel head-on the levels of intense persecution and backlash that comes against us when we do.

Ever since I received Jesus on September 21, 1978, I've witnessed a gradual sliding away from God, and the things of God, not just within society at large, but within the church in particular. This "slide" has intensified as time goes by. What was once thought perverse and unthinkable to tolerate religiously—or even socially—is now thought of to be the norm and not the exception by many. Churches and so-called Christian ministers bend over backwards to appease sinners, spiritual rebellion, heresy, and openly deviate and perverse lifestyles—calling it a "user-friendly" or "seeker-friendly" approach. God forbid we ever "offend" anyone! Very few believers have the courage to defend the unchanging purity of the truth, and the righteousness and holiness of Almighty God. Those who still do are now commonly maligned, ridiculed, and persecuted—being called religious, old-fashioned, narrow-minded, controlling, and manipulative. This is coming not just from the sinners, mind you, but from so-called Christians claiming to represent the Son of God!

This book goes beyond the truths expressed in *Military Mentality*, and presents the very real-world facts about life and death. We're in a fight, and this fight goes on until the Rapture of the church, or until we die and go home to Heaven. We must understand reality as it is on planet Earth. We are at war for God and against Satan. The objects of this conflict are the eternal souls of men, and this fight will go on without interruption, every day for the rest of our lives. There is no holiday truce, no politically brokered cease-fire, no armistice—and no end to the fighting. There is no retreat or surrender to the enemy, and we take no prisoners when we engage him on the battlefields of this world! We fight until Jesus comes. We don't apologize for who we are and Who we represent, and that's it.

The Bible is a military manual, showing the reader how to successfully wage war in the name of Jesus. And to the proportionate degree we choose to make a difference in this war, that will be the degree that we are shot at, attacked, and maligned in return by the enemy. Attack—and counter-attack! That's the way it is everyday, everywhere, until Jesus returns.

Let the enemies of righteousness huff and puff all they want. Let the devil cry, complain, or threaten all he wants. Christianity is not a passive concept, and the Body of Christ is not a reactionary army. We are an aggressive group of dedicated soldiers—always practicing the very real truth that in war, the best defense is a potent and aggressive offense. Jesus has given us the command to *charge* (see Mark 16:15-18)! We have been told to advance, and so we will—but it will always be *under fire!*

May the content of this book inspire and enable you to do just that, successfully to the glory of God. Now more than ever, its time to take up arms and engage the enemy on the front lines everywhere in this great end-time push for souls.

Apostle Mike Keyes, Sr.

P A R T I

Encountering and Overcoming Enemy Resistance

CHAPTER 1

You Are A Soldier!

*You therefore must endure hardship as a good soldier
of Jesus Christ. No one engaged in warfare entangles
himself with the affairs of this life, that he may
please him who enlisted him as a soldier.*
—2 TIMOTHY 2:3-4

There are many wonderful truths revealed in these two verses. In my book entitled *Be Strong! Stay Strong!* we talk about many of the other aspects of these powerful statements, and I encourage you to get hold of that book to find out what they are. For this study however, we're talking about the fact that when you were saved, you were drafted into God's military.

Notice that in both verses the believer is referred to as a "soldier." As good soldiers of Jesus Christ, we're told to endure hardship. Then in the next verse, we're instructed to avoid becoming entangled in the affairs of this life, so that we please Him Who enlisted us as soldiers. Soldiers—that's what we're called, because that's who we are as far as God is concerned! That's you, me, and every other believer worldwide. No exceptions to this. No deferments. No excused absences. No draft-dodging, or refusal to be inducted. Everyone who receives Jesus as Lord and Savior gets enlisted by the Holy Spirit into the army of the Lord.

You're in the Army!

Secondly, notice the word "enlisted" in verse 4. You didn't enlist yourself in God's army—Jesus enlisted you! This wasn't a decision on your part to volunteer, like when someone chooses to walk into a recruiter's office and volunteers to join up with the Army, Navy, Air Force, or Marines. No sir! The choice you made was to accept Jesus as Lord, and receive the free gift of salvation. That was your choice, and yours alone. God has chosen not to force anyone to receive the gift of salvation, so that choice was yours to make. It was completely up to you. However, simultaneously, when you made your choice to receive Jesus, God made His choice to draft you!

The enlistment into God's army was God's choosing *for* you, not unlike years ago in the USA, when we had the military draft. When I was growing up, young men between certain ages of eligibility were drafted into the military. Since this was at the height of the Vietnam War, being drafted into the military was something very few young men wanted to have happen to them. But, whether they wanted to or not, they didn't have a choice about it. When a young man's birthday was called up, he joined up! He didn't have a choice to say no. Now, there was the option to apply for certain legal deferments, and many did that, including me. But if you didn't qualify for any of the approved deferment classifications, you were going into the military, like it or not.

When I turned 18, I applied for a full-time student deferment to the draft, and when I proved to the draft board that I was in fact a full-time university student, my draft status was changed from 1-A to 2-S, which meant I wouldn't be called up into active military duty until after my 4 years of college was finished—if they still needed me.

But before I reached my graduation date in 1973, then-President Nixon instituted the military draft lottery. The first draft lottery that was held on July 1, 1970, dealt with men born in 1951, which included me. According to what we were told, even with the Vietnam War raging on as it was, the military wouldn't need to draft any higher than the number 100 or so. I can remember sitting in my back yard sunbathing and listening to the draft results over the radio. When my birth date was announced, I held my breath and prayed! I was overjoyed to hear that my birthday—November 22—drew the number 253! When that happened, I immediately dropped my 2-S student deferment, went 1-A for my one year of draft eligibility, then when that year was up, moved on with my life without the concern of being drafted or enlisted into the military against my wishes.

But with God, that's not the case whatsoever! You don't do the choosing concerning this—He does. It is His sovereign will that anyone who becomes born-again is *automatically* enlisted in His military. No deferments allowed. No exemptions or exceptions allowed. All go in, no one is left out.

Accept It and Adjust If Necessary

Maybe you don't see yourself this way, and maybe nobody has told you this is what happened when you confessed Jesus as Lord of your life—but this *is* what happened, and this *is* who you really are in Christ, as a child of God. Man or woman, young or old, married or unmarried, educated or uneducated—if you're saved, you're in God's army! If you're a Christian, you've been drafted! This is how God sees you, so this is how you must see yourself. It might take some time to reeducate yourself to this truth, but you must do it because that is who you are, and that is how God views you. It doesn't matter if you ever served in the United Stated Armed Forces or not—you're serving in God's Armed Forces, so understand that and live in the light of that truth.

There Are No Discharges!

Also understand there is no discharge either! You *never* get discharged from this army, because when you made the decision to get saved, you also made the decision to allow God to sign you up *for life!* You don't serve for 3 or 4 years in "active duty," and then get honorably discharged. Not in this army, my friend! In this life on Earth, you're in until you die, or until Jesus comes, whichever comes first. And then, once you leave your flesh and blood body behind, you step out into eternity as a born-again spirit, alive in Christ Jesus, *continuing to serve* as a Christian soldier in God's army.

Realize this fact, and live accordingly. As a Christian soldier, you're serving God Almighty and the Lord Jesus by the indwelling power and presence of the Holy Spirit—forever—in this life and the next. From the day you were born-again, you're in God's army, and you will never leave the ranks! The sooner you see this, understand this, and live in the light of this truth, the sooner God can begin using you the way He wants to in this great worldwide war for souls.

Most of the time, Christians refer to themselves collectively with terms and phrases that fail to address the military aspect of our life on earth in Christ. We very frequently refer to ourselves as the *Body of Christ*. We also like to talk about believers as being the *Church of the Lord Jesus Christ*. Both of those descriptions are absolutely accurate, and right on the money. We are the Body of Christ, and we are the Church of the Lord Jesus Christ. But we need to also see ourselves the way God sees us, and that's as *soldiers in His army*. In a redemptive sense, yes, we are the Body of Christ, and yes, we are the Church. But we're also an army—the army of the Lord, and recognizing that is the first step towards promotion and advancement within the ranks of that army.

The sad truth is that most believers never develop a working understanding about the war, and the armies fighting in it. They love to talk about the soothing aspects of our Lord's character, and that's fine, but they struggle to see Jesus as the Lord of War (see Exodus 15:3)! I'm here to tell you that you're in the military my friend, and it's about time you woke up to that fact. So, get your helmet, get your gear, and get your weapons. Its time to engage the enemy like never before!

CHAPTER 2

No Ordinary Soldier

There was also a lot for the tribe of Manasseh, for he was
the firstborn of Joseph: namely for Machir the firstborn of
Manasseh, the father of Gilead, because he was a man
of war; therefore he was given Gilead and Bashan.
—JOSHUA 17:1-2

The book of Joshua is a book of war and conquest, so I recommend you read it often—several times a year at least. This book, along with the book of Judges, contains a wealth of insight and information on the subject of warfare and spiritual combat. We can learn so much from men like Joshua, Gideon, and others described in those books. What those men faced on the battlefield during their time will reveal certain principles we can apply today in our spiritual fights of faith against the devil and his forces.

This particular verse in Joshua is so obscure you can read right over it and miss a marvelous truth being revealed here. If you read these middle chapters of the book, you discover it can be "slow reading." There's not much "action" in this part of the book; its mostly about the promised land being divided up amongst the twelve tribes of Israel. So-and-so got this parcel of land, such-and-such tribe got this piece of property, and so on. For me at least, its slow and tedious reading through these middle chapters—until we read this verse here, which emphasizes this one important truth:

Because he (Machir) was a man of war, therefore he was given something!

Don't read over that too quickly, or you'll miss something you must understand about God's ability to use you and anoint you mightily in spiritual warfare. Notice that this man Machir is described as a "man of war." As such, also notice that God rewarded him with two prime pieces of real estate: the towns of Gilead and Bashan. Why? For no other reason other than the fact he's described as this man of war! When you read the word "therefore" in this statement, it means that *because* he was a man of war, he was given something from God. You should meditate on that phrase until you get it down into your heart forever.

Because He Was, Therefore He Received!

According to Joshua 17:1, because Machir *was* something, he *received* something from the Lord. Being a "man of war" put him in position for those two pieces of real estate. This also tells me that God wants to handsomely reward those who develop and protect this kind of mindset; what I call a "military mentality."

Because he was . . . therefore . . . he received. Think about that statement. This is a spiritual principle found throughout the Bible, so you should take the time to meditate on this until it sinks in! *Because he was a man of war, therefore he was given something!* Why did he receive those two towns as his inheritance from God? Because he was a man of war. That's it. No other reason is given, so we must assume no other qualifications were necessary as far as God was concerned. What does this tell us? It tells us that God, who is no respecter of persons, is ready, willing, and able to bless and handsomely reward *anyone* who develops and protects this kind of attitude and lifestyle. It tells us that He's not the least bit nervous about people becoming men or women *of war*. In fact, it tells us the opposite—that not only is He not nervous about such an attitude and lifestyle, He is pleased and overjoyed when He finds it! If you don't believe me, ask Machir!

For the eyes of the LORD run to and fro throughout the whole earth, to show Himself strong on behalf of those whose heart is loyal to Him.

—2 CHRONICLES 16:9

God searches back and forth (to and fro) across this earth, looking for people to show Himself strong to! The fact that He has to search for such people tells us they can't readily be found. They're a minority, not a majority within the army of the Lord. This reveals a very important truth never to be forgotten: *every man or woman of war is a soldier, but not every soldier is a man or woman of war.* Let me repeat that, because you need to know this. *Not every soldier is a man or woman of war!*

There is a vast difference between the rank-and-file soldier who has never seen combat, and the hardened veteran who has earned his promotions, medals, and citations with inspirational courage and valor time and again on the battlefield against the enemy. Both are in the military and both are soldiers, but both of them are *not* men or women of war! That's why you don't see every soldier being blessed like we see Machir being blessed in Joshua 17.

Remember, God is looking and searching for His men or women of war, because they aren't everywhere. There are soldiers everywhere you find Christians, because we are all enlisted when we accept Jesus. However, from that point on, those who become men or women of war are those who make the choice—its purely up to him or her!

Become Much More than Just a Soldier!

As a soldier in the army of the Lord, you can be promoted as fast as you want to be promoted—it's not up to God, but totally up to you! How fast you move up the ranks, and how fast you position yourself and qualify for God to show Himself strong to you is all a matter of passion, priority, and commitment to the cause. God wants to promote *every soldier* in His army, because He wants to use every soldier in extraordinary ways, but He can't because most either don't want it, or are too weak or lazy to obtain such recognition and promotion.

When I was born-again September 21, 1978, I rose up quickly through the ranks of Christian soldiers around me. I was absolutely on fire for the Lord, and I couldn't stop witnessing to people about the free gift of eternal life. I was born and raised Roman Catholic, so I had known about the message of salvation all my life—except the part about having to be born-again! No one, in all my years of going to Catholic grade school, then Catholic high school, and attending retreat after retreat, told me about the necessity of opening up my heart, inviting Jesus to come in, and making Him the personal Lord and Savior of my life. So, when God finally got me to that point of time in life, where I found eternal life in Christ, I was so overjoyed I couldn't contain myself.

I tried going to work as before, but I no longer had any desire to do that kind of secular work. All I wanted to do was tell my co-workers about Jesus. From the time I got to work until the time I left at the end of the day, I tried telling everyone on my floor about Jesus. As you can imagine, my efforts were not well-received! But I tried to the best of my ability for the next ten or eleven months, before I finally knew it was time for me to leave the business world and begin preparing for full-time ministry.

During that time, from September 1978 until August of 1979, I devoured the Bible. I hooked up with a good Assembly of God church in Perrysburg, Ohio, and began attending all the classes and Bible studies I could. In addition, the associate pastor was an ardent street-witnessing believer, who took me under his wing to tutor me and teach me how to win souls on the streets one-on-one. Therefore, in a matter of weeks after my salvation experience, I was going out on Friday nights, and all day Saturday, passing out tracts in downtown Toledo, Ohio. I tried talking to anyone who would listen to me about the need to be born-again.

At other times during the week, I faithfully attended evening Bible studies conducted by some of the church's leadership. On my lunch hour at work, instead of going out to eat with my colleagues as before, I stayed in my office at my desk, reading the Bible. The associate pastor and I went to the Toledo Express Airport, and having received favor from the Lord, we were given permission to pass out tracts anywhere we wanted to on airport property. Taking full advantage of this opening, I would go up to the airport early on Saturday morning, whenever I wasn't out of town traveling for my job, and would pass out hundreds of tracts to passengers coming in or flying out from that airport. I even made a master log of all incoming and outgoing flights, so I would know where to be at what time to maximize my tract distribution. By looking at my log, I could tell what airline, what gate, and what time a flight would arrive or depart. I would then be at that gate, to pass out tracts to those waiting to board the plane, or to those getting off the plane upon arrival.

I would go all through the airport, putting tracts everywhere. I would even stand outside the ladies' restroom, patiently waiting until I knew no one was inside, then zip in and put tracts on all the toilets, sinks, and countertops! I would go out into the airport parking lots and put tracts under the windshield wipers of all the cars out there. Then, I would come back around every couple of hours or so, to pick up any tracts thrown down by patrons, and put them back under the wipers of those cars, or of any new cars that had entered since my last pass through the parking lots. When I knew, according to my log, that I needed to get back inside to be at a certain gate at a certain time, I went back inside to share tracts with those passengers coming or going.

I had tracts in my suit coat pocket and in my wallet. I had tracts in the glove compartment of my car. I had tracts in my briefcase. I had tracts in the drawer of my desk in my office at work. Wherever I went, I gave out tracts to people—at restaurants when I finished my meals, at the bank when I would go to deposit my paycheck, in airplanes to fellow-passengers when I flew somewhere for business, in the hotels wherever I stayed when I traveled on business—everywhere, all the time. I averaged about 5,000 tracts distributed each month. And all the time, I was still working my job, still attending church every time the doors opened, and still attending every weekday Bible Study I could get to.

Whenever I was in town on the weekends, the associate pastor, Rev. Ronal Charles, and I would go into downtown Toledo, and pass out tracts to the homeless, to the drunks, and even inside the bars and strip clubs! It was during this time that I got to know about the ministry of Rev. Kenneth E. Hagin, and the new Bible school he had started a few years before—Rhema Bible Training Center in Tulsa, Oklahoma.

To make the long story short, I applied and was accepted as a student at Rhema for the school year beginning in September, 1979. Therefore, I resigned my job at Owens Corning (a very well-paying job I might add), sold most of my possessions in several yard sales, and with a few belongings and an intense hunger for the things of God, moved to Broken Arrow, Oklahoma, and began my studies there.

What I was doing while working a full-time job in Toledo, Ohio, I did as a student and part-time worker in Tulsa, Oklahoma, as well. Whenever I could, in-between classes, study and prayer time, and work, I would go downtown and pass out tracts to the street people in Tulsa. I would go to the big mall (there was only one of them in Tulsa at the time), and pass out tracts, and like I did in the airport parking lots in Toledo, I would cruise around the mall parking lots, putting tracts under the windshield wipers of the cars.

Do What You Can Do!

I wasn't looking for fame or recognition. I didn't care about any of that. All I wanted to do was tell people about Jesus, and at that point in my life, I saw that one of the best ways for me to do that was through street ministry. Walking up to total strangers on the street and trying to witness for Jesus wasn't easy, but I did it and did it as often as I could. Passing out tracts wasn't always fun, but I did it and did as much of it as possible. I never asked anyone for assistance, and I never waited around for somebody to notice me. I just did what I could, and God honored it.

I didn't ask my home church to sponsor my tract distribution. I paid for it all by myself. On my own time, with my own money, I would go through tract catalogs, pick out the ones I liked, and order them. They would come to my house in Bowling Green, Ohio, and then later, to my apartment while living in Broken Arrow, Oklahoma. I had rubber stamps made with the name and address of my home church and pastor in Perrysburg, Ohio, and then again with my home church in Tulsa, Oklahoma. Whenever I had time, I would spread out hundreds of tracts on my kitchen table, and hand stamp them with the local church's address information. Then, as I mentioned before, I would stuff tracts into every conceivable pocket, holder, compartment, or file folder I could carry, and distribute them as the Lord led—averaging about 5,000 tracts per month.

You see my friend, the promotion I received was not up to God, but purely up to me. He will do for you, or anyone else, the very same things He did for me back then, if only we show some kind of drive and desire to see souls saved in these last days. Christians can choose to be lukewarm, mediocre, and unaffected by the teeming masses of unsaved people all around them, or they can choose a passion and lifestyle that gives God something to work with and promote!

The three most destructive and deadly enemies within the army of the Lord today are *lethargy, apathy,* and *laziness.* From the beginning of my walk with Jesus, I purposed never to allow any of these to have or gain a stronghold in my mind or heart. This is why, I believe, God was able to move me up through the ranks as quickly as He did. I was saved in September of 1978. I was enrolled as a full-time Bible School student by September of 1979. I was on the foreign field as a full-time missionary in the Philippines by September of 1980. As you can see, September is a special month for me and Jesus!

But the God who worked with me in those early days is the same God wanting to work with you, or anyone else who demonstrates the kind of seriousness He's looking back and forth across the Earth for. You just need to know that it's not up to God, but completely up to you!

Not every soldier is a man or woman of war. He or she who becomes such does so purely because they want it badly enough, and are willing to sacrifice, adjust, or change whenever necessary to see their fullest potential realized in Christ. Do what you can do—and He'll do what you *can't* do! He already made the first move and did all the hard work for us. Jesus paid the price for our sins, purchased our redemption, and crushed the devil on our behalf. Then He turned and gave all that authority to us, His church—the army of the Lord—and told us to go into all the world and preach the Gospel everywhere to everyone. It's really just a simple command to *charge!* The Great Commission is an order given by the Commander-in-Chief, and we as His soldiers must obey! The only ones *fit enough* to obey are those who are not content being just an ordinary soldier. They want all that God has for them in this army, and they dedicate themselves to the fight in ways that embarrass most people claiming to be Christian!

CHAPTER 3

Press on Under Fire!

Not that I have already attained, or am already perfected;
but I press on, that I may lay hold of that for which Christ
Jesus has also laid hold of me. Brethren, I do not count
myself to have apprehended; but one thing I do, forgetting
those things which are behind and reaching forward to those
things which are ahead, I press toward the goal for the prize
of the upward call of God in Christ Jesus. Therefore let us,
as many as are mature, have this mind; and if in anything
you think otherwise, God will reveal even this to you.
Nevertheless, to the degree that we have already attained,
let us walk by the same rule, let us be of the same mind.
—PHILIPPIANS 3:12-16

These five verses contain some of the most important information you will ever need to know as a soldier in the army of the Lord. Let's take this passage apart verse by verse, and see what Paul was anointed by the Holy Spirit to say to us here.

We Are All Works-in-Progress

In verse 12, notice that Paul freely admits he's a work-in-progress. He says that he hasn't yet "attained," and hasn't yet been "perfected." What does this mean? Simply that he's still a man with "issues" that haven't all been successfully dealt with yet! You know, over the years I've heard a lot of preachers practically deify the Apostle Paul. They refer to him as this super-saint, who was a stalwart in every spiritual area possible. Well, there can be no doubt about this man's accomplishments for the Lord in his life-time of ministry. Subsequent to his conversion experience on the Damascus road, Paul was a man mightily used by God to write much of the New Testament, and be one of the point-men to introduce the gospel to the Gentile world. This man has many rewards and crowns awaiting him on reward day to be sure!

However, Paul struggled with certain areas of compromise and sin, just like all the rest of us. He writes about those struggles in the book of Romans, specifically in chapters six and seven. Listen to what he says about his own process of sanctification:

> *For we know that the law is spiritual, but I am carnal, sold under sin. For what I am doing, I do not understand. For what I will to do, that I do not practice; but what I hate, that I do. If, then, I do what I will not to do, I agree with the law that it is good. But now, it is no longer I who do it, but sin that dwells in me. For I know that in me (that is, in my flesh) nothing good dwells; for to will is present with me, but how to perform what is good I do not find. For the good that I will to do, I do not do; but the evil I will not to do, that I practice. Now if I do what I will not to do, it is no longer I who do it, but sin that dwells in me.*
>
> *I find then a law, that evil is present with me, the one who wills to do good. For I delight in the law of God according to the inward man. But I see another law in my members, warring against the law of my mind, and bringing me into captivity to the law of sin which is in my members. O wretched man that I am! Who will deliver me from this body of death? I thank God — through Jesus Christ our Lord!*
>
> *So then, with the mind I myself serve the law of God, but with the flesh the law of sin.*
>
> —ROMANS 7:14-25

Now the Holy Spirit inspired Paul to write these things, not just for the benefit of the Roman church, but for us as well. God wants us to know that just like you and me, Paul was being mightily used in spite of the fact that he was what we call a "work-in-progress." As we see in reading this passage from Romans, Paul struggled with certain issues in his life that he knew weren't right in the sight of God. The Holy Spirit didn't see fit to reveal to the readers exactly what those areas of compromise, sin, or personal struggle were, but it is enough to know they were there. In writing to the Roman Christians, Paul simply acknowledges that there was this constant struggle within, for doing what was right, as opposed to doing what was wrong. That should be extremely encouraging for all of us, don't you think? I know it is for me!

This is what the Lord does with all of us. If He has to wait around for us to get rid of all the carnal issues in our lives before He can use us in any significant way to fulfill the Great Commission (see Mark 16:15-18), then He won't be using any of us! The fact is that in spite of our personal issues, struggles, or chronic areas of sin and failure before the Lord, God works with us! He uses us! He anoints us! This war rages on, and the Lord needs us out there on the front lines, moving forward and driving the devil back at every turn. Time is very short now, and God isn't waiting around for us to achieve total sanctification before He uses us in this great war. The command to go into all the world to preach to every sinner applies to the believer who just got saved a few minutes ago, as much as it applies to the rest of us who have been in this fight for awhile.

No, Paul wasn't perfect, but he was on the road towards complete sanctification, which is the same road you and I are on too. He was growing and maturing more and more, and heading in the right direction, and that's what we should be doing as well. The fact that Paul was mightily used of God, but had these ongoing recurrent struggles with his flesh at the same time, should be a great source of comfort and encouragement for you and me. I'm not perfect, but God uses me nonetheless. You're not perfect, but God will use you the same way too. It's what I call the "blessings of availability."

Also I heard the voice of the Lord, saying: "Whom shall I send, and who will go for Us?" Then I said, "Here am I! Send me." And He said, "Go, and tell this people:'Keep on hearing, but do not understand; Keep on seeing, but do not perceive.'"

—ISAIAH 6:8-9

The same question God asked Isaiah is the same question He's asking from every one of His children today. The correct answer will open up all of Heaven's exceedingly great and precious promises to whoever makes themselves available for the war effort. To answer God and say "Here am I Lord, send me," is to say you're available, anytime and anywhere He needs you. When you do that for Him, He'll do whatever it takes to provide and protect on your behalf.

When most Christians hear this question from God, their answer is "There they are Lord, send them!" That's why so many live and die without experiencing the fullness of the blessings God promises to all His children. Once again, remember that truth that not every soldier in God's army is a man or woman of war. Machir got those two prime pieces of real estate in Joshua 17:1 not because he was just in the army, but because he was a man of war—someone God could count on in the thick of the fight. No mention is made of Machir's personal life. He may have struggled with his flesh the same way we do, but that's not what God is looking for. As it was for Machir, Isaiah, Paul, or anybody else in God's army, He's not looking for external perfection with the outward man so much as He's looking at the heart of the inward man. If you're available, He'll use you!

Press on!

This is why Paul starts this passage by acknowledging his own short-comings. He says that although he is struggling at times with his own flesh, he presses on. Notice that in the same sentence where he admits the fact that he's still a work in progress, he also says this:

but I press on! That is one of the greatest keys to our success as soldiers first, and then as men or women of war. Pressing on.

As Christian soldiers charging across the spiritual battlefields of this planet, with our enemies doing all they can to steal, kill, or destroy us, we're *commanded* to press on despite the sins and failures of the past. When he talks about "pressing on," he's talking about *moving forward with pressure being applied against you.*

This is one of the problems I see with much of what is being preached and taught from churches in the free-world Western church. So many people are being taught that our lives down here on earth are supposed to be these wonderful, comfortable, and "abundant" lives of pleasure and ease. This is not what is found in the Bible, if you care to read the book from front to back and see the bigger picture. Taking verses out of their setting will not change the fact that in this life, God never promises us an easy life. If you don't believe me, consider the myriads of people over the ages who have bled, suffered, and died as martyrs for the cause of Christ.

Yes, we can have an abundant life, because Jesus died to provide it (see John 10:10), but that abundance isn't for us so much as it is for us to use to help others—and to do so while under fire from an enemy who seeks to stop us at every turn. Does God want us to enjoy life, and enjoy it more abundantly? Of course He does, but He expects us to do so in the light of the spiritual world war currently raging on Earth. We have enemies who are not in sympathy with anything we try to do to assist the Holy Spirit in reaching the lost and proclaiming the truth concerning God's plan of salvation. In whatever way they can, they will try to stop us, that's why we're told to "press on," with resistance being applied against us.

Peter wrote extensively about this to those he was inspired by the Holy Sprit to address. Listen to some of his statements:

> *Beloved, do not think it strange concerning the fiery trial which is to try you, as though some strange thing happened to you; but rejoice to the extent that you partake of Christ's sufferings, that when His glory is revealed, you may also be glad with exceeding*

joy. If you are reproached for the name of Christ, blessed are you, for the Spirit of glory and of God rests upon you. On their part He is blasphemed, but on your part He is glorified. But let none of you suffer as a murderer, a thief, an evildoer, or as a busybody in other people's matters. Yet if anyone suffers as a Christian, let him not be ashamed, but let him glorify God in this matter. For the time has come for judgment to begin at the house of God; and if it begins with us first, what will be the end of those who do not obey the gospel of God? Now "If the righteous one is scarcely saved, where will the ungodly and the sinner appear?" Therefore let those who suffer according to the will of God commit their souls to Him in doing good, as to a faithful Creator.

—1 PETER 4:12-19

Abundant Life from What Perspective?

So much is being heralded as the "abundant life" among Christians in places like the USA, when it's nothing more than greed disguised as prosperity. You won't find those kinds of messages being preached, or those kinds of seminars or conferences being promoted, in countries where being Christian is a crime against the state. For the underground portion of Body of Christ on Earth, they have a much better and much more complete grasp of what it means to press on with resistance being applied against them. We have no shortage of prosperity preaching in the free-world portion of the Body of Christ, which as far as I can see from scripture, is fine as long as we know the spiritual reasons for why we want all this "prosperity." If people genuinely want to have more to give more towards the cause of Christ, then I think God will move Heaven and Earth to supply all their needs (see Philippians 4:19) because He's promised to do so. But if all we want is more to enjoy for ourselves, while sinners all around us are stumbling towards their eternal doom and we're doing nothing about it, then that's not prosperity or the abundant life at all. Its nothing more than selfishness with a thin veneer of fake prosperity!

In other parts of the world, where people are literally risking life and limb to love and live for Jesus, nobody is preaching about the western world's idea of abundance or prosperity. For untold millions of believers who suffer for their faith, just having a job without the fear of daily reprisals from co-workers would be prosperity for them. Or, just being able to live at peace at home, or to go to work or school without the threats of violence and bodily harm would be abundant life for them. In places like the USA, we love to drive the newest and most expensive cars, while for many other believers in other parts of the world, just having a bicycle to ride is prosperity enough for them!

It's always a matter of perspective, and being able to see the "bigger picture." God won't hesitate to abundantly bless and provide for His children, but He expects us to remember His commandments to go into all the world, and carry out our assignments in the name of Jesus as soldiers advancing under fire! Proverbs says it this way:

> *If you faint in the day of adversity, your strength is small. Deliver those who are drawn toward death, and hold back those stumbling to the slaughter. If you say, "Surely we did not know this," does not He who weighs the hearts consider it? He who keeps your soul, does He not know it? And will He not render to each man according to his deeds?*
>
> —PROVERBS 24:10-12

Our job on Earth is to do what verse 11 says to do. This is the sole reason for why God leaves His children on Earth after they accept Jesus as Lord and Savior. By His own choice, God decided to limit His earthly evangelistic activity to partnership with us, and therefore, has issued His commands to go evangelize and reach out to those who, according to verse 12, are "stumbling to the slaughter." We're commanded to advance under fire, so that according to Ephesians 6:10, in God's power and might, we deliver people drawn towards death and hold back people stumbling to their own slaughter.

Being "drawn towards death" is descriptive of an unbeliever's carnal nature, which is in control of their lives, dragging them towards their day of departure, dying unprepared to face the righteous judgment of God. "Stumbling to the slaughter" describes the lifelong process of living without Jesus as Lord and Savior—without real direction and sense of earthly purpose. Our job is to stand in the way, and whenever possible, halt the sinner's forward progress towards their own doom. This is our assignment. This is the Great Commission.

Resistance Training

If you have ever done any weightlifting, or have ever worked out at the gym, you can easily understand the principle of resistance training. All those machines you use at the gym operate on this principle, as well as when you put those weights on the bar. Resistance training is the concept whereby we grow stronger, leaner, or more physically fit by forcing our bodies to work harder. How do we do that? By increasing the level of resistance.

If you want to get stronger physically, you put more weight on the barbell, and increase your repetitions. In short, you make it harder on yourself to lift that bar! You force your muscles to work harder because you've increased the level of weight resistance. And you know that the more you do that, the more positive results you're going to see. The person who increases the frequency of their workouts, and increases the amount of weight on the bar, and increases the number of repetitions, will see greater results than others who don't do such things.

It's the same when using rowing machines, or stair-masters, or some of the other machines you can use down at the gym. I know in my own workouts, when I use the Stairmaster, I get better results when I increase the level of resistance as well as the length of time I'm on the machine. If I want to get stronger faster, I increase the level of physical resistance my body has to overcome. This is the way it is for any physical fitness goal one may set to accomplish. The more resistance you create to overcome, the stronger you're going to become.

For me, my hobby of choice is bicycling. Years ago, I would go jogging as often as I could, but when the constant pounding on my feet, legs, and hips began to adversely affect me, I switched over to bicycling as a better way to train and stay in shape without all the aches and pains that jogging was producing. Now when I say I'm going cycling, understand that I'm not just tooling around the neighborhood at 2 mph on my Huffy bike from Walmart. The bikes I ride are world-class machines designed to keep the rider safe at race speeds, when traveling at speeds faster than 50 mph! These bikes cost thousands of dollars because they're built with very exotic components and composites, making them very strong but very light at the same time. They're made with things like titanium or fiber composites, so that the frames are all one piece, not welded together as most of the family-oriented bikes would be. My bike, for example, is so light I can literally pick it up off the ground with one finger. Yet at the same time, when I'm on a downhill run and my speed is around 45mph (the pros ride 10 or 20 mph faster than that even), I'm absolutely confident, safe, and secure because this bike has been built for just such a scenario.

Well, when I get ready to ride, whether I go solo or with others, the wind directions are always checked. When planning the riding route (which is usually 35 or 40 miles minimum), we're looking at time of day, wind speed, and wind direction. We do this so we can plan our route in such a way that we're riding into the wind as much as possible. Why? Because any serious cyclist knows the wind is a great trainer! The stronger the headwind you're riding into, the more you're going to have to work to keep your speed up. That's resistance training! Of course it's a lot more fun to ride with the wind, but that won't make you stronger on the bike. If we want to do well in an upcoming race or cycling event, we try to ride into the wind when we do our training rides, because we know the stronger the wind, the greater amount of resistance we'll have to overcome. That makes us stronger, and that's the goal. Riding with the wind is easy. Riding against the wind is much harder. But its all a matter of choice concerning what you want out of your ride! If you just want to have fun, ride with the wind. If you want to get aerobically stronger in lungs and legs, ride into the wind for as long as you can.

Around 2002, I decided to get back into the sport of bicycling just to help keep my body physically fit as I got older. I used to do a lot of bicycling when I was in college years before, but hadn't ridden at all since then. When I decided to pick the sport back up, I quickly discovered how out-of-shape I was! But I also discovered that if I was diligent and disciplined to ride—and ride into the wind as often as possible—my level of physical fitness rose dramatically in just a short amount of time. When I first started riding again, it was all I could do to get to the end of the driveway without gasping for air, but after several months of constant and ever-increasing levels of resistance training, I was at the point where it was nothing for me to ride 40, 50, or 60 miles and not even feel tired when I was finished with the ride. In addition, going up the hills was very difficult when I first got back on the bike, but the more I made myself do it, the better I got at doing it. The time came when I could glide up and over even the steepest of hills with very little effort, because through the principle of resistance training, I had forced myself to work harder and harder until my end-results were achieved.

This works for anyone because it's based on laws that never change. It would work for you as much as for me, or anyone else. And this same principle applies to the things of God, and the work of the Great Commission. Paul said that he was pressing on, despite the heavy levels of resistance being applied against him. Even though he had stumbled and even struggled in his life with personal setbacks and sin, he was pressing on. He was moving forward despite the resistance being applied against him.

We must do the same! We're not perfect people any more than the Apostle Paul, but if we're committed to the fight, and God knows He can depend on us under fire, we're going to continue to grow and progress and move forward in Jesus.

CHAPTER 4

One Thing We Must Do

Brethren, I do not count myself to have apprehended;
but one thing I do, forgetting those things which
are behind and reaching forward to those things
which are ahead, I press toward the goal for
the prize of the upward call of God in Christ Jesus.
—PHILIPPIANS 3:13-14

As Paul was admonishing and exhorting the Philippian Christians, he talked about pressing on no matter what. No matter what sins, personal issues, or struggles were being dealt with, he kept pressing on. No matter how severe the levels of persecution thrown against him by the Jews or Romans, he kept pressing on. We must do the same if we're to be the kind of soldiers God can depend upon in the heat of the battle. To be men or women of war, we must discipline ourselves to do what Paul talks about here.

In order to press on under fire, no matter what kind of fire it is coming against us, we must do this one thing described in these two verses. When Paul talks about pressing on, this is how he did it, and this is how you and I are going to do it too.

One Thing with Three Parts

This one thing has three parts to it. You have to take care of all three parts in order to do this one thing. They work together, and you can't do only one or two and expect this to work in your life. You must do all three. When you stop and consider all that Paul went through in his ministry, you can begin to appreciate the power and effectiveness of what these three parts to this one thing can do. When Jesus told Ananias that Paul would suffer greatly for the Name of Jesus, He wasn't kidding (see Acts 9:16)! Yet, in spite of all that the devil tried to do to stop Paul, doing this one thing with these three parts got him through every test, trial, or obstacle thrown against him. No matter how intense the fights of faith became, Paul was always able to keep advancing forward under fire. And unless you're a member of the underground church in some closed country somewhere, the "fire" he faced was much more severe than anything you and I are facing in this day and time.

Read the book of 2 Corinthians, especially chapters one, four, six, and eleven. Read and meditate on the long list of difficulties Paul faced and dealt with in ministry. When you really stop and think about what he endured, it's amazing the man was still standing at the end of it all! But because he applied in his own life what he tells the Philippians to apply in theirs, he reached the end of the line and was able to say this:

> *For I am already being poured out as a drink offering, and the time of my departure is at hand. I have fought the good fight, I have finished the race, I have kept the faith.*
>
> —2 TIMOTHY 4:6-7

There's a real note of victory in that statement! This man was able to advance under fire, and finish his assignment from God. My prayer is that one day at the end of my life, I'll be able to say exactly the same thing. How about you? When Paul exhorted Christians to fight the good fight of faith, he knew what he was talking about (see 1 Timothy 6:12). He charted the course and set the pace for all the other believers to follow. He told them to hang in there and keep on fighting no matter what, because he was doing it himself. He could boldly exhort his spiritual children because he had been where they were now, and had not only survived, but thrived with intense pressure being applied against Him. He was a doer of the word (see James 1:22). He was doing this "one thing." This was also the message the writer of Hebrews exhorted his disciples over as well:

> But recall the former days in which, after you were illuminated, you endured a great struggle with sufferings: partly while you were made a spectacle both by reproaches and tribulations, and partly while you became companions of those who were so treated; for you had compassion on me in my chains, and joyfully accepted the plundering of your goods, knowing that you have a better and an enduring possession for yourselves in heaven. Therefore do not cast away your confidence, which has great reward. For you have need of endurance, so that after you have done the will of God, you may receive the promise: "For yet a little while, and He who is coming will come and will not tarry. Now the just shall live by faith; but if anyone draws back, my soul has no pleasure in him." But we are not of those who draw back to perdition, but of those who believe to the saving of the soul.
>
> —HEBREWS 10:32-39

Notice that in this passage, the believers were experiencing a "great struggle with sufferings." That doesn't sound too edifying or appealing, does it? At least not in the lukewarm, carnal, shallow, superficial, selfish, self-centered, and anemic portion of the Body of Christ located in western world countries like the USA. As these Christians were under fire from all sides, the Holy Spirit was moving to strengthen them in their time of difficulty by reminding them of these important truths.

Don't throw away your confidence in God just because you're under attack! Don't "draw back" and quit. Don't retreat or surrender to the temptations to sin or embrace doctrinal or lifestyle compromise. Exercise *spiritual endurance* against any and all forms of attack or persecution. Stay steadfast and strong in the Lord, and no matter how intense the fights of faith may be in your life, remember that as you continue to advance under fire in the name of Jesus, all Heaven stands with you, and every one of God's exceedingly great and precious promises is yours to appropriate whenever necessary. Even if it seems so, remember you're never alone in these fights. God your Father is with you, the son of God, the Lord Jesus will never leave you or forsake you, and greater is the Holy Spirit in you than the enemies out there in the world. If the Father is *always with you*, the Lord Jesus is *never leaving you* and the Holy Spirit is *living within you*, you're never alone, no matter how much you may feel to the contrary!

Part 1: Forget Your Past

Here is part one to this one thing: forgetting your past sins, failures, and mistakes. Entire books could be written on this one subject alone, because it's where so many of us have fallen prey to the devil's tactics. If you're going to advance under fire for God, you must learn how to forget the negative and remember the positive. You can't let the devil sit on your shoulder for years after some mistake was made or sin committed, condemning you and tormenting you with it. Once you have been forgiven by God, you need to move on and never look back.

If anyone had "skeletons in his closet", it was Paul. Here's how he describes himself before his dramatic encounter with Jesus on the road to Damascus:

> *For I am the least of the apostles, who am not worthy to be called an apostle, because I persecuted the church of God.*
> —1 CORINTHIANS 15:9

> *This is a faithful saying, and worthy of all acceptance, that Christ Jesus came into the world to save sinners; of whom I am chief.*
> —1 TIMOTHY 1:15 KJV

*So I said, 'Lord, they know that in every synagogue I impris-
oned and beat those who believe on You. And when the blood of Your
martyr Stephen was shed, I also was standing by consenting to his
death, and guarding the clothes of those who were killing him.'*
—ACTS 22:19-21

*As for Saul, he made havoc of the church, entering every house,
and dragging off men and women, committing them to prison.*
—ACTS 8:3

*Then Saul, still breathing threats and murder against the
disciples of the Lord, went to the high priest and asked letters from
him to the synagogues of Damascus, so that if he found any who
were of the Way, whether men or women, he might bring them
bound to Jerusalem.*
—ACTS 9:1-2

*I persecuted this Way to the death, binding and delivering into
prisons both men and women.*
—ACTS 22:4

Paul, then called Saul, had a very sordid history concerning
Christianity. He didn't just dislike Christians, he hated them. He
went after them to destroy this "heresy" with a vengeance. He did
his best to arrest, torment, torture, or murder anyone calling on
the name of the Lord Jesus. If anyone had a "past" to be ashamed
of before finding Jesus, Paul would be the one. But yet, listen to
what he tells the Philippians. He's telling them that the first part
to this one thing he practices is to forget your past and move on.
Did he practice what he was preaching? Yes, he did. Listen to how
he talks about himself to the Corinthian Christians after his
remarkable conversion and complete surrender to Jesus on the
road to Damascus:

*Open your hearts to us. We have wronged no one, we have
corrupted no one, we have cheated no one.*
—2 CORINTHIANS 7:2

Wronged no one? Cheated no one? Corrupted no one? Is this the same man we read about in the book of Acts, prior to the Damascus road experience? Yes it is, and no it isn't. What we have here is a man who truly understands what it means to be born-again. When he wrote and told the Corinthians in this very same letter that people who receive Jesus become "new creatures," he knew exactly what that meant (see 2 Corinthians 5:17). Old things were "passed away," and all things became new. Not most things became new, but *all things!*

That old man once called Saul died on the road to Damascus. On the inside, he died. His spirit man was literally recreated by the power of God in response to his acceptance of Jesus as His Lord and Savior, and he was born-again, which is what Jesus told all of us we had to do in order to go to Heaven in John 3:3. The physical body of Saul never changed, but his inner man was made new, just like a newborn baby! Therefore, Paul was telling the truth when he told the Corinthian believers that he hadn't hurt, harmed, or injured *anyone.* He understood the new birth, and the fact that old things had been passed away. He knew his inner man—the real man, called the inward man of the heart—had been born-again (see Romans 7:22, 2 Corinthians 4:16, Ephesians 3:16, 1 Peter 3:4).

The devil will work in this area over and over again, because it's one of his most successful tactics against us. He knows the chances for success are high when he works to keep people bound up with guilt, condemnation, and remorse over past sins, mistakes, and failures committed before a holy and righteous God. Don't let the devil have his way with you in this area! Discipline yourself mentally, emotionally, and physically if necessary, and refuse to return to the scene of your crimes! One of the greatest aspects to our salvation is the fact that when we ask forgiveness from God in sincere and heartfelt sorrow and repentance, He grants it! Over and over again, when He grants forgiveness, He moves on—so let's learn to move on with Him.

Paul learned how to forget his past, and that's what you and I must do if we're to start doing this one thing. It all starts here. If

you can't get past your past, you'll never be able to advance under
fire for Jesus.

*There is therefore now no condemnation to those who are in
Christ Jesus, who do not walk according to the flesh, but according
to the Spirit.*

—ROMANS 8:1

If you're born-again, you're in Christ Jesus. There is therefore no
condemnation over past sins, mistakes, or failures—before or
after receiving Jesus. The past covers what you did before you
accepted Jesus as Lord and Savior, and afterwards as well, right up
to this present moment in time. Thank God for His mercy, which
is new every morning (see Lamentations 3:22-23). Thank God that
Jesus placed His precious blood on the heavenly mercy seat, not
the heavenly judgment seat (see Hebrews chapter 9). Thank God
we have these wonderful promises from the Lord:

*If we confess our sins, He is faithful and just to forgive us our
sins and to cleanse us from all unrighteousness. If we say that we
have not sinned, we make Him a liar, and His word is not in us.*

—1 JOHN 1:9-10

*Seeing then that we have a great High Priest who has passed
through the heavens, Jesus the Son of God, let us hold fast our
confession. For we do not have a High Priest who cannot sympa-
thize with our weaknesses, but was in all points tempted as we are,
yet without sin. Let us therefore come boldly to the throne of grace,
that we may obtain mercy and find grace to help in time of need.*

—HEBREWS 4:14-16

All these verses, and many more like them, tell us the same
wonderful story. When you were saved by accepting Jesus as your
Lord and Savior, all your old sins were washed away. And after you
are saved, every time you go to God and confess your sins, they get
washed away as well. Here's how God deals with our sins when we
come to Him for forgiveness:

"I, even I, am He who blots out your transgressions for My own sake; and I will not remember your sins."

—ISAIAH 43:25

"But this is the covenant that I will make with the house of Israel after those days, says the LORD: I will put My law in their minds, and write it on their hearts; and I will be their God, and they shall be My people. No more shall every man teach his neighbor, and every man his brother, saying, 'Know the LORD,' for they all shall know Me, from the least of them to the greatest of them, says the LORD. For I will forgive their iniquity, and their sin I will remember no more."

—JEREMIAH 31:33-34

"This is the covenant that I will make with them after those days, says the LORD: I will put My laws into their hearts, and in their minds I will write them," then He adds, *"Their sins and their lawless deeds I will remember no more."* Now where there is remission of these, there is no longer an offering for sin.

—HEBREWS 10:16-18

If God forgives and forgets all your past sins and mistakes when you receive Jesus as Lord, then you should too! And if He does that *before* you get born again, as you make the decision to surrender your life to Jesus, how much more would He be willing to do the very same thing *after* you become a child of God? Never forget this one profound truth: if God forgives and forgets all of your sins, failures, and mistakes whenever you come to him as His beloved son or daughter, you should do it for yourself too! Why should we be walking around with the burden of self-condemnation when God isn't holding anything against us? That's just stupid! So many believers have failed to learn to do this, and the devil takes full advantage of that.

Receive Forgiveness by Faith, Not Feelings

When you come to God for forgiveness, you must distinguish between faith and feelings, because you receive forgiveness by faith and faith alone. Your feelings have nothing to do with it, one way or the other. This is something many Christians fail to realize, and the devil uses this ignorance against them. *Forgiveness isn't granted when you feel forgiven! It's granted the moment you ask for it in faith.* Many times I've asked the Lord to forgive me, and my forgiveness was received by faith alone, because I certainly didn't *feel* forgiven. In fact, there have been times when after I asked the Lord to forgive me, it was days before I actually felt better about myself. Even so, that didn't change the fact that the moment I asked for forgiveness, I received it. And when God forgave me, He forgot about the sins I had committed against Him! Listen to this:

> *As far as the east is from the west, so far has He removed our transgressions from us.*
>
> —Psalm 103:12

When you go north until you reach the North Pole, or south until you reach the South Pole, you automatically change directions if you keep going forward. If you're heading north; cross the North Pole and keep moving forward and immediately you're now heading south. You can't keep going north forever, and you can't keep going south forever. But when you're going east and west, its different. If you keep going east, you'll forever be going east. You never pass a certain point where you cease going east, and automatically start going west.

That's why its significant that when God forgives us of sin, He says those sins are forgotten as far as the east is from the west, not as far as the north is from the south! So how long would that be for? *Forever!* Keep going east and you'll forever be traveling east! Think about that for a moment, and receive that truth into your spirit. There is literally no limit or boundaries to the extent whereby God forgives and forgets our sins. He loves us that much!

When the Word of God says that God forgets our confessed sins, how does that actually happen? How does he do that? I don't know, and no one else does either, really. He either does something to Himself to cancel out the memory of what we've done after He forgives us, or He simply chooses never to think about, talk about, or have a continuing issue with anything we've been forgiven from. I can't explain it anymore than you can, but I'm just simple enough to take Him at His word, and praise Him for it! If that doesn't get you running and shouting for joy, what could?

> *But Jesus said to him, "No one, having put his hand to the plow, and looking back, is fit for the kingdom of God."*
>
> —LUKE 9:62

This verse is usually used to refer to people who received Jesus, but then afterwards, allowed the allure of the world and the deceitfulness of sin to distract them and nullify their usefulness for the kingdom of God. That's certainly true, but there's another slant to this verse which is equally truthful, and which applies to what we're talking about here.

If you let the devil browbeat you with condemnation over sins and mistakes of the past, or if you yourself can't move on from the failures of the past, then you're also guilty of "looking back." Those who do that are of no value to the Lord in this end-time war, because instead of advancing under fire, they're slumped over in their foxhole, crying and feeling sorry for themselves.

> *For a righteous man may fall seven times and rise again, but the wicked shall fall by calamity.*
>
> —PROVERBS 24:16

Notice the tense of the verb in this statement. It doesn't say the righteous man *fell* seven times, implying that he's done falling. No, it says the righteous *may fall* seven times, implying an ongoing, chronic pattern of failure that may *still be an issue* in that person's life. The message here is one of not looking back and camping at your sins or failures, but instead, receiving your forgiveness, getting back up from where you've fallen, and making up your mind to keep moving forward with God instead. And the reference to falling "seven times" indicates a consistent application of this truth. Even when the believer has fallen for the seventh time (or seventy-seventh time for that matter), he or she doesn't choose to sit there on the ground feeling sorry for himself.

> *Do not rejoice over me, my enemy; when I fall, I will arise; when I sit in darkness, the LORD will be a light to me. I will bear the indignation of the LORD, because I have sinned against Him, until He pleads my case and executes justice for me. He will bring me forth to the light; I will see His righteousness.*
>
> —MICAH 7:8-9

If you've been saved for longer than ten minutes, you already know what I'm about to tell you is true. *It's not a matter of "if" we fall because of sin, but "when, where, and how often!"* It's like bicycling, which is my hobby of choice when I have the time. In the bicycling community, when talking about bike crashes, we have a saying that goes like this: *There are two kinds of bicyclists: those who have crashed, and those who are going to!*

It's just something you must understand about riding a bike. You're *going to fall.* So you go into the activity of bike riding with the right mindset about falling. You don't stand there looking at the bike, refusing to get on because you're paralyzed with the fear of falling, and *after* you've fallen, you don't sit on the road crying for two weeks either (unless you crash at 30-miles-an-hour on a downhill descent—then you've got everyone's permission to cry for the pain of it all if you wish!).

So it is with Christians. We're not perfect, and we make mistakes and commit sins. All of us do, no exceptions. But even though we get knocked down through sin, compromise, or disobedience, we don't have to sit there crying and feeling sorry for ourselves. Notice what Micah tells us to do. Even as you're flat on your back in humiliation and defeat, you look up at your adversary, and tell him to quit rejoicing because *the fight isn't over!* Even if we're "sitting in darkness" through sin or failure, we can choose to get up, knowing the Lord will plead our case for us, and knowing that once forgiven, we never have to look back in condemnation, shame, or embarrassment! Ever! *When I fall (not if) I will arise!* That's an act of free will. That's a choice.

Even though he has been knocked down, a Christian who confesses his sins and receives forgiveness can move on and never look back. He gets up and gets back in the game. He reengages the enemy. He puts his helmet back on, picks up his weapon, and rejoins the fight. And the good news is that there is no "cut-off" point, or no "limit" to God's willingness and eagerness to forgive us when we sin. It doesn't matter if this is the seventh time you've confessed your sins, or the seventeenth time, or the one-hundred-and-seventeenth time. God *wants* to forgive you! He *wants* to cleanse you! He is for us, not against us. It's the same principle Jesus taught Peter and the disciples:

> *Then Peter came to Him and said, "Lord, how often shall my brother sin against me, and I forgive him? Up to seven times?" Jesus said to him, "I do not say to you, up to seven times, but up to seventy times seven."*
>
> —MATTHEW 18:21-22

You and I must do the same, which is what Paul was doing throughout the course of his life and ministry. Many times the devil tried to stop Paul and kill him, but Paul just wouldn't cooperate!

Have you noticed like I have, that when we sin, fail God, or disappoint Him in some significant way, not only do we ourselves feel terrible, but our flesh wants everybody else to have a pity party with us? And have you also discovered like I have, that very few people want to participate? No matter what's going on in your life, the world continues to spin with or without you. It's our carnal human nature to want everybody to sit and cry with us when we're going through a rough patch of some kind, but that's not how things are in the real world.

As much as some people may make themselves available to help you, counsel you, encourage you, pray for you, and even pray with you, they aren't going to stop their lives just so they can sit and stroke your hand all day long! They may do their best to help you move on with your life, but you need to realize they want to live their lives, not yours. Life goes on—with or without you. People are not going to allow their lives to come to a screeching halt just so you can continue to be melancholy and morose over your past or present failures or mistakes. Everybody has their own lives to live, even those who try their best to console the downtrodden.

I have found this out by experience, and you'd be wise to know it and understand it as well. Most people are too busy with their own issues to stop their world to camp with you at the site of your disappointment, tragedy, or difficulty. Thank God for those who do choose to stay with you and help to the best of their ability, but at the end of the day, it's your life and you're going to have to decide to get up, dust yourself off, and get back in the war! Remember—we're not just advancing, we're advancing under fire.

Charging While Wounded

When you're being shot at, you're going to get hit, sooner or later. In this great fight of faith for Jesus in this world, you're going to be attacked and you're going to get wounded, and sometimes those wounds are severe. Sin happens. Failures happen. Disappointment happens. Tragedies happen. In many ways we need God's forgiveness and mercy, which is new every morning. Well, that's why its there! So ask for it, receive it by faith, get up off your knees, quit feeling sorry for yourself, and get back out there and make the devil pay! When we're told to advance under fire, you need to know you'll be doing that as a *wounded soldier* more often than not! Even when you're hit, bleeding and in great pain, you've got to keep moving forward.

When the devil has hit you and successfully attacked you, you can't just stand there in the middle of the battlefield feeling sorry for yourself. You might be shot to pieces, so to speak, but don't just give up and collapse in a pile of self-pity. Remember Micah. You may have fallen for the "seventh" time, but get up! The bleeding will stop. Your wounds will heal. You'll be fine. God will never leave you or forsake you. The battles go on, and we need for you to go on too!

Paul moved on, and as a result, was confidently able to tell the Corinthians he had never done anything wrong before the Lord. That's how you walk in the light of true forgiveness. That's how you forget the past and move on. If the devil brings up some old event, mistake, or sin from your past, just remind him that you've confessed that to God, and received your forgiveness. Don't let him condemn you over that anymore. When he tries to remind you of past failures, remember that's nothing more than an old "photograph" of someone who doesn't exist anymore, doing something that's been washed away by the blood of Jesus. You've been forgiven. You're free. You're moving on and not looking back. Shove that truth back in the devil's face a few times, and he'll realize this old tactic against you isn't working anymore! I heard someone once say that when the devil tries to remind you of your past, remind him of his future! That's good advice.

Make Sure You're Not Playing Games with God

One more important truth needs to be understood here on the subject of receiving forgiveness and forgetting the past. When it comes to the business of offering forgiveness to those who ask for it, the only thing God won't do is allow Himself to be mocked. There's a big difference between the person who is really sorry for the sins they've committed, and has no intention of allowing that sin a permanent place in their life, as opposed to the person who thinks he can just receive God's forgiveness whenever it suits him, with no intention of stopping or halting the sinful lifestyle.

> *Do not be deceived, God is not mocked; for whatever a man sows, that he will also reap. For he who sows to his flesh will of the flesh reap corruption, but he who sows to the Spirit will of the Spirit reap everlasting life.*

> —GALATIANS 6:7-8

The person who thinks their sinful lifestyle is somehow "covered" by God's love and grace is, according to this verse, *deceived*. This is a very popular heresy circulating worldwide these days, and you need to be wary of it. There is much error being taught about the subjects of love and grace, and it is overthrowing the faith of many in these last days, exactly as the false prophets and heretics in Paul's day overthrew the faith of many back then (see 2 Timothy 2:16-19).

Many false prophets, false teachers, and false apostles declare that since God is love, there couldn't possibly be something as evil as an actual spiritual being called the devil, or a place as horrible as an actual and eternal lake of fire for unrepentant, unsaved people. And according to them, because the Bible says that where sin abounds, grace much more abounds, we're supposed to believe that no matter what sins are being committed by people who have no intention of stopping, that somehow God's grace will save the day for them, and these unrepentant sinners will all be welcomed into Heaven along with the true believers by a loving and merciful God. The Bible says otherwise. Here's what the Bible says about those lies: the day of judgment for these heretics and false teachers is coming, and it will be terrible indeed.

God is not mocked. He is holy, righteous, pure, and in His time, removes and banishes all sin and sinners from His presence forever—period. Yes, He is love, but because He is love, He must also *hate!* Go study your Bible on the word "hate," and you'll find out that our God of love is also a God who hates.

He's putting up with sin on the earth for a season of time now because of Adam's 7,000-year lease, but that time is quickly coming to a close. Think about it for a moment. One sin of disobedience and rebellion by Adam thousands of years ago, not thousands of sins, brought a curse on this earth that we're still living with today. Many people want to excuse sin, trivialize sin, apologize for sin, and justify sin, because the world as we know it today is a cesspool of perversion, evil, and rebellion against God. They think that because *we've decided* what is and what isn't heinous and evil in the sight of God, that He is compelled to go along with our charade! Nothing is farther from the truth.

I tremble when I think of how holy God is, and what awaits those people on judgment day, who think they can enjoy the pleasures of sin, and then flippantly go to God whenever its convenient to ask Him for forgiveness—with no intention of ever stopping or altering their sinful ways. God has a word for such people.

Woe to those who call evil good, and good evil; who put darkness for light, and light for darkness; who put bitter for sweet, and sweet for bitter!

—Isaiah 5:20

When God says "Woe to you," you're in deep trouble mister! Thank God for His mercy, patience, and willingness to forgive and forget our sins. Without that, none of us would make it to Heaven. Just make sure you're not playing games with God. He knows your heart, and he knows what your true intentions really are. You can look good on the outside, but God knows you from the inside! Don't be deceived into thinking *any* decision to entertain *any kind* of sin will be winked at, tolerated, or overlooked by a holy, pure, and righteous God, just because some idiot disguised as a preacher tells you He does.

If you're doing your best to stay clear of sin, and are quick to run to God the moment you've fallen in sin—asking for forgiveness in sincere sorrow and desire to repent—then that forgiveness is yours every time you ask for it. On the other hand, if you're just hiding your sins behind a cloak of doctrinal heresy that has become very popular these days, which allows people to live any way they want without any eternal consequences, then you need to wake up and *repent before its too late!*

Part 2: Moving on by Reaching Forward

The second part to this one thing deals with the decision to reach forward. First, we forget the past, but then we reach forward to the future. Paul said to reach forward to the things "ahead of us." That means we utilize the helmet of hope, and discipline our minds to only consider and think about the great things going on for Jesus, and the part we're playing to fulfill the Great Commission.

But let us who are of the day be sober, putting on the breastplate of faith and love, and as a helmet the hope of salvation.
—1 THESSALONIANS 5:8

Hope is such a powerful weapon! The Bible calls it our "helmet" which as such, must never be taken off (see 1 Thessalonians 5:8). It's a very important part of our spiritual armor, included in the classic list of spiritual weapons and armor given to all believers, found in Ephesians chapter six. In Ephesians 6:17, we're told to take (put on) the helmet of our salvation, which according to 1 Thessalonians 5:8, is hope. *The helmet of our salvation is the hope of our salvation.*

Hebrews 11:6 says that without faith, its impossible to please God, but in that same passage, it says that faith is the substance of things hoped for, the evidence of things not seen (see Hebrews 11:1). So when we've made the decision to move on and forget the past, we must know what to replace those old thoughts with. We replace them with thoughts that line up with God's word, and God's promises to cover and protect our lives at every turn.

This is a choice. You don't look forward to the things ahead because you always feel like doing so. You might still be dealing with feelings of grief, sorrow and condemnation over things you've been forgiven for, but that doesn't matter. By faith, you choose to move on, look ahead, and embrace the plan that God has for your life and ministry.

"Call to Me, and I will answer you, and show you great and mighty things, which you do not know."
—JEREMIAH 33:3

Instead of calling on God so you can continue going back over sins of the past already forgiven, call upon God and expect Him to show you great and mighty things *to come*—things you don't even know yet! I guarantee you won't be disappointed! God's plan for you is to keep advancing under fire. To do that, you must know that no matter what fight of faith you're going through right now, God's still got a great plan beyond today's difficulties or yesterday's failures, tailor-made for you to accomplish for His glory on Earth in this life.

> *For I know the thoughts that I think toward you, says the LORD, thoughts of peace and not of evil, to give you a future and a hope.*
>
> —JEREMIAH 29:11

Notice that God wants to give you "a future and a hope." Hope always deals with the future, or according to Philippians chapter 3, with looking ahead. God thinks about you all the time, and contrary to the way people think about each other, it's not about all the times you've failed Him. He's washed all of that away with the blood of Jesus, so when He thinks about you, He's thinking about your future—the plan He has for your life. Psalm 139:17-18 says that if you tried to number the times He's thought about you in particular, its more than all the grains of sand on Earth's beaches. That's a lot!

God knows you better than you know you. If you keep that helmet of hope on your head, you're going to consistently look ahead, embrace and agree with the plans and purposes God established for you before you were even born. Quit looking at past mistakes, whether they be before you got saved, or after. The past is one minute ago, one year ago, ten years ago or more. The moment you realize you've let God down through sin or failure, go to Him and ask for forgiveness. Receive it by faith, and get your eyes back on the horizon with the Lord Jesus. Don't let the enemy knock that helmet of hope off your head, and don't you do it to yourself either!

One more point to emphasize here is the importance of maintaining your fellowship with God through consistent acknowledgement of sin and the subsequent requests for forgiveness. Another popular heresy currently making the rounds worldwide is this idea that because we were forgiven of all sins by God through the death and resurrection of Jesus, there is no longer a need to ask God for any forgiveness regarding any sins committed after receiving our salvation. This is a serious error that must be exposed and refuted.

Maintaining a daily communion with God is essential to our ability to reach forward to the things ahead of us. That daily communion requires a constant searching of our hearts by the Holy Spirit, who then reveals to us the sins or failures we need to bring before our heavenly Father in sincere sorrow and repentance.

Search me, O God, and know my heart; try me, and know my anxieties; and see if there is any wicked way in me, and lead me in the way everlasting.

—PSALM 139:23-24

This prayer from the psalmist David applies to you and I as much as it did for him back in the Old Testament. The need for vigilance against sin is something that *never* goes away, no matter what time period or dispensation you care to talk about. It doesn't matter if I'm living in the Old Testament or New—I need to have God constantly searching my heart; revealing to me any area that is out of line with His Word and with His holy nature. Then its up to me to bring that issue to the Lord in prayer, asking for my forgiveness, receiving it by faith, and moving on by reaching forward.

If we say that we have no sin, we deceive ourselves, and the truth is not in us. If we confess our sins, He is faithful and just to forgive us our sins and to cleanse us from all unrighteousness. If we say that we have not sinned, we make Him a liar, and His word is not in us.

—1 JOHN 1:8-10

This letter was written to Christians, not unbelievers. We're told to acknowledge our sins, confess them to God, receive our forgiveness and move on. To say we don't need to do this now because of the work of Christ on the cross is *self-deception*, exactly as it says in verse 8.

To reach forward, you need to confess your sins to God and receive His forgiveness first. There is no shortcut around this. That's why Paul told the Philippians that they needed to forget the past before they started reaching forward towards the future. You can't reach forward without letting go of the past, and to do that spiritually, you must allow God to search your heart, reveal your sins and shortcomings, and let you request His mercy and forgiveness. Are all our sins forgiven because of our Lord's death and resurrection? In a legal sense, yes. In an everyday vital sense, no. The *penalty* for all our sins was paid for, but a person still has the choice to reject the free gift of salvation, in the same way a Christian still has the choice to hold on to their sins and not bring them to God.

> *He who covers his sins will not prosper, but whoever confesses and forsakes them will have mercy.*
>
> —Proverbs 28:13

Notice you are the one here told to confess and forsake the sins. Not God! Jesus paid for all men's sins, once for all (see Hebrews 9:26-28), but people still have to choose to respond.

For example, I can choose to buy you a nice birthday present, wrap it up, and bring it to your birthday party. That present belongs to me because I bought it, not you. However, it's my intention to offer it to you as a gift. You didn't buy that gift, I did. Therefore, it's up to me to choose to give it or not. If I wanted, I could keep the present for myself and never give it. But I want to give you a nice present, so I wrap it up and take it to your party so I can give it to you. But as the birthday boy or girl, you still have the right to refuse my gift. You can choose to take it, or not take it. I have no control over that part of this exchange, do I? I chose to buy the gift, not you. I chose to offer the gift, not you. But only you can choose to accept it.

That's the way it is for receiving the free gift of salvation, and that's the way it is for walking in the light of daily forgiveness before God. Having our sins paid for by Jesus is the first step, but the second step is up to us, because of our free will. We still have to choose to accept the gift, or in the case of daily fellowship with God, choose to come to God and confess our sins in godly sorrow and repentance. Failure to understand this will prevent you from forgetting the past and reaching forward to the future.

Press Toward the Goal for the Prize

The third part of this one thing deals with the determination needed to keep moving forward under fire. In verse 14, notice Paul uses that word "press" a second time. You find it in verse 12, and again in verse 14. Remember that word "press" indicates a decision to move forward with pressure being applied against you. What are we pressing towards? The goal. What's the goal? The prize of the upward calling of God in Christ Jesus.

We want to stand before the Lord someday in Heaven, and hear Him say to us: "Well done, good and faithful servant" (see Matthew 25:21-23). So no matter how you're being attacked, continue moving forward. One of the best ways to do that is to keep thinking about the day to come, when you're going to be judged for the life you've lived. That's the helmet of hope we're told to wear as part of our daily spiritual armor. A committed soul-winner will be attacked many times in many ways throughout the course of life. Anyone who is even just a casual reader of the New Testament can see that. That's why we're told to "press on" towards the goal.

> *If you faint in the day of adversity, your strength is small. Deliver those who are drawn toward death, and hold back those stumbling to the slaughter. If you say, "Surely we did not know this," does not He who weighs the hearts consider it? He who keeps your soul, does He not know it? And will He not render to each man according to his deeds?*
>
> —PROVERBS 24:10-12

Verse 10 of this passage is one of my favorites. If we faint in the day of adversity, our level of spiritual strength is small. The word "faint" simply means to quit, give up and accept defeat. And how about the word "adversity?" *The American Heritage Dictionary of the English Language* defines that word as: 1. A state of hardship or affliction; misfortune. 2. A calamitous event.

An interesting thing to note are the synonyms of adversity: c*atastrophe, disaster, trouble, misery,* and *affliction.* The antonym for this word would be—you guessed it—*prosperity!* So we could render this verse this way, without violating the truth or context of God's Word: *If you quit, give up or accept defeat in times of catastrophe, disaster, trouble, misery, or affliction, your level of spiritual strength is small.*

Wow! We need to really consider this, because it's not a question of "if" the devil attacks, but "how often and how severe" his attacks are going to be! So many of us are self-deceived (see James 1:22), thinking we're much stronger than we really are. To really find out how strong you are, you've got to face the enemy on the field of battle and defeat him. Then and only then will you really know how strong you are in Christ. Until that happens, your idea about how strong you are is just a hollow confession which will be shattered in the wind when you find yourself surrounded with the enemy closing in on all sides.

Its important to know why verse 10 precedes verses 11 and 12 in this passage. Verse 11 declares our sole reason for being left on Earth after accepting Jesus as Lord and Savior. It's not for the pursuit of creature comforts of this world or this life, but instead, for the business of winning souls in the name of Jesus. And in the pursuit of that battlefield command, we're going to have to be as strong as necessary to continue advancing under fire to reach the multitudes in this world who still don't know what we know about God's plan for salvation.

This then leads us to verse 12, which reminds us that down deep inside our hearts, every Christian knows this is his or her assignment from God. No matter what else may be going on in a believer's life, he or she must always remember that we will stand in judgment one day for how we did—or didn't—get involved in the great commission of Mark 16:15-20.

Notice the progression of these three verses. Verse 10 talks about the importance of being strong enough to withstand any and all attacks of the enemy—to continue advancing under fire regardless of how severe the battle rages all around us. Verse 11 then tells us why it's so important to be that strong, so that we can deliver those "drawn towards death," holding back those "stumbling to the slaughter." Delivering people from death, and holding people back from the slaughter is the one reason why we're left on Earth after rebirth. Jesus has done all that was necessary to get rid of the sin issue for all of us, and once that was done, gave us His authority to go into all the world and preach to anyone and everyone in His name. He's the head, but we're His Body, and therefore it's really up to us to obey God and make ourselves available to Him. That's why He commands us to be strong in Joshua 1:9, and in other places throughout the Bible as well. He knows what we're in store for when we commit to the fight, and He wants us strong enough to advance with bullets whizzing by, bombs exploding all around us, and shrapnel flying through the air.

And when (not if) wounded, we'll have the inner-strength to keep going forward—pressing towards the mark for the prize of the upward call of God in Christ Jesus. Millions of people are lost today, stumbling towards the slaughter, drawn towards the eternal death that awaits every sinner who dies without Jesus. We have to have what it takes to charge the battlefields of this Earth, and reach them before it's too late. We must be pressing towards them to reach them, because that's how we press towards the goal of God's upward call in Christ Jesus.

A Christian who is truly strong (not just thinking he is) will never fall backwards, but always forwards. We'll all make mistakes, commit sins, and disappoint God, that's why the first of these three things deals with moving on from failure. But after failing God in some way, the soldier who is worth something to the war effort will never quit or give up. Falling forward is still advancement. Falling backwards is not. We're never to retreat under fire, but to advance under fire.

But also for this very reason, giving all diligence, add to your faith virtue, to virtue knowledge, to knowledge self-control, to self-control perseverance, to perseverance godliness, to godliness brotherly kindness, and to brotherly kindness love. For if these things are yours and abound, you will be neither barren nor unfruitful in the knowledge of our Lord Jesus Christ. For he who lacks these things is shortsighted, even to blindness, and has forgotten that he was cleansed from his old sins. Therefore, brethren, be even more diligent to make your call and election sure, for if you do these things you will never stumble; for so an entrance will be supplied to you abundantly into the everlasting kingdom of our Lord and Savior Jesus Christ.

—2 PETER 1:5-11

According to verse 11 in this passage, there's an "abundant entrance" made available to the Christian, a triumphant way into God's everlasting kingdom in Christ Jesus. We're not just talking here about barely making it into Heaven; being a believer who never did anything of significance for God in this life. No, it's "abundant" because it's a promise of rewards, honor, and recognition one day in Heaven.

If we exercise diligence to remain strong, focused, and razor-sharp for God in this life, we're never going to become "barren nor unfruitful in the knowledge of our Lord Jesus Christ." We'll be acknowledged by God before all of Heaven, and the rewards we receive will be ours for eternity. But that kind of awards ceremony is reserved only for those who hung in there, fight after faith fight, and never quit.

Notice that the word diligence is found at the front of this passage, and at the end as well. We see it in verse 5, and again in verse 10. This passage is therefore something like a spiritual hamburger. Diligence is the top bun (verse 5), and the bottom bun (verse 10), and everything in the verses in between are the meat and condiments.

Do not rejoice over me, my enemy; when I fall, I will arise; when I sit in darkness, the LORD will be a light to me. I will bear

the indignation of the LORD, because I have sinned against Him,
until He pleads my case and executes justice for me. He will bring
me forth to the light; I will see His righteousness.

—MICAH 7:8-9

In light of our need to press towards the goal of the upward call of God, let's reexamine our passage from Micah 7:8-9. When you get knocked down in some fight of faith somewhere along life's way, don't just lay there and let the devil taunt you and condemn you. Do what Micah did. When the devil or his cohorts are laughing at you, mocking you, and saying you're defeated, fire the Word of God right back in his face! As he stands over you on the canvas in the ring, even while you're still flat on your back, tell him not to rejoice over your fall, because even though you may be wounded, you're getting up and the fight will resume. Tell him that you've taken his best shot, and it hasn't stopped you! This is a magnificent object lesson in how to counter-attack the enemy after he has seemingly dealt you a severe blow of some kind.

Read these two verses carefully. In verse 9, Micah admits he has sinned before the Lord, and bears the indignation from God that goes with it. That would be akin to admitting sin, failure, and disobedience before the Lord. But (and here is the shouting part!), God doesn't just leave us wounded and fallen like that on the battlefield. He pleads our case and executes justice for us, as He will do for any of His beloved children. He brings us back from the brink, and shows us His light once again. As a wounded soldier, He brings us into the MASH tent, forgives us, loves us, cleans us up, gets us back on our feet, and then sends us back to the front lines ready to fight on in His name! Oh Hallelujah! If this doesn't cause you to leap for joy, what could?

Among other things, Jesus is our Great High Priest in Heaven today (see Hebrews 3:1). He doesn't just sit up there at God's right hand, bored with nothing to do, waiting for the time of His return to Earth. No! He actively works with God on our behalf, and works with us on God's behalf, to enforce the New Covenant and carry out the Great Commission. That's why He is identified as the "mediator" of the New Covenant (see 1 Timothy 2:5, Hebrews 9:15, and 12:24).

In verse 8, notice the confession of faith being made in the midst of the fight. "Don't shout for joy too quickly devil, because when (not if) I fall, I *will* arise." That's a confession of faith, a decision made to keep on fighting. The Holy Spirit is telling us what to say to our enemy when it looks like he has us on the ropes, so to speak. "When (not if) I sit in darkness, the Lord *will be* a light to me." Most definitely, when we've committed sin and failed our God in the heat of the fight, we're going to feel like we're sitting in the darkness. I know I have felt this way many times over the years. *However, notice it's our confession of faith that changes the situation, not God's.*

And isn't this exactly what happened when Jesus became sin for us on the cross, died that horrible death, descended into Hell for those three days and nights, and then in the pit of Hell itself, was born-again and rose triumphant over death, Hell, and the grave? When Jesus died, He died as our sin substitute. He never committed any sin, but took upon Himself all of our sins, and was punished for it in our stead. For those three days in Hell, you can be sure the devil and all his demons were jumping for joy, thinking they had finally defeated God and forever doomed not only the Son of God, but all of humankind as well.

But what a shock and surprise on the third day, when by the power of God, Jesus became the first begotten from the dead, and by force took the keys of death away from the devil, and made an open display of him—defeated and vanquished! Hallelujah once again! Just writing about this gets me so excited I could run through a troop and leap over a wall (watch out David, I'm coming through!).

You know, the devil is subtle, sly, and deceptive in every way, but he's also quite predictable if you understand his tactics, as it tells us to be in 2 Corinthians 2:11. If you give him enough rope, he'll hang himself every time, just like he did with Jesus at Calvary. It might take some time, but hang in there. No weapon formed against you can succeed against you as long as you continue moving forward in Jesus' name (see Isaiah 54:13-17). That's why in James 1:2-4, the Bible tells us to count it all joy when (not if once again) we encounter various kinds of temptations, testings, and trials, knowing the testing of our faith works patience, which when finished, will make us perfect and complete, lacking nothing. God doesn't tell us to count it all tragedy, difficulty, adversity, and defeat, does He? No, He tells us to count it all joy! Why? Because the joy of the Lord is our strength (see Nehemiah 8:10).

That's the kind of strength that brings you through to victory, pressing on towards the goal for the prize of the upward call of God in Christ Jesus.

CHAPTER 5

Having the Mature Mindset

Therefore let us, as many as are mature, have this mind;
and if in anything you think otherwise, God will
reveal even this to you. Nevertheless, to the degree
that we have already attained, let us walk
by the same rule, let us be of the same mind.
—PHILIPPIANS 3:15-16

Continuing with our study of Paul's instructions to the Philippian church, we see powerful truths revealed in verses 15 and 16, which will help us advance under fire successfully in life and ministry for the Lord.

Notice the first word of verse 15: "therefore." In other words, if we want to be able to advance under fire for God, even with intense pressure to compromise being applied against us, we must understand the importance of maintaining the mindset outlined in verses 12 to 14. We must develop the discipline to forget the things behind, reach forward to the things ahead, and press toward the goal for the prize of the high calling of God in Christ.

Notice Paul tells the readers to "have this mind." He wants them to see the importance of developing and protecting this kind of thinking—doing the one thing with these three parts consistently. He admits he's not perfect, and we must admit we're not perfect either (I'm sure you've figured that part out by now!).

But even though we're "works-in-progress" for God's glory, we can—and should—have this mindset in order to continue to grow, progress, and advance in life for Christ.

The Litmus Test for Spiritual Maturity

If we're told to "have this mind," that means it's possible not to have this mind. You can think other ways if you want. But if you do, you'll never be able to proceed and grow in Christ, and you'll never reach a place of true spiritual maturity. Notice verse 15 again. Paul declares that if you have this mindset, you're a mature believer. He says, ". . . as many as are mature, have this mind. . . ." So this is not just a suggested set of mental guidelines for the believer to follow, but in fact, a *command* from God! God wants *all believers* to grow up and move beyond spiritual infancy and baby-hood. How can this be accomplished? Read this verse and you'll know! By being a doer of verses 12-14. By learning to be a disciplined thinker—forgetting the past, reaching forward to the future, pressing towards the goal. This is how Paul did it, and this is how we're going to do it too.

If this is the litmus test to indicate true spiritual maturity, can you see that the majority of Christians are *not spiritually mature at all?* Not even close! I've been saved since September 21, 1978, and in full-time ministry since September, 1979, and I can tell you the greater majority of people I've encountered in my many travels for Jesus aren't anywhere near this level of spiritual thinking. The vast majority of believers I've met are spiritually immature because they don't think this way, and that includes ministers and missionaries as well.

People can think of themselves as mature in Christ all they want, but if they're not thinking this way, as described in these verses from Philippians, they're not mature at all—they just think they are. That's called self-deception, according to James 1:22. You can now begin to see why so many Christians struggle in all kinds of ways in this life, and then wonder why God isn't using them the way they think He should, or answering their prayers like He promises to in the Bible. It's not God's fault, it's our fault. But also notice that God will do His best to correct us and turn this situation around.

He says this to the Philippians, ". . . and if in anything you think otherwise, God will reveal even this to you." What does that mean? It means He expects you to learn how to think like He does, and have the "mind of Christ" (see 1 Corinthians 2:16). It also means that God is ready to teach us and show us the way to spiritual maturity. In essence, God wants us to learn to think like He does, to synchronize ourselves with Him, becoming anointed and effective co-workers in Christ for the cause of Christ, which is the Great Commission. Basically, God is telling us how to "get on the same page" with Him mentally, so He can use us the way He wants, and so that we can overcome, repel, and advance despite any and all attacks thrown against us by the devil.

This is most important! God tells us here how to think to position ourselves for mighty accomplishments in His name, as we progress in this life. When we fail to forget the past, reach forward to the future, and press towards the goals God sets for us, we're choosing to remain at a lower level of thought—a mindset that prevents God from using us and protecting us the way He wants. We're not operating as a mature believers when we fail to do the one thing with those three parts. Instead, we're acting, living, and operating just like the vast majority of Christians out there, who may love the Lord dearly, but will never become "useful" to the Lord (see 2 Timothy 2:21), because they won't (not can't) rise to God's prescribed level of thinking.

So if we want to be someone God can use, and someone God can depend on in the midst of spiritual attacks against the Body of Christ, we must become people with this kind of mindset. If you don't think this way, notice Paul says that God will "reveal" this to you! That means He's going to pull you aside and let you know that until you change the way you think, you're not "on His page," and He's therefore unable to use you, anoint you, bless you, and protect you the way He promises in His Word. It's not a question of God's love for us, or our love for Him. It's a question about *usability!* God is spiritually unable to work with those who never rise to this level of spiritual thinking. This is what He's trying to get us to see here from this passage in Philippians.

Nevertheless, to the degree that we have already attained, let us walk by the same rule, let us be of the same mind.

—PHILIPPIANS 3:16

And then as a final word of instruction and reminder to the brethren, Paul tells them that to the degree that they've already attained, they are to walk by the same rule and be of the same mind. In other words, developing this kind of mature mindset is the first half of the battle—staying in this kind of mindset is the second half. Getting there is the first step, staying there is the rest of your life. It's like the slogan we've adopted in our ministry, a phrase God gave me some time back to help me lead my troops effectively into battle in the Name of Jesus. *Be Strong! Stay Strong!* We use this phrase often in our sermons, Bible studies, publications, and conversations, which reminds us of the importance of achieving the victory *and* protecting the victory once we've reached our goals and objectives according to the Word of God.

The Lord is telling us that if the mature mindset got us this far in our fights of faith, it will carry us all the way to victory—for the rest of our lives! It's like the old saying that goes like this: *What got me to the dance is going to keep me at the dance!* Once you've developed the discipline to think this way, you have to understand the rest of your life will be the mental battleground where the enemy constantly seeks a way to convince you to abandon this mature mindset. This will require as much discipline as it took to alter your immature mindset in the first place! Getting there is important, but staying there is critical to your ongoing usefulness to Jesus and the Great Commission.

Soldiers in Christ, at war and advancing under fire, must remember the importance of these three parts to this one thing. It's crucial to our spiritual well-being, and being "meet for the Master's use" in the times of spiritual conflict. According to James 4:7, when we resist the devil, he *will* flee from us, that's why we must protect this mature mentality and not allow the devil to creep back in, bit by bit, with ungodly thoughts that erode the foundation and strength of this mindset. If you can't tell he's at work against you, trying to move you away from this kind of godly thinking, you won't make it a point to resist him, and that means he'll be standing next to you instead of fleeing from you!

We must not allow the enemy to drag us back to an old, immature, and vulnerable mentality that prohibits God and empowers the devil. Spiritual vigilance is imperative if we're to obtain, then hold on to the mature mentality that God speaks of in this passage. The moment you find yourself drifting away from this mental mindset, stop and reconsolidate your defenses! Somehow the devil has come in and gained a foothold in your mind that you must recognize, attack, and get rid of. That can happen in a myriad of ways, but no matter how that foothold was successfully established, you need to be alert and able to see it, address it, and reject in Jesus' name—before spiritual damage is done to you, and to others around you.

CHAPTER 6

All Things Can
Be Overcome

*[Love] bears all things, believes all things, hopes all things,
endures all things.Love never fails.*
—1 CORINTHIANS 13:7-8

In context, these verses are part of the great love dissertation
from 1 Corinthians chapter 13, which talks about the *agape* love
of God. From verse 1 to verse 8, these are the classic verses that
show us how we should be thinking, talking, and acting if God's
love dominates our lives like it should. But in verses 7 and 8, we
see a parallel truth that has significant bearing upon the importance of learning how to advance under fire for Jesus.

Notice the phrase "all things" in verse 7. It's hard to miss
because it's there four times. Why four times? For emphasis, obviously, but what is the truth the Holy Spirit wants to emphasize here?

It's simply this: no matter how severe or intense the attacks
may be against you from the devil, his demons, the world system
he controls, or your own dead-to-sin flesh, *you can continue to move
forward in Christ.* As long as you have, and protect, that mature
mentality from Philippians 3:12-16, you can overcome any obstacle, any attack, any subtle or deceptive attempt to defeat or
destroy you. You can continue to progress spiritually, no matter

what's going on in your life in terms of spiritual attack. Under pressure, you can continue to make a significant impact for Jesus in this life on earth, because *greater is He in you than the devil who is in the world* (see 1 John 4:4).

On your worst day, you still have the ability to kick the devil from pillar to post, not because you necessarily feel like it, but because of who you are in Christ! Think about it for a moment. When the devil came to tempt Jesus (see Matthew 4:1-10 or Luke 4:1-4), it was after a 40-day fast in the desert. Please let that sink in! Not just the 40 days of fasting, but doing so in the desert (think hot, hostile, tough, challenging, difficult, unforgiving, remote, isolated—that's what a wilderness desert would be like). It's tough enough doing a fast for that length of time, much less doing it out in the wild desert. Mark's gospel says that while in the wilderness for those 40 days, he was *with the wild beasts* (see Mark 1:13).

> *Then Jesus was led up by the Spirit into the wilderness to be tempted by the devil. And when He had fasted forty days and forty nights, afterward He was hungry. Now when the tempter came to Him, he said, "If You are the Son of God, command that these stones become bread." But He answered and said, "It is written, 'Man shall not live by bread alone, but by every word that proceeds from the mouth of God.'"*
>
> —MATTHEW 4:2-4

When those 40 days of tough and difficult fasting in that hostile place were finished, Jesus *was hungry.* So, guess who shows up with a temptation centered around food? Ol' Split-Foot himself! According to Matthew's account of this incident, the first thing the devil did was try to tempt Jesus using food as his tool, since he knew Jesus was physically hungry. So it would be safe to say that at that moment, the devil thought this would be the most vulnerable area—if any type of temptation would be successful against Jesus, right?

Well, even though this was a bonafide temptation (meaning Jesus was as capable of failing this test as any one of us—or it wouldn't have been a valid test), Jesus was still able to use the

Word of God to slice and dice the devil out there in that dry, hot, hostile environment, with no support or encouragement from anyone. He was alone out there, with all of hell set against Him, and still, He was able to take that temptation and shove it right back in the devil's face!

"Yeah," someone might say, "but that was Jesus!" As though He was somehow operating on a different level than we, and therefore, better able to withstand this onslaught of the enemy. Nothing could be further from the truth!

In John 14:12-14, Jesus Himself told us the works that He did we could do also—and should do also! Not just the works He did, but greater works too! Successfully resisting temptation to sin, fail, quit, or give up on God, as we see Jesus do here, would definitely be included in the "works that He did that we can do also." If not, it would be unjust of God to judge and condemn us if our abilities to resist demonic attacks were any less than our Lord's.

The Bible says Jesus was tempted in all points as we, yet without sin (see Hebrews 4:15). *Amazing, isn't it!* For more than 33 years on Earth, Jesus never sinned, although He was tempted in every way we are. That truth alone is enough for me to fall at His feet in worship and praise—forever! What an accomplishment—for God and for us! No wonder God says He is the only one *worthy* to sit at His right hand forever.

All Things Means All Things

With divine love in control, we have the ability to bear *all things.* We can believe *all things.* We can hope and endure *all things.* So it doesn't matter what the devil throws against you—you can successfully repel the attack and still continue to advance for the glory of God!

No temptation has overtaken you except such as is common to man; but God is faithful, who will not allow you to be tempted beyond what you are able, but with the temptation will also make the way of escape, that you may be able to bear it.

—1 CORINTHIANS 10:13

There is no test, trial, or temptation too big, too overwhelming, too severe, or intense, that you can't successfully resist it! God will not allow it! In other words, the devil can't launch any attacks against us that we can't successfully resist. That means whatever you're facing today in the form of a demonic attack, you *can* successfully resist it and advance under fire!

So when God tells us that we can endure anything, stay in faith and believe for anything; continue to stay strong in hope at all times, no matter what, and endure any test or trial (or combinations thereof), He means it! All things mean all things—no exceptions! No special cases that exempt us from the standards and commands laid out in God's Word! Everybody is on an equal playing field. Anything the devil tries against us can be resisted and overthrown. Nothing is out of bounds, or beyond our abilities to resist. *The Amplified Bible's* translation of 1 Corinthians 13:7 sheds additional light on this truth.

Love bears up under anything and everything that comes, is ever ready to believe the best of every person, its hopes are fadeless under all circumstances, and it endures everything [without weakening].

—1 CORINTHIANS 13:7 AMP

Praise God! No amount of enemy fire can stop you! With bullets flying by, bombs exploding all around, shrapnel flying through the air and fellow soldiers falling all around you, you can continue to advance in the Name of Jesus! No excuses! No exceptions! No exemptions! You can do it Christian, because God said so!

CHAPTER 7

Get Back Up!

If you faint in the day of adversity, your strength is small.
Deliver those who are drawn toward death, and hold back
those stumbling to the slaughter. If you say, "Surely we
did not know this," does not He who weighs the hearts
consider it? He who keeps your soul, does He not know it?
And will He not render to each man according to his deeds?
—PROVERBS 24:10-12

These are some of my favorite verses in the Bible, especially verse 10. Too many times we have surrendered in defeat to the enemy, when if we had only exhibited perseverance and patience, we would've seen our way through to victory. The fact is, most Christians aren't nearly as strong as they think they are! I know I wasn't—for a long time.

When I first got to the Philippines in September, 1980, I was full of excitement, anticipation, enthusiasm, and zeal for the Lord. I was also much weaker in spirit than I thought I was. That became painfully apparent during the first two years of ministry, which many times entailed extended trips into the mountains and remote areas of the country.

More than once, I was so far into the mountainous interior of islands like Negros, Cebu, and Leyte, that the people I came to had never even seen a white man before. There were times when

I was so high up in the mountains that clouds would be rolling through the church while service was going on. I'd be preaching and a cloud would come in and everybody disappeared from sight! I kept on preaching in this grey mist and fog, knowing the people were still there because I could hear them saying "Amen" to my message points! (I write much more extensively about all of my many physical and spiritual trials during the early years of my ministry in my book entitled *Be Strong, Stay Strong*). The point for you today as you read this book is this: the things I'm sharing with you have been learned through experience—the hard way in many cases.

When I first started out in ministry years ago, like so many others in the Body of Christ, I labored under a false illusion of spiritual strength. When I arrived in the Philippines, young, single, fresh from Bible school and full of zeal for God, I quickly found out I was not as strong as I thought I was. As a result, I found myself scrambling spiritually just to stay alive and keep going for Jesus!

It's no coincidence that verse 10 precedes verses 11 and 12 in this passage from Proverbs. Notice that before God starts talking about our responsibilities to witness and win souls for Him, He addresses this issue of spiritual strength. Why? Because if you're not strong in spirit, you'll never be able to continue to advance under fire when the going gets tough. You'll quit and give up, because it's much easier to do that than to persevere under pressure and temptation. That's why God says that if you faint (give up and quit) in the day of adversity, your level of spiritual strength is really very small.

Those who have really built themselves up for God in terms of spiritual strength have the mindset to face, and overcome, every obstacle or hurdle the devil throws against them when they go out and try to tell people about Jesus.

In verse 12, we see the weak ones trying to offer excuses for their failure to be mighty soul-winners for the Lord. But unfortunately, there won't be any excuses that hold any water with God on judgment day! Like it says in 1 Chronicles 28:10, we're told to *be strong and do it!* In other words, get out there and make something happen for Jesus. Be a player, not a spectator or sideline critic. Quit whining and complaining and murmuring about how hard things are!

Our job is to hold back those stumbling towards the slaughter, and rescue souls from the brink of eternity in hell without Jesus. To do that, we're going to have to learn how to advance under fire, or else we'll never amount to anything of significance for the Lord in this life. That's why, in the same chapter, God goes on to offer instruction to those who have fallen, stumbled or otherwise failed God in this business of sharing their faith and leading people to the Lord.

> *For a righteous man may fall seven times and rise again, but the wicked shall fall by calamity.*
> —PROVERBS 24:16

When we purpose to advance for God under fire from the enemy, there will be times we fail God. It's happened to all of us. In fact, those who are doing the most for the Lord have probably failed God more than most along the way! The more we do or want to do, the more opportunity we're going to have to stumble and fall through sin, mistakes or the like.

We're not perfect, as I've said earlier in this book, so we're going to learn a lot through the mistakes we make. When that happens, we can sit in our bunker or foxhole, feeling sorry for ourselves and letting the devil condemn us, or we can ask the Holy Spirit for help to learn from our mistakes, and get back up to re-engage the enemy!

We may fall "seven times," but we're told to *rise again!* Thank God I learned this lesson early on in my ministry, and therefore I've been able to keep advancing under fire time and again, receiving forgiveness for sins, mistakes, broken vows, broken promises, disobedience, and all manner of failure before a holy and righteous God. As already noted, it's exactly what Micah told his enemies when he was tempted to falter as a result of his mistakes, sins, and failures. Let's take another look at how he handled this opportunity for failure:

Do not rejoice over me, my enemy; when I fall, I will arise; when I sit in darkness, the Lord will be a light to me. I will bear the indignation of the Lord, because I have sinned against Him, until He pleads my case and executes justice for me. He will bring me forth to the light; I will see His righteousness.

—MICAH 7:8-9

When the devil is trying to gloat over your latest failure in this great fight of faith for the souls of men, you can quote these verses to him, and like Jesus, shove his accusations right back in his face! We're told to tell our enemies not to rejoice over us when we fail God, or when we fall into sin. Instead, we're to remind him that God is still our Heavenly Father, and Jesus is still our Advocate and Surety in Heaven.

Are we to feel sorry for our sins and failures? Of course! That's why verse 9 tells us to bear the "indignation" of the Lord. However, we don't stay there. We acknowledge our sins (like David did in Psalms 51:3-4), ask for forgiveness and receive it by faith, not feelings. We present ourselves to Jesus, our High Priest, Advocate, and Intercessor before the Father, and let Him plead our case based upon *His righteousness, not ours.* By doing that, we can, as it says in verse 9, come forth from our darkness (failure or sin) into the light of His love, mercy, patience, and forgiveness. We come forth to see His righteousness, and rejoice for the fact that what our enemy says about our situation is irrelevant!

Notice in these two verses, the one who has failed God is the one making the statements of faith. It is the one who has sinned who declares what God will do to deliver him and bring him forth to the light. The devil isn't saying anything here—because as we read these verses we can see that he's the one being rebuked by those who have committed the sin and whom he's trying to defeat!

Soul-Winners Will Be Attacked in Many Ways

No matter how many times, or in how many ways, you're attacked by the enemy in this life, understand the importance of coming boldly to the throne of grace to find the help necessary in those times of need (see Hebrews 4:16). When you've failed God, broken some promise you've made to Him, or just yielded to the temptation to sin in some way, go to Him immediately, ask Him for mercy and forgiveness, and receive it by faith. When you've just been hit from all sides with simultaneous attacks of the devil, go to God, cast all your cares upon Him and commit yourself to the One who cares for you (see 1 Peter 5:7).

> *You will keep him in perfect peace, whose mind is stayed on You, because he trusts in You. Trust in the LORD forever, FOR IN YAH, THE LORD, IS EVERLASTING STRENGTH.*
>
> —ISAIAH 26:3-4

There are many good reasons to read God's Word every day. One important reason we should feed upon God's Word daily is because it helps us keep our minds focused upon Him, not our problems. This creates the kind of "perfect peace" that no demon or devil can penetrate. Reading the Bible helps you get back up when you've been knocked down. It enables you to continue to advance under fire.

Personally, I know how important this is. One special reason why I must read the Bible in times of spiritual attack is to remind myself that everything I'm facing in this Christian life is something every writer in the Bible faced before me. None of the men who were used by God to write the Bible had an easy life. They faced the same kinds of temptations and trials we face today, and in many cases, to a much greater degree. One of my favorite passages along this line is from the book of Acts.

> *From Miletus he sent to Ephesus and called for the elders of the church. And when they had come to him, he said to them: "You know, from the first day that I came to Asia, in what manner I always lived among you, serving the Lord with all humility, with many tears and trials which happened to me by the plotting of the Jews;* **how I kept back nothing that was helpful, but proclaimed it to you, and taught you publicly and from house to house, testifying to Jews, and also to Greeks, repentance toward God and**

*faith toward our Lord Jesus Christ. And see, now I go bound in the spirit to Jerusalem, not knowing the things that will happen to me there, **except that the Holy Spirit testifies in every city, saying that chains and tribulations await me.** But none of these things move me; nor do I count my life dear to myself, so that I may finish my race with joy, and the ministry which I received from the Lord Jesus, to testify to the gospel of the grace of God.*

—ACTS 20:17-24 [EMPHASIS MINE.]

Paul knew how to advance under fire. If you read the first, fourth, sixth, and eleventh chapters of Second Corinthians, you'll see what kinds of "enemy fire" he contended with as he served Jesus in ministry. This is what Jesus Himself said to Paul when he first got started in ministry (see Acts 9:16). Yes, the same man who said there remains a rest for the people of God (see Hebrews chapters 3 and 4) is the same man who talks about being in such dire straits he *despaired even of life* (2 Corinthians 1:8). I pray you can appreciate the ongoing struggle in Paul's life.

When reading the Pauline epistles, as well as the book of Acts, you can clearly see the struggles of a man determined to serve Jesus, confronted consistently with a devil determined to stop him and his ministry. He was the one inspired by God to write the majority of the New Testament, teaching people how to walk in love, how to walk by faith and not by sight, how to exercise dominion and authority, and much more. But he's also the one taken aside by the Lord to plainly be told he would suffer greatly for the name of Jesus. Satan himself assigned a "thorn in the flesh," an evil spirit, whose sole assignment was to harass and buffet Paul wherever he went. Therein is our challenge, my friend! Should Satan assign thorns in the flesh *to you,* are you able to keep moving forward under the kind of fire that Paul, and millions of others since him have faced?

Then Peter began to say to Him, "See, we have left all and followed You." So Jesus answered and said, "Assuredly, I say to you, there is no one who has left house or brothers or sisters or father or mother or wife or children or lands, for My sake and the gospel's, who shall not receive a hundredfold now in this time—houses and brothers and sisters and mothers and children and lands, with persecutions—and in the age to come, eternal life.

—MARK 10:28-30

So many today warp, twist, and distort the message on biblical prosperity. Using verses like these, they leave the impression upon the ill-informed that prosperity is a goal unto itself. Opulence is exalted as prosperity, while the vast majority of the world's population is dying lost without Jesus. For so many, prosperity is nothing more than greed in disguise.

Do I teach prosperity? Absolutely, but before God and in all good conscience in the sight of the Lord, I do it for the right reasons, so we can become prosperous for the right reasons. Prosperity is promised for one main reason in this life—soul-winning. It takes money to win souls, and fulfill the Great Commission, that's why God wants us to prosper. It isn't about us, its about us helping someone else find Jesus. Knowing this helps keep the whole "prosperity message" in its proper place and context.

Notice in this passage that along with the hundred-fold return, Jesus also promises persecution. How may prosperity teachers devote time in their books, CDs, seminars, and conferences to that portion of the verse? Very few.

I'd like to tell you that if you want to prosper for the right reasons—that is, to increase your ability to finance and fund the Great Commission, then get ready for the persecutions, because they're coming your way! Jesus said so. The devil will attack you in special ways if he sees financial prosperity manifesting in your life. So, if you take a hit financially in your life, don't let it frighten you or intimidate you. Get back up, get back in the game, and let the Lord continue to use you to pull resources out of the world and put them into the hands of the saints.

But you have carefully followed my doctrine, manner of life, purpose, faith, longsuffering, love, perseverance, persecutions, afflictions, which happened to me at Antioch, at Iconium, at Lystra—what persecutions I endured. And out of them all the Lord delivered me. Yes, and all who desire to live godly in Christ Jesus will suffer persecution. But evil men and impostors will grow worse and worse, deceiving and being deceived. But you must continue in the things which you have learned and been assured of, knowing from whom you have learned them, and that from childhood you have known the Holy Scriptures, which are able to make you wise for salvation through faith which is in Christ Jesus.

—2 TIMOTHY 3:10-15

Notice that along with the doctrine, lifestyle, purpose, faith, patience, and love, we're told to *carefully follow* Paul in the area of persecutions and afflictions. We're to follow in his footsteps, as he followed in the footsteps of Christ Jesus (see John 15:20 and 16:33). He told them what we all need to hear and know. *If you desire to live godly in this life for Jesus, you will suffer persecution.* In other words, you are going to get shot at, and the more you do, or want to do, for Jesus, that will be the proportionate degree of persecution that is ramped up against you. Notice in verse 14 above, Paul admonishes the brethren to *continue in the things you've learned and been assured of.*

What are we assured of in this life? Jesus will never leave us, or forsake us (see Hebrews 13:5). He is with us always, even to the end of the age (see Matthew 28:20). We're not alone in our fights of faith—ever! We have the confident assurance that no matter how intense the battles may be in our lives, all of Heaven is standing with us; ready to back us up when we boldly declare our faith, exercise our dominion, and use the name of Jesus as we're told to, as often as necessary, wherever necessary.

Help Others Get Back Up

We're not only to learn how to advance under fire for ourselves, but we're told to help others do the same. We're to exhort, comfort, encourage, and support those who are undergoing the withering fire of the enemy, and do whatever we can in the name of Jesus to help them navigate through these storms to find the safe haven of God's harbor in their lives.

In Acts 14:22, Paul bluntly told the saints that this business of advancing under enemy fire was, in fact, the "gate pass" into the bliss and eternal rewards of Heaven! *Through many tribulations* we enter the kingdom of God! It comes with the job, so just accept it, and be prepared for the attacks coming against you. Don't wilt under pressure, quit, or give up. As God told Solomon when he was given the assignment to build the sanctuary for the Lord, *be strong and do it* (see 1 Chronicles 28:10)!

Soul-winners are attacked, frequently and with intensity. If you get knocked down, get back up. And as often as you get knocked down, keep getting up! That's the way it is here on planet Earth until Jesus comes back. Understand it. Accept it. Get used to it. Learn to thrive in the midst of it.

CHAPTER 8

The Hard Is What
Makes It Great!

I have fought the good fight, I have finished the race,
I have kept the faith. Finally, there is laid up for me the
crown of righteousness, which the Lord, the righteous Judge,
will give to me on that Day, and not to me only
but also to all who have loved His appearing.
—2 TIMOTHY 4:7-8

Every so often, filmmakers in Hollywood actually make a movie that's enjoyable to watch. For me, one such movie is *A League of their Own*, which is a movie about the short-lived Women's Professional Baseball League, created during World War II. In this movie, there is a scene where the team's most talented player and her manager have a confrontation about her decision to quit and go home as the team is about to enter the playoffs. Her husband has just come home safely from war in Europe, and now (for various reasons you'd have to watch the movie to appreciate), the young couple intends to return home to Oregon and start a family, which means of course that the team will be playing without their star catcher as they enter the playoffs.

When confronted and questioned about the timing of her decision to leave the team at this critical juncture in the season, the ball player, played by Geena Davis, tells her manager, played by Tom Hanks, that the reason she's quitting now is because "it just got too hard." To which Hank's character responds: "It's supposed to be hard! If it was easy everybody would do it. *The hard is what makes it great!"*

That kind of thinking is foreign to many in the Body of Christ, especially those who live in parts of the world where Christianity is established and freedom of religion is allowed. In the western world, free world portion of the Body of Christ, what I call "hardship Christianity" is a completely foreign concept that believers fail to understand.

Ask any believer in a closed country like communist China, or any of the Muslim-controlled countries in the world, especially in the Middle East. Ask any Christian living and working for Jesus in Muslim-controlled areas of our home island in the Philippines, which is Mindanao. Or, ask any Christian who actively seeks to win the lost and see them discipled into a close walk with the Lord, no matter where they live. They'll all say the same thing. Living for Jesus is glorious and wonderful on one hand, but extremely challenging and even dangerous on the other. This is the true message of the New Testament, all of it written by men who, at the time, were literally risking their lives in service to the Master. If we're going to amount to anything of significance for Jesus in our lifetime, we must know and understand this, otherwise we'll be unable to return enemy fire, much less advance under enemy fire.

In the Philippines, our staff and Bible school staff, faculty, and students meet periodically for what we call the RBTC Circle. It's an opportunity to discuss issues, present projects, work out difficulties and keep everyone on the "same page," so to speak. In one such circle meeting recently, I addressed the complaining I had been hearing from many of the students, about their workload during that particular trimester of study. Some of the students felt like we were piling too much work on them, with many research assignments and unannounced tests and quizzes, in addition to their mandatory participation in our early-morning devotions (which start at 5:30 a.m. Tuesday through Friday weekly), mid-day prayer (30 minutes of reading scripture and praying after lunch Monday through Friday weekly), and other similar things as well.

I talked to them about doing a "gut check" in their hearts about what they were doing in our school in the first place. I began asking them questions. What did they expect when they enrolled in our Bible school? Who told them graduating from this school was going to be easy? And after graduation, who told them ministry would be easy? What did they think would happen when they graduated and went out into the world to pioneer a work for the Lord? Did they think everything would just fall into their lap, and favor and good fortune would automatically follow them wherever they went?

I reminded them that even if a Christian is never called into full-time pulpit ministry, we are *all* full-time ministers representing Jesus and all of Heaven. As such, I reminded them that we're going to be shot at—over and over again—by the enemies of our soul, and that they needed to be prepared to successfully resist and repel those attacks without growing weak, weary, or ready to quit and give up over time.

I also reminded them that serving Jesus in ministry is a privilege, the highest honor that can be bestowed upon men from God. I reminded them that we didn't choose the ministry assignments we had from God, but rather, God was the one who selected us, placed us, and positioned us (see and John 15:16 and 1 Corinthians 12:18). I reminded them that while with us in our school, part of our responsibility as faculty and staff was to make their time with us both as enjoyable *and* as challenging as possible.

I believe they were successfully challenged, inspired, and if necessary, corrected during that particular circle meeting. Time will tell, as it does for all of our graduates and field personnel.

In my classes at our Bible school, as an example, I give unannounced quizzes and tests. At the beginning of my course, on the first day, the students are told when the mid-term and final exams are, but that's all. They're told that all other tests or quizzes are given without any advance notification. I might go one or two weeks without a surprise test, but then, they might get three tests, three days in a row. They never know when.

Why do I do this? Because they need to learn what I've learned since 1980, when I left the United States with a one-way plane ticket to the Philippines and $20 in my pocket. The devil doesn't send us e-mails, text messages, tweets, Facebook posts, and other assorted social networking announcements, alerting us to the next series of coordinated attacks planned against us. So whenever I teach, I intend to make sure my students learn this now— before they leave our school. By doing that and other things along the same lines, I will do my best to teach them to be ready at all times for enemy assaults against them, because the enemy will always do his best to hide and camouflage his plans against us until the day he launches his attacks. The Holy Spirit is within us at all times, ready to show us "things to come" (see John 16:13), but that won't prevent the attacks themselves. If we suck it up, take the hit from the enemy and keep moving forward regardless, this is acceptable and pleasing to God (see 1 Peter chapters 2, 3, and 4).

I've also sent our students out for weekend outreaches with enough money to get them to their assigned places of ministry, but with no money to get back to class on Monday. I do this on purpose. Their assignment is not only to preach and teach the Word of God to the people they're sent to, but also to believe God for the money to get back on time for their 8 a.m. class Monday morning. Anyone late for class has their grade docked accordingly. I've talked with students of mine from the first Bible school where I did this after coming to the Philippines in 1980, and these many years later, they've told me that the lessons they learned through those exercises are still helping them to walk by faith and not by sight in service to our Lord and Savior.

There is a story about a group of new army recruits, who were enduring exceptional hardship at the hands of their Drill Sergeant in boot camp (basic training). For a long time, day after day, the recruits were pushed to the breaking point in terms of physical and mental endurance. Finally, one of the new recruits asked for an explanation. "Why are you so tough on us Sergeant?" asked the exhausted young soldier. "Are you angry with us? Do you hate us? Why are you so hard on us?" The Drill Sergeant snapped back at the new recruit with this answer, "Because if we're all in battle someday against a determined and ruthless enemy, and I see your dead, blown-apart carcass on the side of the road, I'll know it wasn't my fault!"

When students graduate from our Bible school, they are as prepared to advance under fire as we can make them. If they fail out there on the field of spiritual battle, it won't be our fault! It's not going to be because we failed to do our best to make them ready for success. With God's help, we'll have done everything in our power not just to teach and train them, but also to push them, challenge them, and demand excellence from them, so that they *know* that if they will not quit, God will see them through any and all tests, trials and tribulations that await them in the future.

One of the things we purposely do in our Bible school is challenge our students, training them to excel and succeed in spite of what we do to make it hard for them to do so! The platform and philosophy of our Bible school is threefold. First, our emphasis is on *challenge*. Second, we require *commitment*. Third, our goal for the students is *preparedness*. (To read the complete philosophy of our school, go to www.mkmi.org, and click on the appropriate tab.)

Seeing the Whole Picture

I understand what Jesus said about our burden being easy, and our yoke light (see Matthew 11:30). There are many statements like that in the New Testament, exhorting the believer to place all care, trust, and worry in the hands of God, and rest and relax in pure faith before Him, such as Hebrews chapters 3 and 4. I say "amen" to all of that. I believe that and preach it myself. But there is the other side to this issue, which the scriptures also talk much about, which is the issue of advancing under fire for the Lord.

If serving Jesus was easy (and remember, we're *all* full-time ministers for Jesus, even if we're never called to be an apostle, prophet, evangelist, pastor, or teacher), everybody who did it would say so, but we know that isn't the case. As I said before, ask anyone who has ever decided to make an impact for Jesus in their areas of assignment, life, or influence. Ask anyone who's been in ministry for any length of time. It isn't easy on the frontlines of world evangelism, no matter who you are or where you are. The devil is always looking for ways to distract, discourage, defeat, diminish, and destroy our ministry work. We are living in a world system invented, controlled, and dominated by the devil (see 2 Corinthians 4:4), and we're living in a flesh and blood body that is still dead-to-sin and doesn't want to obey God (see Romans chapter 7).

Add to that the wonderful opportunity to meet, minister, and fellowship with people at all levels of spiritual growth and maturity, and you can readily see how challenging it is to stay in the game—sharp, focused and determined—to cross the finish line of your life in a blaze of passion, excellence, and glory for the Lord.

It's hard advancing under fire! It's not easy. If it were easy, everybody would be able to do it. But the reason they don't is because it's not easy, it's hard—very hard! But then again, that's why the Word of God is so full of promises of reward for those who overcome! The hard part is what makes our life in Christ great! God doesn't promise rewards to those who haven't overcome anything—He promises rewards to those who *have*. In addition, the more they've overcome, the greater their rewards will be.

Read about those seven churches in Revelation chapters 1 and 2, and see that at the end of every admonishment from Jesus, there is a reward promised for the overcomers. Overcoming is not easy, because it entails a fight of some kind—encountering spiritual resistance to what we're trying to do for the Lord. An overcomer, therefore, is one who has been shot at in many ways, many times, and has still prevailed for the Lord. They've not quit, given in, or given up. They've stayed the course, and like Paul, fought the good fight of faith all the way to the finish line of their lives. That's what makes them special, and that's why they'll get the rewards someday in Heaven.

Living for Jesus Is Special

Being called by God to represent Him in this earth as His son or daughter is special, and being called into full-time ministry is even more special. If I was offered the job of President of the United States, I would turn it down in an instant, because I know my job for God is far more special, precious, important, and significant in the eternal scope of things. But with the special status of being a child of God—a Christian serving Jesus and fulfilling the Great Commission, comes the difficulties, challenges, and obstacles that make it hard. It's just the way things are.

When resistance is encountered, there are some things we can, and should, change in this world with our faith. But other things are the way they are until Jesus comes back, and nothing you do can change it. Your faith, as strong as it might be, can't remove or eliminate the testings, trials, and obstacles that Satan, his world system, or our dead-to-sin flesh brings against us. The difficulties, challenges, and obstacles of being a righteous person in an unrighteous world are things that will never change until Jesus returns and sets up His millennial reign. So until He does, we need to understand these truths and live accordingly.

No, I'm not suggesting we just sit back and let the devil pummel us from pillar to post anytime he wants. No, I'm not inferring we should just let ourselves become spiritual doormats for the devil, the world, or other ungodly people to walk all over. We have dominion, we have authority, we have weapons for spiritual warfare, and we've been told to go into all the world and take territory and personnel for Jesus. We're commanded to be proactive, not reactive. We're commanded to be *more than conquerors* (see Romans 8:37). We're told that *greater is He in us than the devil in the world* (see 1 John 4:4).

> *And for me, that utterance may be given to me, that I may open my mouth boldly to make known the mystery of the gospel, for which I am an ambassador in chains; that in it I may speak boldly, as I ought to speak.*
>
> —Ephesians 6:19-20

We're told, in many places throughout the New Testament, to go forth and attack the strongholds of the enemy worldwide. We're not to be passive, tentative, weak, or indecisive. We're to be bold witnesses for Jesus, glorifying God, bringing people to Jesus and tormenting the devil simultaneously.

But never forget the challenges that go with the assignment! Never forget the importance of knowing how to advance under fire. Never forget the awesome responsibility we've been given to represent the Lord Jesus Christ on this Earth in our lifetime. Never forget how precious and special His calling is. And because of all of that, never forget that we will be repeatedly attacked from every conceivable angle, over and over again, throughout the course of our lifetime on Earth. That's why it's the hard stuff that makes our life great in Jesus! It's what's makes us special, and worthy of the kinds of eternal rewards waiting for us in Heaven someday soon.

CHAPTER 9

Fellowshipping with Jesus

*Yet indeed I also count all things loss for the excellence of
the knowledge of Christ Jesus my Lord, for whom I have
suffered the loss of all things, and count them as rubbish,
that I may gain Christ and be found in Him, not having
my own righteousness, which is from the law, but that which
is through faith in Christ, the righteousness which is from
God by faith; that I may know Him and the power of
His resurrection, and the fellowship of His sufferings,
being conformed to His death, if, by any means,
I may attain to the resurrection from the dead.*
—PHILIPPIANS 3:8-11

I would like to point out the four basic goals Paul established for himself in ministry. They are found in verse 10 of the passage quoted above. First, he had the desire to know God. Second, he wanted to know the power of our Lord's resurrection. Third, he wanted to know the "fellowship" of our Lord's sufferings, and fourth, he had the desire to be conformed to His death. These four things represent the heartfelt desires of Paul in life and ministry. These are the things he was using his faith for, above all else. And if we're going to learn how to effectively advance under fire, these should be the things we use our faith for as well. The list isn't long, but it is profound.

1. To know God.
2. To know the power of our Lord's resurrection.
3. To know the fellowship of our Lord's sufferings.
4. To be conformed to His death.

Are these the desires of your heart? Are these four things at the top of your things-to-believe-God-for list? For most Christians, the answer would be no. Yet, if you're going to develop the kind of strength needed to advance under enemy fire, these four desires need to take priority in your life when you're using faith to obtain things from God.

We could talk about all four of these desires at length, but for the purposes of this book, I'm only going to highlight desire number 3: *knowing and fellowshipping with the Lord's sufferings.*

When most people think about "fellowshipping with Jesus," they're thinking about a back and forth exchange with the Lord in times of prayer. That's a part of what it means to fellowship with the Lord, but Paul reveals a deeper dimension of what true fellowship with Jesus would entail. It's coming to a place in your heart and life where it's not enough just to talk with Jesus—as wonderful as that is. To want this kind of "fellowship" with Jesus means, according to the context of Paul's statements to the Philippian brethren, you actually have a desire to experience the kinds of suffering Jesus experienced on Earth while He was here.

Now of course, this doesn't refer to our Lord's substitutionary work on the cross, being made sin for us, and taking upon Himself the sin, and sins, of the world as the Lamb of God. That suffering was something He did *for* us because we couldn't do it ourselves. But in writing to the church at Philippi, Paul expressed a heartfelt desire to fellowship with the sufferings our Lord endured as the last Old Testament prophet, sent to fulfill the Mosaic Law, delivering life-changing messages that pointed to Him as *the way, the truth, and the life* (see John 14:6), as well as the confrontational, scathing indictments against the religious hypocrites of His day (see Matthew chapters 23 through 25 as examples of this).

Simply put in context, the suffering Paul speaks of here refers to religious persecution—whatever the devil tried in his attempts to stop Jesus from fulfilling God's plan and purpose. These are also the tactics the devil will try against us, which we'll get into in more detail in part 2 of this book. To "know the fellowship of our Lord's sufferings" is to experience persecution as Jesus did, right up to and including the levels of physical pain and anguish He endured on the cross. But again let me emphasize for clarity's sake—we're not talking about the substitutionary work of Christ on the cross. That work was a work that only He could do, and having paid the price for our sins, He will never have to go through that again (see Hebrews 2:9—once for all he tasted death for every man). He was made to be sin *for us,* so that we could become the righteousness of God in Christ (see 2 Corinthians 5:17). Paul is not talking about that kind of suffering here. That was a kind of suffering you and I will never have to go through because only the spotless Lamb of God could do what Jesus did, thank God!

But on the other hand, Jesus was attacked and persecuted in all sorts of ways, from the time He started His ministry until the time he breathed His last on that cross. The kind of suffering being referred to here is the persecution and challenges that Jesus faced every day.

Oftentimes, people don't think about this aspect of our Lord's ministry. They focus on the miracles, the sermons and the parables, but fail to realize that all of that was taking place in an atmosphere charged with persecution and resistance at every turn. Nothing came easy for Him, because Satan knew who He was and what He was here to do. As a result, things didn't always go smoothly for the Lord on a day-to-day basis. He always came through each attack victoriously, but it was a fight of faith, just like it is for you and me. That kind of suffering we *will* experience—guaranteed! Anyone wishing to live godly in Christ Jesus *will be persecuted* (see 2 Timothy 3:12).

Jesus Himself said it very plainly. The servant is not above his master. He was persecuted in His life and ministry on earth, and as His followers, we will be too (see John 15:20). All through the

Bible, we see the people of God being persecuted for their faith, and around the world today, millions of believers are being attacked and persecuted at every turn. Christians living in countries like the United States of America sometimes lose sight of that truth, and that's why so many are spiritual weaklings, disqualified for any meaningful ministry on Earth.

You Will Get What You Ask For!

If you ask the rank-and-file believer for a list of things they believe God for, how many would answer like Paul, in Philippians 3:10? How many would tell you that above all else, they're standing in faith to know God, *and* to know the power of His resurrection, *and* to know the fellowship of our Lord's sufferings, *and* to be made conformed to His death? *Not very many!* Why? Because it requires a level of commitment and sacrifice that they're just not willing to make. It's just too hard. And yet, this is the place we can come to if we really want to learn how to master our ability to advance under fire.

A mature believer who wishes to develop a greater ability to advance under fire will understand the value and importance of *wanting* to know and fellowship with the sufferings of our Savior. That's right, I said "wanting" to. Not just enduring it or going through it with the right attitude, but more than that. The mature Christian soldier actually comes to a place in life where they desire to experience the same kinds of persecution that Jesus experienced! Be careful my friend! If you ask for this, and stand in faith for this, you're going to get it.

Are you there yet? Most Christians are not, because most are just not that dedicated to the war effort. Many believers try to avoid persecution at all costs just because it's extremely unpleasant. Others, who are more mature, understand the fact that the sufferings of Jesus just come with the territory, so to speak. They don't want it, but understand it will come because of who they represent, and where they're doing their work for God. Therefore, they work at developing the ability to go through persecution and suffering in faith and patience—advancing under fire as we all must do.

But finally, we have this group of believers that Paul was a part of here, which is a very small group indeed. These are what I consider to be the most battle-tested and battle-ready soldiers in the army of the Lord. They are the elite. They are the ones who are going to get the highest rewards in Heaven—the rewards the rest of the Body of Christ loves to sing about, talk about and dream about!

Anyone who wants to serve Jesus *will* be persecuted. That's a fact of life. We're righteous people living in an unrighteous world, so we're going to be shot at. But can we actually come to this place of focus and maturity in our prayer closets? Can we actually stand in faith for God to grant us our request—which is to know and fellowship with our Lord's sufferings? Paul did it, and many others throughout Christian history have done it too, especially those living in closed countries where being Christian is a crime worthy of all sorts of persecution and suffering, including martyrdom.

Obviously, this is not easy to do. Coming to this place in your heart and life requires the kind of "gut check" very few of us are willing to make. Nevertheless, God has put it out there as a goal that can be reached, so we can get there with the help of the Holy Spirit if we really want to. And as we have already found out, the "hard" is what makes it great, and makes it special. Make no mistake about it: standing in faith for fellowship with our Lord's sufferings *will* bring you to a place of "outreach intensity" reserved only for the few willing to pay its price. But it's in that place that you can truly become valuable and useable in ways that others cannot (see 2 Timothy 2:21).

Take a long look at verses like these, and note the segments I've emphasized. They speak for themselves.

*Beloved, **do not think it strange** concerning the fiery trial which is to try you, as though some strange thing happened to you; but **rejoice to the extent that you partake of Christ's sufferings**, that when His glory is revealed, you may also be glad with exceeding joy. **If you are reproached for the name of Christ, blessed are*** *you, for the Spirit of glory and of God rests upon you. On their part He is blasphemed, but on your part He is glorified. But let none of you suffer as a murderer, a thief, an evildoer, or as a busybody in other people's matters.* **Yet if anyone suffers as a Christian, let him not be ashamed, but let him glorify God in this matter.**

—1 PETER 4:12-16 [EMPHASIS MINE]

That exhortation was from Peter. Now take a look at one from Paul, quoted from several different translations.

Only let your conduct be worthy of the gospel of Christ, so that whether I come and see you or am absent, I may hear of your affairs, that you stand fast in one spirit, with one mind striving together for the faith of the gospel, and not in any way terrified by your adversaries, which is to them a proof of perdition, but to you of salvation, and that from God. **For to you it has been granted on behalf of Christ, not only to believe in Him, but also to suffer for His sake,** *having the same conflict which you saw in me and now hear is in me.*

—PHILIPPIANS 1:27-30 [EMPHASIS MINE]

For you have been given not only the privilege of trusting in Christ but also **the privilege of suffering for him.** *We are in this fight together. You have seen me suffer for him in the past, and you know that I am still in the midst of this great struggle.*

—PHILIPPIANS 1:29-30 NLT [EMPHASIS MINE]

*For he has graciously granted you the privilege not only of believing in Christ, but of suffering for him as well—***since you are having the same struggle that you saw I had and now hear that I still have.**

—PHILIPPIANS 1:29-30 NRSV [EMPHASIS MINE]

Finally, note what Jesus told Ananias about Paul, before he even got started!

But the Lord said to him, "Go, for he is a chosen vessel of Mine to bear My name before Gentiles, kings, and the children of Israel. For I will show him how many things he must suffer for My name's sake."

—ACTS 9:15-16 [EMPHASIS MINE]

Right at the beginning, before Paul ever delivered one sermon or brought one person to Jesus, the Lord showed him how many things he *must* suffer for the name of Jesus. Jesus didn't say he *might* have to suffer for the name of Jesus, He said he *must*. Why? Because there is something about suffering that sharpens our sword like nothing else can!

Peter, himself a man who knew what it meant to suffer intensely for the gospel of Jesus Christ, says that the person who suffers in the flesh has ceased from sin (see 1 Peter 4:1). Why? Because when you're suffering for Jesus and the message of the gospel, the lust and powerful allure of the flesh isn't nearly as appealing as when things are all just the way our flesh wants them to be. Just take a trip and visit with brethren in closed countries who worship Jesus secretly because of intense persecution. Take a look at their lives and you won't find much fluff—shallow, superficial attitudes or petty offenses. You also won't find people struggling with the lusts of the flesh like you do in free-world societies and cultures. These people understand the meaning of "fellowshipping with His suffering." They understand it, embrace it, and accept it – and have swords far sharper than most of us in other parts of the world.

Paul was told he *must* suffer greatly for Jesus—and from Philippians 3:10, we see he accepted the challenge with all his heart. It was one of the four basic drives of his life in ministry—to fellowship with our Lord's sufferings. He didn't try to find ways to avoid it, or work around it, or rebuke it and make it go away. No! He *embraced* the challenge, and in fact, made it one of the pillars of his life of faith, believing for it, and using his faith to experience it!

You won't find many Christians today in countries like the USA who understand this, and fewer who stand in faith for it! That's why, in many respects, the Body of Christ in the USA (and other countries where freedom to believe has long since been established) is a sick, anemic, weak, and emaciated spiritual organism—unfit for front-line duty in the army of the Lord, and totally unable to advance under fire in the name of Jesus.

The Holy Spirit Will Lead You Where He Led Jesus

Why did the Holy Spirit lead Jesus out into the wilderness to be tempted by the devil just before the start of His earthly ministry? Have you ever thought about that? I have—many times.

> *Then Jesus was led up by the Spirit into the wilderness to be tempted by the devil.*
>
> —MATTHEW 4:1

I want you to really meditate on this passage with me for a few minutes. This account is also recorded in Mark 1:12, and Luke 4:1. Right at the beginning of our Lord's public ministry, He was led into the wilderness by the Holy Spirit, to be tempted by the devil. Why? *To be tempted by the devil.* Give it a minute! Let that sink in!

Many times people love to point fingers at those who fall into sin or make mistakes in life, judging them and saying the testing, attacks, trials, and difficulties came their way because of sin in their lives, or because they made a wrong turn somewhere and "got off" into error. While that is certainly the case in some instances, it isn't here.

The Holy Spirit was the One doing the leading. Did the Holy Spirit get His directions mixed up? Was He intending to lead Jesus elsewhere, but accidentally led Him into the wilderness? No, of course not! The Holy Spirit knew exactly where He was and what He was doing when He led Jesus into the wilderness to be tempted by the enemy. And how about Jesus? Did he commit some sin or violate some command from God, and ended up under attack from the enemy as a result out in the wilderness? No, of course not! Jesus knew no sin and made no mistakes—ever. So we see the perfect third Person of the Trinity leading the sinless second Person of the Trinity out into the wilderness, for the express purpose of being tempted and tried by the devil.

Let me just say, that doesn't line up with a lot of our modern-day theology, especially in full-gospel and charismatic circles. But if you're going to know how to advance under fire in this life for Jesus, you *must* understand what God was doing with Jesus by having the Holy Spirit lead Him out into the wilderness as He did.

Also take note of where Jesus was being led for this temptation of the enemy. *The wilderness.* That's symbolic—it speaks of the difficult places we encounter in life. They are places no one likes, no one wants, and everybody tries to avoid. In the natural, the wilderness was not some oasis or paradise full of pleasure, comfort, and ease. The wilderness was a hard, hostile, unforgiving place that could kill you in a heartbeat. Nobody ventured out into the wilderness. Out there it was hard, difficult, and challenging. Spiritually, the wilderness represents all those obstacles, unexpected hurdles, difficulties, challenges, and heartaches that come against us from the enemy in many forms and fashions.

Would you like to know why the Holy Spirit led Jesus into the wilderness to be tempted by the devil? Like it or not, here it is. *Nothing toughens you up like being put out into the toughest of environments, to be attacked by the toughest foe you will ever face.*

God knows what Jesus knew, and what you and I need to know. Nothing else strengthens us faster, or maximizes our potential better, than being led to a place of conflict in difficult circumstances against the arch-enemy of God and us. And furthermore, nothing else will prepare you to successfully hold your ground and *advance under the withering fire of persecution that has yet to sweep over this earth in the not-to-distant future.* If you think things are hard and difficult now, just wait around and see how bad things are going to get!

That's why Jesus told Ananias that He would show Paul all the things he *must* suffer, because of what Paul was being assigned to do for the rest of his life. Paul got the message, and lived in the light of it for the rest of his life. If you read the book of 2 Corinthians, pay special attention to chapters 1, 4, 6, and 11. In those chapters, more than anywhere else, Paul lists the many sufferings and hardships he encountered in life after entering full-time ministry for the name of Jesus. And as you read those four chapters, ask yourself how prepared you would be, if you were called upon to suffer like he suffered for the name of Jesus.

It's interesting to note that *after* this wilderness test, Jesus entered into full-time ministry *in the power of the Holy Spirit,* with a miracle anointing so strong that multitudes were being drawn to Him just to see the healed and meet the miraculous, if for no other reason (see Matthew 4:25, Luke 5:15, and many more)! This kind of anointing did not rest on Jesus until *after* He had been proven under the toughest of circumstances out in the toughest of environments. The same thing happened to Paul, and to many others in the church over the centuries, who through hardship, suffering, persecution, and difficulty, rose to unprecedented heights of power, anointing, and "usability" for Jesus on the front lines of world evangelism! Paul taught this lesson to his spiritual sons and daughters as well!

> *You therefore* **must endure hardship** *as a good soldier of Jesus Christ.*
> —2 TIMOTHY 2:3 [EMPHASIS MINE]

Paul told Timothy, his beloved son in the faith, that he *must* endure hardship if he were to be a worthy, dependable soldier in the army of the Lord. Must endure hardship! Not maybe, or possibly, but *must*! There is just a note of urgency and importance to that statement. By using the word "must," Paul is telling Timothy that there is no other option here—no other way. He must do this. There is no choice, and it's important to do this. He *must* know how to endure hardship.

We Live in A Fallen World Cursed by Sin

If you've heard me preach over the years, you've heard me say this many times, and in this book, you'll see me state this truth repeatedly for emphasis. We are born into a world cursed with the curse of sin, and therefore, we're living in a world where bad things happen to good people. And more specifically, bad things happen to good *Christian* people! It's a fact of life no one can deny. Yes, we have authority over the devil, and we are told to exercise it consistently. I do, and I hope you do too. Yes, through faith we can obtain all of those exceedingly great and precious promises we find throughout the Bible, from the front to the back. I'm doing my best to walk by faith and not by sight, and I hope you are too. Yes, we have been promised an abundant, victorious life in Christ. I believe that and I hope you do too.

However, there is a balance to all of that. There is the other side that very few of our charismatic circles want to talk about, or to understand. It deals with what Paul had a desire to do—to fellowship with our Lord's sufferings.

Like it or not, we're going to experience hardship and difficulty in life. Why? First of all, because the world we're born into is a world cursed with sin, and a world at war. Secondly, because we're commanded to go into that cursed world at war and preach a righteous message to unrighteous people. We see imperfection, disabilities, and physical handicaps all around, and we see death, suffering, and human tragedy everywhere. In the midst of all of this, we're commanded to shine the light upon people who have been living in the darkness all their lives—and many of them aren't going to like it (see John 3:19)!

A World of Suffering

This is why we *must* be able to suffer hardship and advance under fire with the right frame of mind! God needs us to hang in there and fight our way through this life without getting offended and allowing the devil to deceive us by blaming all our woes and sufferings on God.

One important fact to remember—there was no suffering of any kind on the recreated and replenished Earth described in

Genesis, *until* Adam sinned and opened the door for the devil. And, when the devil is thrown into the bottomless pit at the beginning of our Lord's 1,000 year millennial reign, all the suffering that was instituted after man's fall goes away also, *until* he is released for a short season one last time before being banished to the lake of fire for all eternity. And when that has taken place, God says there will be no more pain, sorrow, tears, or suffering—what He calls the "former things" (see Revelation chapters 20 and 21). So, what does that tell us about who is responsible for all the pain, sorrow and suffering in the world today?

Once in the Philippines, one of our churches experienced untold suffering and tragedy. Just a few days before Christmas, several days of intense rain produced a flash flood that roared through many towns and villages in the city of Iligan in the middle of the night, destroying thousands of homes and killing hundreds of men, women, and children. We have churches in that city, and many of our church members lost everything in one night. When we sent relief teams to assist and aid the victims as best we could, one of our brethren testified that he lost *all four* of his children in the great flood. Try to imagine going to sleep as normal one night, with your loved ones by your side or in the next room, and wake up to a torrential river of mud and water that has literally taken all your family away! This man's children were never found—they were killed in a very cruel and difficult-to-comprehend tragedy.

Stories like this are repeated by the thousands all over the world every week, month and year. Perhaps you yourself have experienced similar tragedies and unexpected opportunities to become bitter at God! I hope for your sake you held it together and kept moving forward under fire for Jesus.

In my own family, I was the second of five children my mother gave birth to. However, for all practical purposes, all my life I grew up in our home as the oldest sibling because my older brother was born with severe mental disabilities. He was seven years older than I, and so when he was committed to a state hospital in Columbus, Ohio, at the age of ten, I was only three years old. So as I grew up, every month or two my parents would travel down to Columbus from Cleveland to visit my older brother John (we never called him John—he always preferred we call him Jack). Honestly, as a kid growing up, even though he was my older brother, I hated going on those trips! Not so much because I didn't want to see him, but because of all the other horrible things I saw at the place where he was being cared for.

Back in the 1950s and 1960s, there wasn't the vast array of social programs and facilities available to help such handicapped people as there are today. Back then, if you were like my brother, Jack, they pretty much just put you in a room with lots of others like you (or worse), and forgot about you. This is how my brother lived for many years, and this is why I hated going to see him so much. From the age of eight, I remember going on these visits with my parents to get my brother and take him out of the state "hospital" in Columbus for a few hours. We'd check him out of the facility and go somewhere to have lunch with him, spend a couple of hours together, bring him back, and then go back home to Cleveland. It was a full day's trip—we'd leave home on Saturday morning after an early breakfast, see Jack, and be back home late that same night.

In that state facility, I can remember seeing things that were so horrible it would be hard to try to describe with words. Most of us never see the kinds of deformities that some people are born with, but I saw them firsthand because of where I went to visit my brother. First of all there was the smell of the place. This was a big campus with many buildings, all of them old and filled to the brim with severely handicapped and/or deformed people. Some were babies, some were adults, but all were totally unable to function on their own. The smell of the place was so offensive to me that these many years later, I can still smell the place in my mind. It was horrible.

Then there were the physical and mental deformities. Dear God—it's hard to imagine people being born with such handicaps, but this is what happens in a fallen world cursed by sin. I will never forget one particular person I saw on one of our visits to see Jack. I forget the exact reason for why we were where we were, but I remember being in a large room with many metal beds with bars on the sides. It looked like a room full of cribs where you would put little babies, except these beds were large enough to handle full-grown adults.

The room wasn't big enough to contain all the beds, so they had placed beds along the corridor where we were to pass. With my parents, I walked past bed after bed where inside, I saw the most shocking deformities. Words can't describe them—they were so unbelievable to see! I stopped at the side of one such bed, just staring at what I saw in fear and unbelief. In the bed was the head of a full grown man attached to the body of a little infant baby, and the body didn't have any arms at all, just "flappers" that protruded out from the tops of his shoulders. I can see him in my mind to this day, decades later. I couldn't move I was so afraid. He kept flapping his "hands" back and forth, all the while staring at me with deep, piercing eyes. I don't remember how old I was— somewhere around nine or ten—but I'll never forget him as long as I live. That image is forever etched into my mind.

And you know what? A mom and dad somewhere gave birth to every one of those poor souls in that room, and in countless rooms like that worldwide since the beginning of time. I've often tried to imagine what it must be like for parents who have to face that kind of heartbreak for their child. What an opportunity to get bitter and angry at God! And yet, we see this sort of thing all the time, don't we?

We see children born with severe mental impairment or physical disabilities—or both. Parents give birth to children who will never be normal, and who will require special care and treatment until the day they die. Through no fault of their own, others are born into war-torn countries that have produced epic levels of death and suffering from fighting, famine, or genocide. Then there are the natural disasters that kill or injure multitudes— victims of circumstances beyond their control, just by being in the wrong place at the wrong time as hurricanes, typhoons, floods, tsunamis, earthquakes, volcanic eruptions, and the like bring death and destruction to their doorstep. And let's not overlook the many good people who are victimized and punished for things they've never done (just ask Joseph about that in Genesis chapters 39 and 40). And finally, never forget the fact that many who experience things like these are born-again, God-loving, and God-fearing people!

Discover Your Potential

Being born into the greatest free country in the history of the human race is not just a blessing, but a responsibility to help others as well. Not everyone is as fortunate as we are in this world, and for some reason, there are many who can't seem to understand that. That's why I believe this message must be proclaimed and understood now more than ever. More than anyone else, it's the job of the Christian to learn how to suffer hardship wherever and whenever, and through the midst of it all, to keep telling the lost about Jesus.

We'll be shot at my friend—in many forms and in many ways. Not just after we get saved and start our work for Jesus, but beforehand as well, as people born into a world that's twisted and racked with the curse of sin. Some of us will even die for our faith in these last days, like how they died for their faith in generations gone by. I have been told that there were more people martyred for their faith in Christ during the 20th century than in all the previous nineteen centuries combined! I, for one, believe the truth of that statistic—it comes with the territory. But remember the truth revealed in how Jesus was led by the Spirit into the wilderness to be tested by Satan? Nothing else sharpens your sword, or prepares you for enemy attack like being attacked in the wilderness by the enemy.

Why did the Holy Spirit lead Jesus out into the wilderness like that? So that Jesus would discover what God wants all of us to know. That on our worst day, in the most trying of circumstances, we can still whip the devil up one side and down the other! On our worst day, we can still slap and torment the devil at every turn. Jesus was in the wilderness for 40 days fasting. That wasn't easy! (Many of us can't handle a 40-minute fast, let along a 40-day fast). And what did the devil tempt the Lord with first, at the end of those 40 days? Food! He tempted Jesus to turn rocks into bread to satisfy His hunger. That sounds just like the devil, doesn't it? Waiting until we're seemingly at our weakest point, then coming in with a strong temptation to hopefully stir up very particular areas of the flesh. But what did Jesus find out? The same thing you and I need to find out. *Greater is He in us than he that is in the world* (see 1 John 4:4)!

The Bible says that Jesus grew in wisdom, knowledge, and understanding, just like anyone else (see Luke 2:52). Jesus spent the first 30 years of His life studying the scriptures in preparation for those final three-and-a-half years of public ministry leading up to His horrific experience of becoming our sin substitute and dying in our place. Yet, before He launched out as the last prophet of the Old Testament, He needed to learn this one last, vital truth before He struck out into public ministry in enemy territory. He needed to know how strong He really was! He needed to learn that on His worst day, the devil was still no match for Him! That's why God purposely led His Son into the wilderness by the Holy Spirit so He could be tempted and tested by the enemy. *And that's why the Holy Spirit will do the very same thing with you and me from time to time throughout our life in Christ, as the situation warrants it!*

What are we talking about as the subject title for this book? *Advancing under Fire!* Not retreating under fire, or surrendering under fire, or being killed or severely wounded under fire! No! To *advance* under fire! To take the devil's best shot, and keep going forward! To take the devil's best punch, but get back up and keep punching back! Even if wounded, we keep moving forward. No retreat, no surrender, and no quitting allowed. If that's you, then don't run from adversity—embrace it! Be like Paul, and actually use your faith to experience the kinds of attacks that made Jesus, and Paul, and Peter, and John, and all the other great men and women of God great!

We Are the Violent!

And from the days of John the Baptist until now
the kingdom of heaven suffers violence,
and the violent take it by force.
—MATTHEW 11:12

Developing and protecting a "violent" spiritual attitude is one key element every Christian must understand when talking about the ability to advance under enemy fire. This is the kind of mindset that God likes, and looks for in all of us. And no matter what type of "temperament" you may have, this is something that the Lord has "hard-wired" into each and every human being. Someone might say, "Well, I'm not that type of person," and that may be true on the surface, *but deep down you have this ability because you're made in the image and likeness of God* (see Genesis 1:26-28). If God possesses this mindset, you possess it too! You just have to let the Holy Spirit teach you how and when to tap into it to use it when encountering enemy resistance.

Of course, I'm not talking about being violent in an unscriptural way towards people around us. Never! We're not talking about being purposely rude, or intentionally abrasive with our fellow brothers and sisters, or with the populace in general. We're certainly not talking about any level of physical mistreatment either. What this verse addresses is the inevitable confrontations we have with our *spiritual* enemy—Satan. Let me break down this statement for you, and show you what Jesus meant by what He said here.

This Is A Violent War We Wage

The first thing to take note of here is that God's kingdom (of which all believers are a part) suffers violence. That Greek word used for the English word "violence" is a word that has an interesting definition. Reflexively, it refers to a personal decision to press into something, forcibly if necessary. Like people pushing and shoving to get into a subway train during rush hour—many people forcing and crowding their way into a very small space. Jesus made mention of this kind of mindset in another exchange He had with His disciples and those who followed Him.

> *"The law and the prophets were until John. Since that time the kingdom of God has been preached, and everyone is pressing into it."*

> —LUKE 16:16

The word Jesus used for the English word "pressing" in Luke 16:16 is the same Greek word He used in Matthew 11:12, when he spoke of entering the kingdom of Heaven with "violence." Here is how *Vine's Expository* defines that word:

> PRESS (VERB) *3. biazo (NT:971), in the middle voice, "to press violently" or "force one's way into," is translated "presseth" in Luke 16:16, KJV, RV, "entereth violently," a meaning confirmed by the papyri. Moulton and Milligan also quote a passage from D. S. Sharp's Epictetus and the NT, speaking of "those who (try to) force their way in"; the verb suggests forceful endeavor.*

To summarize, in Matthew 11:12, Jesus is saying that if you want to enter into the kingdom of Heaven (i.e. get saved), the devil is going to try and stop you. He's not just going to let you waltz your way into God's kingdom without putting up a fight. Colossians 1:13 tells us that when we accepted Jesus as Lord and Savior, God transferred us out of the kingdom of darkness, and into the kingdom of His Son, Jesus. The devil is going to try and prevent that transfer with as much violence as he thinks necessary. If that fails and you get saved anyway, from the time of your new birth experience, you can expect the devil to look for any and all ways possible to slow you down or stop you from advancing altogether.

Therefore, you're going to have to force your way into any blessing offered to you from God in His Word! Sometimes things go smoothly when we appropriate God's blessings in our lives, but more often than not, it will be a spiritually violent encounter! When that happens, you will have to do what Jude talks about, which is to *earnestly contend for the faith* (see Jude 3). The enemy will fight you tooth and toenail, so to speak, and make it as hard as he can on you in every area of life. Of course, the devil can't stop anyone from making the decision to receive Jesus as Lord and Savior, and he can't stop any Christian from using faith to appropriate the promises and blessings of God. Our free will is the ultimate weapon Satan has no answer for. But, he can (and he will) put intense and violent pressure to bear against you, in the hopes of forcing you to make the choices that cut God off and which continue to empower him at the same time. *This is what it means when Jesus says His kingdom suffers violence.*

The World Is A Painful Place

This is also why there is so much suffering, pain, violence, and heartache in the world today. We live on a violent planet, where the "god of this world" is a twisted, perverse, and evil adversary, engaged against us in a violent struggle for the eternal souls of men.

It's so sad to see ignorant people running around saying over and over again: "…if God is love, why is there so much hate, death, and suffering in the world?" Or: "Why are deformed babies born?" On and on with questions like: "If God is love, why are people afflicted with incurable diseases, and why do bad things happen to good people?" To be sure, sometimes people have a sincere and searching heart when asking such questions, and are genuinely looking for answers to satisfy their inner confusion. But on the other hand, there are those out there who are looking for any excuse possible to avoid surrendering their hearts to the Lord.

Unbelievers who choose not to serve God love to bring these things up, whenever they try to justify themselves and suppress the truth about who Jesus is and why He came. But the Bible says that in the heart of *every* man, God has stamped an awareness of the truth, and therefore, to deny the truth and embrace a lie (which runs the gamut from false religions on one side, to atheism on the other) is to purposely ignore what their spirit already knows (see 1 John 2:21). That's why no one will have a plausible excuse for rejecting Jesus on the day of the Great White Throne judgment (see Revelation 20:11). Whether the unbeliever was a sincere seeker of truth, or just a person unwilling to give their heart in submission to Jesus, all those who die without being born-again will suffer the same fate in the end—eternal separation from God in the lake of fire (see Revelation 20:11-15).

For us as representatives of Heaven and defenders of the truth, the answer for all of these alibis and excuses is simple. God gave man dominion *and* free will (see Genesis 1:26-28), and man (Adam) chose to give that dominion over to the devil—thus legally empowering Satan to go berserk upon Earth, and bring as much misery and suffering to bear against us as he can. And even though Jesus purchased back Adam's authority when He rose from the dead (having the keys to hell, death, and the grave demonstrates that—see Revelation 1:18), the devil still has the right to operate on Earth because Adam's "lease" was for a duration of 7,000 years, and we're a long way from the termination of that lease. (End-time teachers tell us we're about at the 6,000-year mark of Adam's original lease—the one he signed over to the devil through his sin of treason in the garden of Eden). That's why *after* Jesus rose from the dead and took back the authority Adam gave to Satan, the enemy is *still* referred to as the "god of this world" (see 2 Corinthians 4:4).

As the "god of this world," Satan makes it his business to inflict pain, misery, sorrow, suffering, and death on all humankind, whenever and wherever possible. That's why this has been a planet of pain from Adam until now. Period.

The War Goes on Until Now

This state of affairs will never change until Jesus comes back, and removes Ol' Split-Foot from the earth (see Revelation chapters 20 and 21). For us, as long as we live on Earth in this life, we are in the middle of this global conflict whether we like it or not, or believe it or not. That's what the words "until now" mean from Matthew 11:12.

In the natural world with the normal order of things, people need rest. A human being was not designed by God to operate and function without a fair amount of rest. To cite an old but effective advertising campaign about portable batteries—we're not a bunch of "Energizer bunnies" that just keep going and going and going. God was the One who set the tone for this when He chose to "rest" on the seventh day from all of His creative work in Genesis chapter one. Therefore, it's unhealthy to just keep working all the time, without taking time to stop and rest. It's also unscriptural—that's why even Jesus knew the importance of taking time off to rest physically.

> *And He said to them, "Come aside by yourselves to a deserted place and rest a while." For there were many coming and going, and they did not even have time to eat. So they departed to a deserted place in the boat by themselves.*
>
> —MARK 6:31-32

For Jesus and His team, this was the Bible-days equivalent for what we call today "taking a vacation." For people who work for a living, the whole idea of a vacation is to stop, get away, relax for a while, and get rejuvenated, so they can return to work and be as productive as they should be. That doesn't mean everybody's vacation turns out to be a peaceful time of rest and recuperation, but that's what the concept is supposed to be about. Work is good—God calls laziness a sin. But too much work and no play is bad—that's not balanced and not the way God intended for us to live. The truth is this: everybody *needs* to take a vacation from time to time! It's good for the body and soul. If you don't take the time to rest, sooner or later you'll get sick and shut down.

On my wall in my office in the Philippines, I have, among other posters, one which shows a vacant white lounge chair sitting in the white sand on the tropical beach, with a beautiful blue sky and turquoise blue water all around. The caption below has four words: *Retreat. Relax. Reflect. Renew.* I look at that poster often, because it reminds me that as busy as I am in this ministry, I *must* take time off to stay healthy, so I can continue operating at peak physical efficiency. (This is especially true as we all grow older!)

Our Enemy Never Rests

But when it comes to the spiritual warfare we're a part of, understand the fact that our enemy is a spirit, and this war is first of all a spiritual war, not a physical war. We are spirits that live in bodies that possess souls. We must never forget this. In my book entitled *Be Strong, Stay Strong*, I point out the importance of keeping these things in mind day in and day out. Why? Because when it comes to the attacks launched against us in this life, its critical to remember they *always* originate from the spirit world, where our enemy's headquarters is situated. No matter what form the attack may take, whether it be a disease, a deformity of some kind, sickness, persecution, poverty, etc.—the true source for that attack is always spiritual, not physical. That's why the attacks will keep on coming for the rest of our lives with no break whatsoever, because spirits don't need the kind of rest we need as human "beings," which by biblical definition are human spirits living in their physical bodies. Overseeing enemy operations from the spirit world, the devil doesn't need a vacation and isn't going to take one! He's totally committed to our destruction. Until he's thrown into the bottomless pit, Satan will *never* take a break, take a vacation or offer a ceasefire of any kind. There are no prisoner exchanges either!

God's not willing to lose anyone who is a part of the family of God, and the devil isn't willing to let anyone go without a fight. The war goes on . . . and on . . . and that is what Jesus means when He uses the phrase, *until now!*

On New Year's Eve many years ago, not long after Ethel and I were married, someone tried to kill us while we slept in our bed. This took place in Ozamiz City, where at the time we were living in a rented house—our compound had not been built yet. This house had two upper bedrooms, one facing the street and the other facing the rice fields behind the house. There was a common wall between the two rooms, and our bed's headboard was butted up against that common wall. We were using the front bedroom for sleep at the time, and the back bedroom was being used as my office. We went to bed early that night, even though there was the usual level of noise and commotion going on throughout the city with firecrackers going off, soldiers firing their guns into the air, and people running around acting like idiots, as they do around the world on New Year's Eve.

When we got up in the morning on New Year's Day, I walked into the back bedroom to do some office work, and noticed wood splinters all over the floor. I thought that was odd, because I could tell by how the splinters were laying on the floor that something had propelled them on to the floor in a violent manner. When I followed the pattern of splinters with my eyes, they led me to the bedroom wall facing the rice fields at the back of our house, where I saw that a small hole had been made. When I got down on my knees to look more closely, it was clear that whatever had come through the night before had penetrated both wooden walls—the outside exterior wall and the inside bedroom wall. This is what had created the mess of plywood splinters I now saw on the floor.

In addition, when I got down to the level of the hole and examined the scene, and followed the line of sight across the room, I saw a second hole in the common wall that this bedroom shared with our bedroom. It was now obvious that something had been propelled through three walls – the outside wall, the inside wall and the common wall between these two rooms. I got a knife from the kitchen and began to dig into the hole in the common wall. To my amazement, I found and dislodged a bullet from the wall! It was pulled from wall just a few inches away from where my head had been as I slept the night before.

It was obvious the bullet had been shot by somebody up in a tree on the other side of the rice fields, taking careful aim, no doubt with the intent of killing either me or my wife. This was no accidental or stray bullet that randomly found our house. Whoever it was, they knew approximately where we were positioned in bed as we lay there sleeping. Somebody knew we slept on the second floor of this house, where our bedrooms were, because they had to climb a tree on the other side of the rice field to line up their shot. The shooter took time to scope out our house, observe our comings and goings, and plan this attack diligently. I don't remember the year this took place, but I know it was before February 2, 1987, because that is when our son Mike was born, and this took place before that. Yes the devil tried, but praise God, we're still here! (I've kept that bullet in my desk drawer all these years, from then until now. I look at it from time to time, to remind myself of the things I'm sharing with you here).

I've had Muslim Imams jump up on stage (this happened in our Zamboanga City crusade in 1988) and try to stab me with a hollowed-out Bic pen as I preached my salvation message to the people. I jabbed my finger in his face, and using the name of Jesus, backed him up across the stage until he fell backwards off the platform and into the crowd (the pointed pen was inches away from my stomach as I confronted this deluded soul). I've been in jungle settings (on the island of Negros) where we held crusades by campfire, with me in the middle and the people standing all around the light provided by the fire. However, the farmers and village people weren't the only ones attending—many Communist rebels surrounded us on all sides, hiding in the shadows just beyond the light of the fire. We knew they were there because the metal on their AK-47 rifles were reflecting the campfire's light. Nobody tried to stop me, and nobody tried to shoot me. They just listened to the message, and disappeared into the darkness when the time came for me to pray for the lost and the sick.

We live and work in a violent world, and many people are not in sympathy with who we represent, and what we're doing in His Name. For a Christian, there are only two ways out of this spiritual conflict. First, you can die physically and leave your body behind while you go home to Heaven. Or, you can hang around until Jesus returns for the rapture of the Church, and go up in the air to meet Him there. Take your pick, but it's one or the other! Until you die or the rapture takes place, you're in the war and you're under attack—*until now*. That being the case, *you need the violent mindset to survive and thrive* while you're moving on with your life in Christ!

God Sees Us This Way Now

As far as God is concerned, we are *already* the Violent! This is not something He says we will be someday, but something which we are now! Now from our perspective, we may not think of ourselves as the Violent, but God says we are. We may not see ourselves that way and we may not be acting that way, but that's how God sees us and that's how He describes us. So if that's the way God wants us to be spiritually, then that's the way we should be if we wish to be pleasing to Him—period.

> *Now the Angel of the Lord came and sat under the terebinth tree which was in Ophrah, which belonged to Joash the Abiezrite, while his son Gideon threshed wheat in the winepress, in order to hide it from the Midianites. And the Angel of the Lord appeared to him, and said to him, "The Lord is with you, you mighty man of valor!" Gideon said to Him, "O my lord, if the Lord is with us, why then has all this happened to us? And where are all His miracles which our fathers told us about, saying, 'Did not the Lord bring us up from Egypt?' But now the Lord has forsaken us and delivered us into the hands of the Midianites." Then the Lord turned to him and said, "Go in this might of yours, and you shall save Israel from the hand of the Midianites. Have I not sent you?"*
> —JUDGES 6:11-14

When God's angel came to Gideon with the assignment to deliver the Israelites from Midian bondage, notice how he was addressed. The angel called Gideon a "mighty man of valor." But look at how Gideon responded to that noble salutation. In the midst of this magnificent moment, when Gideon is face-to-face with an angel sent from God, calling him a mighty man of valor, all we hear in reply is complaining and mumbling about a lack of divine power, and an accusation that the Jews have been abandoned by God! All I can say is, *thank God He's merciful, patient, and kind with us, especially in times of expressed stupidity like this!*

What's going on here? God is identifying Gideon according to how God sees him—as a mighty man of valor—in spite of the fact that Gideon is full of doubt about God's abilities, and is presently hiding his work in the winepress for fear of the Midianites! This doesn't sound much like a mighty man of valor, does it? And its obvious Gideon doesn't see himself the way God sees him, either. This is how it is for most believers. God sees them as mighty men or women of valor, while they wallow in doubt, double-mindedness and fear. God calls us "more than conquerors" in Romans 8:37, but how many Christians out there *feel* like it, or *think* they are? First John 4:4 says the Holy Spirit in us is greater than any evil spirit or false prophet, but do we all walk around living in the light of that truth? Hardly! Most believers are as afraid of the devil as unbelievers are. All of this has to do with developing and protecting the right mindset—one that agrees with God's mindset about each one of us.

God says we are the Violent, so that's who we are! That's it. Believe it because He said it—then ask for God's help in learning how to live life and contend with the enemy in light of this truth.

If We're the Violent, Be Violent!

One of my favorite individuals in the Bible is Caleb, the Kennizite. We read about him back in the Old Testament, thousands of years before Jesus came to Earth. He was one of the few back then who knew how to please God with violent faith, which is why God called him out and commended him openly in front of everybody else.

> *But My servant Caleb, because he has a different spirit in him and has followed Me fully, I will bring into the land where he went, and his descendants shall inherit it.*
>
> —NUMBERS 14:24

Contrary to what many Christians think about God, He isn't the least bit nervous or upset around violent people like Caleb. In fact, He applauds that kind of violent mentality and attitude, and wants it to be our normal operating procedure when dealing with the devil. According to *Strong's Concordance*, the name Caleb comes from a Hebrew root word which means "dog," and specifically, a rabid, unpredictable, and aggressive type of dog! We're not talking about some loving, drooling, tail-wagging, domesticated pet here. We're talking about the kind of dog that people usually think of when they think of Pit Bulls gone mad. Mean, strong, and very unpredictable. Violent, vicious, and lethal. That's the kind of dog the name Caleb implies from the Hebrew language, and that's the way God has wired *all* us from the inside out! *He expects us* to have the "different kind of spirit" that Caleb exhibited thousands of years ago—the violent kind of spirit.

Remember when Joshua was dividing up the Promised Land amongst the twelve tribes, after they had come in to take possession? Caleb approached him and in no uncertain terms, reminded Joshua that God made a promise to both of them years ago—a promise he remembered, quoted, and expected to be honored.

> *As yet I am as strong this day as on the day that Moses sent me; just as my strength was then, so now is my strength for war, both for going out and for coming in.*
>
> —JOSHUA 14:11

This is the attitude God loves! If you read the thread of conversation here, you'll find that when Caleb made these statements to Joshua, he was 85 years old, and it had been *45 years* since God promised to bring him into the Promised Land. That means he was a 40-year-old man when God made that promise to him. Now, we expect people to be physically strong at the age of 40, but just as strong at the age of 85? And strong at 85 for what? Enthusiastic participation in early-bird dinner specials at Denny's for old and slow people? Faithful attendance at Bingo parties at the local Senior Citizen's Center? Active counseling as a member of the local Dementia and Alzheimer's support group? No! *For war!* And you can be sure the battles this man fought back then were every bit as violent as any you might see a soldier fight in today's army. This is why God declared that this man had a "different spirit." What an attitude! Truly, he is one of my Bible heroes that I'm going to look for when I get to Heaven (after I spend time at the feet of Jesus, of course)!

The fact that God loves this kind of mindset is news to most believers. In my travels and encounters in full-time missionary ministry since September, 1980, it's been my observation that this kind of violent attitude is foreign to most Christians. So many have become so preoccupied with "walking in love," they've forgotten there is a balance to true, biblical love. Yes, we have the great love chapter of 1 Corinthians 13, as well as other obvious commands throughout the Word of God to develop our *agape* love walk. But an objective and thorough study of the New Testament will also show that Paul (the author of the thirteenth chapter of 1 Corinthians by the way), wasn't afraid to engage the enemy of our souls with vicious tenacity whenever the situation required it.

The Apostle Paul wrote much of the New Testament, and was quite aware of the importance of walking in love, as well as living by faith. Yet, he never hesitated to get up in people's faces, and call down divine judgment on anybody being used by the devil to try and stop his forward progress in ministry. An example of this would be Acts chapter 13, where Paul confronts the sorcerer Elymas, who was trying to dissuade Sergius Paulus, the local proconsul, from believing in the Gospel. Once the sorcerer got into the mix and was actively trying to stop Paul from ministering to a man who was very interested in hearing what he had to say, he got right in this guy's face and called blindness down on the man! That's the kind of "violence" that resides deep down on the inside of all of us, even if you've never tapped into it or used it against our adversary. Trust me and trust God—it's there within you! I remember several incidents in our ministry that amply illustrate this truth.

In one case, we were holding an outdoor Miracle Crusade in the city of General Santos, on the island of Mindanao. Ethel was not with me for this crusade because the Lord hadn't yet orchestrated our courtship and marriage. That was still several years off. For this crusade, I was working with a number of students from the Bible school in Tagbilaran City on the island of Bohol, where I was serving as their principal and faculty member. At that time, our crusades were usually seven days in length.

On the first day of the crusade, the devil sent a local witch doctor to try and disrupt the services. Obviously, it was his intent to use this person to destroy our credibility publicly in front of all those who were attending. There was a crowd of about 400 in attendance, and the meetings were being held in the city's central park, on an outdoor stage that was about 5-feet-high off the ground. This demonic puppet was actually a witch "doctor-ette," since it was a young woman and not an older man, which is usually the kind of person the devil selects and uses in this way. The order of the service that day called for a time of praise and worship by our crusade band, then a salvation and healing message, followed by an altar call and prayer for the sick. I was sitting on the stage behind the singers and musicians. The band had just finished the praise and worship portion of the service, and had gone off the stage to mingle down at ground level with the people. I was preparing to be introduced and take the microphone, when all of a sudden this young woman ran up the steps onto the stage, grabbed one of the microphones and started using it to curse people with sickness, and call down rain from the sky to disrupt the proceedings.

Back in those early days, I didn't have my own staff of trained and anointed crusade workers. I traveled alone, and usually for assistance, as it was that day, I would work with a group of local volunteers and youth from the cooperating churches. Therefore, when this lady started calling down rain and putting curses on people, my helpers didn't know what to do. They were just standing there watching her, not sure of what to do next. As I sat there and saw what was happening, the Lord's indignation and anger rose up within me. The Lord spoke clearly to my heart and said: "Do something about this, *NOW!*"

This was not the time to go back behind the coconut tree and start praying for wisdom and guidance from God! The service was being threatened and the people were beginning to scatter in fear. So, I jumped up from my chair, walked up to her from behind, and grabbed her by the arms, up near her shoulders. I spun her around so she was now facing me, then I put both hands on the front of her blouse, right up under her arms. I then picked her up off the ground, and threw her backwards off the stage—literally. She landed on her rear end about four feet away and five feet down the steps off the platform. When she hit the turf, she let out a meek, weak scream, and the people all stepped away from her. She got up and ran off—never to be seen or heard from again for the rest of our crusade!

A few minutes before, she was defiantly holding our microphone and boldly pronouncing curses on the people and rain from the sky. Now, after this violent confrontation, she was the object of laughter and ridicule from all the people she had been trying to curse. I went back to the microphone, called for my interpreter, and delivered a powerful message about the love of God, and the free gift of salvation. Everyone attending the meeting in the park that day got saved, and many were healed. Plus, it never rained a single drop!

The Violent Know How to Channel Their Rage

Are we to go around looking for people to curse, insult, kick in the shins, or throw off the bus? Of course not! We walk in love, and as God's official representatives, do our best to present a loving, forgiving, merciful, patient, and tender Jesus to those who need salvation. On the other hand, when push comes to shove spiritually, we're not backing down, and we don't hesitate to shove the devil's tools and tactics right back in his face. People can be ugly (including Christians), which is something we'll talk about in greater detail later in this book, but as obnoxious as they may be sometimes, learn to curb your anger if at all possible towards them—at least until they've given you no choice. This was the message Paul shared to the Ephesian brethren, and to all the other churches he was responsible to oversee.

> *Finally, my brethren, be strong in the Lord and in the power of His might. Put on the whole armor of God, that you may be able to stand against the wiles of the devil. For we do not wrestle against flesh and blood, but against principalities, against powers, against the rulers of the darkness of this age, against spiritual hosts of wickedness in the heavenly places. Therefore take up the whole armor of God, that you may be able to withstand in the evil day, and having done all, to stand.*
>
> —EPHESIANS 6:10-13

I'm sure Paul wasn't going around, believing God for more violent encounters like the one with sorcerer Elymas. In fact, he was the one inspired by God to write Romans 12:18, which tells us that if *at all possible, live peaceably with all men.* So, his first approach with people was always one of love, patience, kindness, and forgiveness. He wasn't anxiously anticipating the next demonic confrontation with enemies of the Gospel, but on the other hand, he knew that if the devil was going to use people to try and stop his forward progress in ministry, he might have to get violent with them in the same way he would get violent against the devil himself. *This is how Jesus expects all of us to operate in His Name as the "Violent."*

The Violent Take Whatever They Want from the Devil

Jesus said the Violent take "it" by force. What would be the "it" He refers to here? Anything pertaining to the things of God that are necessary for us to fulfill the Great Commission of Mark 16:15-18. That would include money, equipment, personnel, health, healing, and anything else we would need to be or to have in order to carry out our particular assignments in this life pertaining to the business of spreading the Gospel to the ends of the earth.

Who do we take these things from? From the god of this world, who is the devil (see 2 Corinthians 4:4). We take them with violence because Satan is *never* going to give up anything from his kingdom, just so you can go win more souls for Jesus! He will fight you all the days of your life, and do his best to hold on to anything and everything you want or need to obey God. Jesus called him a liar and a thief (see John 8:44 and John 10:10), and the originator of both. So he's not going to give back whatever he has stolen from you my friend—not unless you just rip it out of his slimy hands!

In my book *Be Strong, Stay Strong,* I talk extensively about our Lord's teaching regarding the "Strong Man" and the "Stronger Man" (see Luke 11:21-22). In that story, Jesus tells us the strong man is the devil, and the stronger man is the Christian. The strong man holds people in bondage against their will, until the stronger man comes along and forces the strong man to let his captives go free. In the New Testament, Jesus was the first "stronger man," but not the last! All of us in the Body of Christ are now the stronger men (or women) of God! That is another way of identifying us as the Violent for Christ. We're stronger men and women of God, and we're the Violent for the Lord. As such, we take back anything the enemy has taken from us—and we *force* him to let the captives go free in the name of Jesus. Period. When do we do this? Anytime we want, or anytime it's necessary! It's not up to the devil as to when he's going to release the spiritually captive, or give over the money, health or whatever else he's stolen from us. And it's not even up to God—He has already declared us to be the Violent, and told us to go into the entire world and preach the gospel to every creature. *It's all up to us!*

I remember one time I was dealing with one particular lying spirit from hell, who was sent against me to try and torment me with his lies. Day and night for quite some time, this imp would whisper in my ear his lies, in the hopes of tormenting me and bringing fear into my life. After a long time of this, I went to the Lord in my prayer closet, and asked: "How long is this going to go on?" His answer was shot back to me almost before I could get the question out of my mouth. He said in reply: *"As long as you let it!"* Once I realized that it was all up to me to deal with this lying spirit, I took authority over him, rebuked and bound him up, and took back my peace of mind that he was stealing from me. That was many years ago, and I've never forgotten that simple exchange between me and Jesus. It has helped me time and again in dealing with the devil's latest attempts to steal, kill, or destroy things in my life.

> *Now it happened, as we went to prayer, that a certain slave girl possessed with a spirit of divination met us, who brought her masters much profit by fortune-telling. This girl followed Paul and us, and cried out, saying, "These men are the servants of the Most High God, who proclaim to us the way of salvation." And this she did for many days. But Paul, greatly annoyed, turned and said to the spirit, "I command you in the name of Jesus Christ to come out of her." And he came out that very hour.*
>
> —ACTS 16:16-19

I believe that this story here shows us that even the great Apostle Paul put up with things longer than he should have. In this passage from Acts, we see this girl possessed with an evil spirit of divination following Paul's group, harassing them as much as possible. Notice verse 18. This she did *for many days.* Although we don't know how many were the many days, we can be sure from the context that it was quite a long time. I've heard some Bible teachers say that the reason why Paul waited for such a long time before casting the devil out of the girl was because the gift of discerning of spirits only operates as the Holy Spirit wills it, not as we will it. That may be true, but we have no scripture verse to verify and confirm that. We do know the *whenever* the Holy Spirit activated that particular gift for Paul, it enabled him to see into the spirit realm and deal with this tormenting spirit. I agree with the premise that all nine gifts of the Holy Spirit operate or manifest as He wants, not as we want, so it's entirely possible this was the reason it took Paul so long to finally turn and cast that devil out of the girl.

But it's also entirely possible that the reason he waited so long before dealing with this evil spirit was because, like me and you and so many of us, he just temporarily forgot that as the Violent of God, he had the authority *and* responsibility to initiate the confrontation to ultimately set this person free! It's entirely possible that instead of him waiting upon God, or the Spirit of God, God was in fact waiting upon him! We'll never know for sure, but I believe this explanation is as scriptural and as plausible as any. No matter what the reasons may have been for the deliverance delay in Paul's ministry that day, from Matthew 11:12, Jesus is telling us that *we take what we want from the enemy anytime its needed or necessary.*

What We Take, We Take by Force!

We take what we want to fulfill our role in the Great Commission, and we don't ask the devil if it's okay or if he likes it or not. As the Violent, we take "it" *by force!*

> *And he cried out with a loud voice and said, "What have I to do with You, Jesus, Son of the Most High God? I implore You by God that You do not torment me." For He said to him, "Come out of the man, unclean spirit!" Then He asked him, "What is your name?" And he answered, saying, "My name is Legion; for we are many." Also he begged Him earnestly that He would not send them out of the country. Now a large herd of swine was feeding there near the mountains. So all the demons begged Him, saying, "Send us to the swine, that we may enter them." And at once Jesus gave them permission. Then the unclean spirits went out and entered the swine (there were about two thousand); and the herd ran violently down the steep place into the sea, and drowned in the sea.*
>
> —MARK 5:7-13

Whenever you have to or need to, throw the devil out of your way! Make him obey! Force him to submit, and to surrender whoever or whatever he is holding as the thief that he is.

In this story, we see Jesus coming upon a man who was possessed by a legion of demons. In those days, a "legion" referred to a group of soldiers in the Roman army numbering approximately 6,000. So, this poor soul was actually being possessed by thousands of evil spirits—totally unable to set himself free. It would be safe to say the demons inhabiting him weren't about to let him go free either! They possessed this man, and enjoyed driving him crazy.

But here comes Jesus, and in a moment of time the whole situation changes. Suddenly the demons, who moments ago had been in total control of this man's life, *were now pleading and begging Jesus that He wouldn't start tormenting them!* Incredible!

Do you think this poor man wanted to be demon-possessed, live in the tombs, cutting himself and going crazy? Of course not. Do you think the Legion of demons possessing him had any intentions of letting him go, so he could live a normal life and serve God? No. But because the Violent can take whatever they want in service to Almighty God, Jesus is now the One in total command of the situation, and was dictating the terms for the release of this man's soul. The demons had absolutely no ability to stop Jesus from giving this man his life back. *They didn't want to let him go, but Jesus was about to take him by force anyway!*

And remember that before He left, Jesus specifically told us that the works He did we could do as well (see John 14:12-14). So this is not just a case of Jesus doing things we admire but can't do ourselves. This is a case of God's Violent taking action and ripping this man's soul away from the clutches of Satan and all of these evil spirits. Jesus didn't ask them for permission to release this individual—He violently demanded it! And what He did there is what we're supposed to be doing now in His name!

If you're going to advance under enemy fire, you'll need to know you can (and should) take whatever you want or need as a member of God's congregation of the mighty (see Psalm 82:1)! *This is what Jesus referred to when telling us to take personnel or territory by force!*

CHAPTER 11

Know How the Devil Works

Lest Satan should take advantage of us;
for we are not ignorant of his devices.
—2 CORINTHIANS 2:11

The first thing a believer must do when learning how to advance under fire is to have a working knowledge of the tools and tactics of the devil and his demons. We should never be ignorant of the enemy's devices, because in Hosea 4:6, we're told that God's people perish for a lack of knowledge. In other words, *what you don't know can kill you!* At the very least, what you don't know about the devil's devices will give him *free ammunition* to use, and an open invitation to attack you whenever and wherever it's convenient for him. Having a lack of knowledge regarding Satan's devices in this area will open doors to the enemy that you don't want opened!

Satan's Top Priority

No matter what the devil tries to do to keep you from advancing for the kingdom of God in the name of Jesus, he'll always seek to camouflage himself for as long as he can. This is his number one priority—*anonymity!* Since the beginning, the devil has worked very hard at the skills of covert operations, and he's become a master at doing it. For example, the vast majority of humans living on Earth today are on their way to an eternity in Hell, but they don't think so! Rev. Lester Sumrall, one of the greatest missionaries of the 20th century, once said: *half the world doesn't believe the devil exists, while the other half lives under his oppression and bondage daily.*

For the unbelievers, their problem is simple—they're not yet children of God. They need to receive Jesus as Lord and Savior and become born-again. Until that happens they are at the devil's mercy, and the bad news for them is that he doesn't have any. However, this kind of spiritual deception is not just confined to sinners or unbelievers. It's rampant within the Body of Christ as well.

Even though the devil has legally and officially been put far below the feet of every member of the Body of Christ (see Ephesians 1:17-23), that fact does not give us consistent victory over the enemy. Our Lord's victory over Satan was complete, but the devil is still here and he will still try to steal all that he can from us. The victory Jesus handed to us legally must be fought for, acquired, enforced, and protected day-to-day. The devil is still around, and he's still the master thief with an unending array of disguises!

The devil knows that believers won't take action against him when they don't know action is required! He knows we have all dominion and authority over him on Earth through Christ Jesus, so he tries to sow the lie that we *don't* have dominion and authority over him on Earth. That way, he can successfully deceive us into voluntarily allowing him to work in our lives, and that's what the majority of Christians do—daily! That's why we must have—and maintain—a working knowledge of the tools, tactics, and devices of Satan. If we know who he is and how he works, he won't be able to use our ignorant free will against us.

Not A Comprehensive List

In part 2 of this book, I've listed some of the main ways the devil will try to come at you. This is not a comprehensive list—there are other devices and tactics he may use against you that aren't listed here. However, based on my Christian walk with Jesus since I was born-again on September 21, 1978, and upon the fact that I've been in full-time ministry since September, 1980, these would be the ones I think represent the bulk of his work to steal, kill, and destroy in our lives.

I am not going to give each of these tactics a detailed study because that's not the main focus on this book. There are already many books written by anointed men and women of God that address these subjects in far greater detail. My purpose is to list and discuss them within the context of this book—establishing a working awareness of the devil's tactics, tools, and operations against us. Armed with this information, we can effectively overcome in each area of attack, and continue to advance for God under enemy fire.

Eight Major Areas of Attack Against Us

From the Word of God, and from experiences accumulated since I entered full-time ministry back in 1980, here are what I would consider the eight major ways in which we are attacked by the devil. (Feel free to add your own "addendums" to this list if you've got experience and testimonies in other areas where the devil has launched attacks against you.) He attacks us:

1. Carnally (temptations to stir up our flesh);
2. Mentally (lying thoughts designed to create confusion and pressure);
3. Financially (not having enough to pay the bills);
4. Doctrinally (false doctrines and heresy creeping in);
5. Relationally (gossip, slander, and false rumors);
6. Physically (sickness and disease);
7. Socially (national, religious, or cultural persecution);
8. Theologically (unanswered questions).

This list isn't given in relative order of frequency or importance. The devil may test you in any one of these areas individually, or in multiple areas simultaneously. And depending upon his assessment of your level of spiritual strength, and his degree of success against you, he may choose to isolate his attacks in one or two particular areas repeatedly.

One on this list is not any more deadly than another, but any of them can be used successfully to bring you down if you don't know how to defend yourself. Understand this list for what it is: *these are strategies and tactics of the enemy designed to kill you, or at the very least, neutralize you concerning the Great Commission* (see Mark 16:15-18). Using any or all of these in demonic combinations, the devil's goal is to inflict as much pain in your life as he possibly can for as long as he can, and make you worthless and of no value to the Holy Spirit for the spread of the gospel. You must know this if you're going to advance under fire with any degree of regularity and consistently.

In the following chapters, we'll take a brief look at each of these areas of attack. As I said earlier, my purpose in discussing this list with you is simply to provide a fundamental, working knowledge of each of these demonic tactics. This will enable you to recognize these tactics for what they are, and develop the basic skills to effectively overcome them, so you can continue to advance under enemy fire.

PART II

What to
Watch For

CHAPTER 12

Carnal Attacks: Temptations of the Flesh

Let no one say when he is tempted, "I am tempted by God ";
for God cannot be tempted by evil, nor does He Himself tempt
anyone. But each one is tempted when he is drawn away by
his own desires and enticed. Then, when desire has conceived,
it gives birth to sin; and sin, when it is full-grown,
brings forth death. Do not be deceived, my beloved brethren.
—JAMES 1:13-16

In verse 16 of this scripture, if the Apostle James tells the Christians (the beloved brethren) not to be deceived in this matter, then it's possible to be deceived in this matter! Unfortunately, multitudes of believers have allowed exactly what this passage warns us not to allow—deception in the area of carnal (fleshly) attack.

A human being is tri-partite in nature and composition. We are spirits possessing souls and living in physical bodies. We are eternal spirits, living in temporal bodies. When we talk about people dying and being buried in the cemetery, understand what got buried and what didn't. The body died, but not the spirit or the soul. We put dead bodies in the ground, but the person who occupied that body isn't there—they went either to Heaven or

Hell, depending upon their spiritual condition at the point of death. If they were Christian, they went home to Heaven. If they weren't Christian, they went home to Hell. The body will be reunited with the spirit at some prophetic point in the future, but for now, it's enough for us to know that our bodies didn't get saved when we did!

When you were born-again, your spirit was re-created by the power of God, and the Holy Spirit took up residence within you. Your flesh, however, didn't change one bit. It was spiritually dead before you got saved, and it stayed that way after you got saved. Therefore, one of the primary ways the devil will attack us in this life is through temptations of the flesh. This passage in James says it all too well—each of us is tempted when we are drawn away *by our own desires and enticed*. Where do these "desires" come from? From our flesh, which still has the sin nature it has always had since birth.

Our Three Enemies

If we're to successfully and consistently advance for God under fire from the enemy, we must remember who our enemies are! If you read further on in James, our three enemies are listed for us in James 4:1-7. They are:

1. The devil and demons working with and for him (vs. 7);

2. The world system, which Satan founded and exerts control over (vs. 4);

3. Our flesh and blood bodies, which the devil attempts to entice, influence, and thereby control (vs.1).

I was born-again on September 21, 1978, and began to walk with Jesus and study the Word of God. Two years later, in September, 1980, I left the United States and flew to the Philippines to start full-time missionary work for God. From back then until now, based upon what I've seen, I'm convinced that of these three enemies we face in this life, the flesh is by far the most difficult to control and subdue on a consistent basis. This is what Paul addressed to the Corinthians:

> *Do you not know that those who run in a race all run, but one receives the prize? Run in such a way that you may obtain it. And everyone who competes for the prize is temperate in all things. Now they do it to obtain a perishable crown, but we for an imperishable crown. Therefore I run thus: not with uncertainty. Thus I fight: not as one who beats the air. But I discipline my body and bring it into subjection, lest, when I have preached to others, I myself should become disqualified.*
>
> —1 CORINTHIANS 9:24-27

Paul was one of the strongest and most heavily anointed soldiers for Christ in the New Testament. He wrote two thirds of the New Testament, and was the leader in bringing the gospel message to the Gentile world, to Kings, Heads of State, and to the Jews (see Acts 9:15,16). But even he knew the importance of disciplining his body, bringing it into subjection to his spirit, and controlling the lusts of flesh. Many Christians erroneously deify Paul, practically to the point of idol worship, but He was just like the rest of us – he struggled to maintain control over his flesh consistently. Read Romans chapters 6, 7 and 8, and see how he describes the difficulties he has in keeping his own flesh "in subjection ". Note this one particular passage:

> *For what I am doing, I do not understand. For what I will to do, that I do not practice; but what I hate, that I do. If, then, I do what I will not to do, I agree with the law that it is good. But now, it is no longer I who do it, but sin that dwells in me. For I know that in me (that is, in my flesh) nothing good dwells; for to will is present with me, but how to perform what is good I do not find. For the good that I will to do, I do not do; but the evil I will not to do, that I practice. Now if I do what I will not to do, it is no longer I who do it, but sin that dwells in me.*
>
> —ROMANS 7:15-20

We don't know what areas of the flesh Paul had problems control-ling, because the scriptures are silent about that. We can, however, see that there were definite areas in his life that he struggled to control—just like you and me!

Multiple passages throughout the New Testament tell us that the greatest war we wage daily is the war between our spirit man and our carnal man. Our born-again spirit on the inside wants to serve God, but our dead-to-sin flesh wants to go on sinning, just like before we were born-again. The devil knows this, and tries to take advantage of this fact as often as possible.

Did God Really Say That?

When the devil tries to entice our flesh, he will first try convinc-ing us that the penalties for carnal indulgence aren't as bad as the scriptures say they will be. This is what he did when he approached Eve right at the beginning, in the Garden of Eden. By questioning God's word to Adam and Eve about the conse-quences of disobedience, Satan was seeking to minimize the devastating effects that sin would have on them – and through them, on us. In Genesis 3:1-4, using the first recorded temptation as our template, we can see that the initial objective for the devil in getting us to yield to fleshly temptation revolves around the integrity of God's Word.

> *Now the serpent was more cunning than any beast of the field which the LORD God had made. And he said to the woman, "Has God indeed said, 'You shall not eat of every tree of the garden'?" And the woman said to the serpent, "We may eat the fruit of the trees of the garden; but of the fruit of the tree which is in the midst of the garden, God has said, 'You shall not eat it, nor shall you touch it, lest you die.'" Then the serpent said to the woman, "You will not surely die. For God knows that in the day you eat of it your eyes will be opened, and you will be like God, knowing good and evil."*
>
> —Genesis 3:1-5

First of all, notice the use of the word "cunning" in verse 1. The devil is a fallen being that's both stupid and brilliant simultaneously. No matter how "cunning " you may be, thinking you can overthrow God is about as stupid an idea as you could possibly have, and he was the author of that idea. On the other hand, even in his fallen state after the attempted coup in Heaven, he retained much of the brilliance he had originally as Lucifer, who was described as a created being that "was the seal of perfection" (see Isaiah 14:12-15 and Ezekiel 28:12-19).

Being the cunning enemy he is, the devil first worked to plant in Eve's mind the suggestion that God really didn't mean what He said to her and her husband. "Has God indeed said . . . ?" That opening question in their verbal exchange reveals the all-important tactic the devil is still using today against us. If he is to successfully entice our flesh to sin, he must first start by making the temptation easier to yield to. He does that by using lies or half-truths to hide the real and true consequences when we let our flesh have its way.

In Eve's case, the devil was working to hide the consequences of her disobedience to God's Word by presenting the half-truth that eating the forbidden fruit wouldn't produce the death that God said it would. First Timothy 2:14 says Eve was deceived (tricked by this ploy), but her husband was not. Eve was deceived because she listened to and believed the devil's slick lie, but Adam knew exactly what God meant when He said they would surely die on the day they ate that forbidden fruit. He knew God wasn't talking about physical death, but rather, spiritual death. At any point in this exchange, he could've ended this conversation with the serpent, and pulled his wife away to explain what the terrible consequences would be if they did eat the forbidden fruit, but he didn't. Instead, he made the decision to forsake God and submit to the devil by willfully and deliberately eating the fruit he was told to avoid.

There are many kinds of sinful temptations when it comes to our flesh, and we must be vigilant against all of them. The flesh is constantly trying to pull us away from God and back into sin, so we cannot give place to it at any time for any reason.

The Flesh Is Never Satisfied

The main characteristic of the flesh that we should never forget is this: *it is never satisfied.* Whatever you yield to concerning the lusts of the flesh today, it will not be enough tomorrow. Giving in to your flesh today will only compound your problems tomorrow. Progressively, the flesh will take over more and more of your life with each decision you make to yield to it.

Giving in to some "small" temptation today will not placate or satisfy your carnal nature, my friend, and you must remember that. No matter what you give in to and let your flesh have today, it will want more than that tomorrow! The flesh will continue to take back more and more of a place in your life until it finally kills you and takes your soul to hell. Understand that! Give it one donut today, and before you know it, you're consuming dozens of donuts daily!

A Little Bit At A Time

This is how pornography gets hold of so many, as an example. Normal people don't start out hooked on hardcore porn. It starts with a temptation to look at something that, according to what our warped and perverse society tells us, isn't harmful at all. And then with each successive decision to yield to the lust of the eyes in this area of carnal temptation, the flesh will continue to create an appetite for more and more perverse and degrading forms of pornographic imagery. That's why porn is categorized as either "soft" or "hard." Ask anyone who has been set free from pornography addiction and they will tell you very few porn addicts start out where they end up. Most of the time, addiction starts by yielding to the lust of the eyes and flesh for something much "softer" or "less offensive" socially or culturally.

There are many good books and resource material available that describe this downward spiral in much greater detail, so we will not elaborate in that area now. Just understand how everything gets going in the wrong direction, because the pattern will repeat itself for just about any vice or sin you care to mention. Tobacco, alcohol, drugs, impure thinking, pride, covetousness, and many others—take your pick. Concerning your flesh, the old saying is true: *If you give it an inch, it will take a mile.*

In whatever area you give place to for your flesh, it will want a bigger piece of your life in that same area from then on. Little bit by little bit, like tentacles, the flesh will once again regain complete and total authority in our lives *if we let it.*

Unfortunately for the work of Christ on Earth, most Christians let their flesh control them to one degree or another, and therefore disqualify themselves from any meaningful service in the army of the Lord. They are what Paul called "carnal Christians."

And I, brethren, could not speak to you as to spiritual people but as to carnal, as to babes in Christ. I fed you with milk and not with solid food; for until now you were not able to receive it, and even now you are still not able; for you are still carnal. For where there are envy, strife, and divisions among you, are you not carnal and behaving like mere men? For when one says, "I am of Paul," and another, "I am of Apollos," are you not carnal?

—1 CORINTHIANS 3:1-4

For to be carnally minded is death, but to be spiritually minded is life and peace. Because the carnal mind is enmity against God; for it is not subject to the law of God, nor indeed can be. So then, those who are in the flesh cannot please God.

—ROMANS 8:6-8

Now the works of the flesh are evident, which are: adultery, fornication, uncleanness, lewdness, idolatry, sorcery, hatred, contentions, jealousies, outbursts of wrath, selfish ambitions, dissensions, heresies, envy, murders, drunkenness, revelries, and the like; of which I tell you beforehand, just as I also told you in time past, that those who practice such things will not inherit the kingdom of God.

—GALATIANS 5:19-21

Notice that according to Romans 8:8, *those who are in the flesh cannot please God.* As a Christian, to be "in the flesh" means you are controlled by your flesh, not your spirit. In that state, believers are not pleasing to God and cannot be "meet for the Master's use" (see 2 Timothy 2:21). In other words, God wants to use every Christian in evangelism and outreach, but can't. He can only use the ones who consistently "keep their body under" (see 1 Corinthians 9:26-27), like Paul did. Sad to say, but most Christians are carnally-controlled and not spiritually-led, which is why they have a very hard time advancing under fire when the devil is working to stir up their flesh through various temptations, testings, or trials.

Also notice that according to Galatians chapter 5, the works of the flesh encompass much more than sexual sin or fleshy vices. It involves a whole array of carnal, sensual activities or motives of the heart. And according to verse 21, this list isn't a sum total of all that the flesh can get us into trouble over! The phrase "and the like" simply means this isn't an all-encompassing list—there is more.

It Starts with Obedience!

Your ability to advance under enemy fire depends in large part on your degree of obedience to the things of God, the Word of God, and the perfect will of God for your life. *Disobedience is the root of all carnal sin.* Get out your concordance and run your references, and find out how prevalent this issue of disobedience is throughout the Bible. Some examples from the Old Testament would include passages like the one from Deuteronomy chapter 28, which list the covenant blessings we are entitled to as the seed of Abraham in Christ. People love to quote all the promises from verse 1 to verse 14, but fail to take note of the word "if" when they do. In reading those 14 verses, you find the word "if" is a prominent prerequisite for obtaining those covenant promise in your life. "If" means those promises are *conditional.* It means that if you aren't obedient to God's Word, you won't be eligible for the blessings and benefits listed in those 14 verses (see Deuteronomy 28:1-14).

In like manner, Isaiah tells us that if we are willing *and obedient,* we'll eat the good of the land (see Isaiah 1:19-20). In 1 Samuel 15:10-28, Saul was told that from God's perspective, obedience was much more important than animal sacrifices, and that continued disobedience reveals the root of the problem within the heart. To summarize what God used Samuel to tell Saul: God wants your heart much more than your works, and obedience is the litmus test that confirms your love and allegiance to the Lord. In short, *obedience proves your love for God is genuine.*

For New Testament believers, Jesus said that to prove our love for Him, we would need to keep His commandments (see John 14:15). That's obedience! Paul wrote about these things extensively as well:

> *And you He made alive, who were dead in trespasses and sins, in which you once walked according to the course of this world, according to the prince of the power of the air, **the spirit who now works in the sons of disobedience,** among whom also we all once conducted ourselves **in the lusts of our flesh, fulfilling the desires of the flesh** and of the mind, and were by nature children of wrath, just as the others.*
>
> —EPHESIANS 2:1-3 [EMPHASIS MINE]

Notice how the Holy Spirit connects the issue of disobedience in verse 2 with the issue of fleshly lusts in verse 3. Let me say it again: *disobedience is the root cause for all carnal, fleshly sin.* People obedient to God and His Word can't be successfully tempted to yield to the lusts of their flesh consistently, because chronic disobedience to God's Word is how we empower the devil to stir up our flesh in the first place!

> *Let no one deceive you with empty words, for because of these things the wrath of God comes upon the sons of disobedience. Therefore do not be partakers with them.*
>
> —EPHESIANS 5:6-7

When you purpose to obey God's Word and perfect will for your life, you insulate yourself against your flesh! You elevate your spirit-man to a place of consistent superiority over your carnal flesh, so that the devil can never successfully entice your flesh and lead you into sin. This is what Romans 8:6 refers to when it says to be carnally-minded is death, but to be spiritually-minded is life and peace. When you are spiritually-minded, obeying God is top priority in life, and the thought of offending or dishonoring God through disobedience is so repulsive that you want no part of it. At that point the temptation loses all of its allure, so the flesh has no ability to pull you in the direction the temptation is suggesting! This is how Paul overcame his carnal struggles, enabling him to keep the faith and finish his race. It works the same way for you and I.

Be Vigilant Concerning the Opposite Sex!

When you look at the list of the works of the flesh in Galatians chapter five, you'll see that the first four deal directly with sexual sins—adultery, fornication, uncleanness, and lewdness. That should tell us something about the power and allure of sexual lust and temptation. Warnings about this are all through the Word of God, yet even so, we see multitudes of professing Christians falling prey to this kind of sin in these promiscuous last days. From the front to the back of the Bible, we see the terrible consequences when people engage in sexual sin.

In the Old Testament, Job made his fair share of mistakes regarding the source and reasons for the attacks against him and his family, as outlined in chapters one and two. Nonetheless, he did manage to recognize the power of sexual temptation and take the necessary steps to protect himself. In Job 31:1, it tells us he made a "covenant with his eyes" so that he wouldn't "think upon a maid." That means he did what he had to do to control the lust of the eyes with regards to the opposite sex. We need to make similar covenants with our eyes, given the sexually perverse, licentious, and promiscuous culture that exists in these last days.

Sodom and Gomorrah have nothing on many of the nations of the world today.

We know what happened to David when he was in the wrong place at the wrong time, unable to control the lust of his eyes when he saw Bathsheba taking a bath (see 2 Samuel 11:2). The sorrow and suffering caused by that one act of sexual sin affected lives for generations to come, from one end of the kingdom to the other, inside and outside David's immediate family. It gave the devil a great and open door to steal, kill, and destroy (see 2 Samuel 12:14).

In the four gospels, Jesus said that if we just look on a woman to sexually fantasize about her (the implication is for all those of the opposite sex, male or female), we've already committed the sin of adultery in our hearts (see Matthew 5:28). This is why, with the Internet being the prime source of information and communication now, the perverseness of pornography is so destructive and widespread—spiritually wounding or even destroying multitudes of strong men and women of God worldwide (see Proverbs 7:26). What once was a sin of the flesh reserved only for dark alleys, peep shows, and sleazy porn shops, is now just one or two clicks away on anyone's computer anywhere in the world! If ever there was a time to keep the spirit man in control of the flesh, now would be that time!

In the New Testament, Paul had to deal with perverted sexual sin frequently in his ministry travels throughout the Roman Empire, including the Corinthian church.

I can hardly believe the report about the sexual immorality going on among you, something so evil that even the pagans don't do it. I am told that you have a man in your church who is living in sin with his father's wife. And you are so proud of yourselves! Why aren't you mourning in sorrow and shame? And why haven't you removed this man from your fellowship?
—1 Corinthians 5:1-2 NLT

If this was an issue in the generations gone by, how much more is it an issue to be vigilant against in these last days? *Keep yourself pure!*

Keep yourself clean! First and Second Peter are great books for further study on this topic. Read through those books and take note of the many references to words like "holy," and "pure," in verses such as these:

> But as He who called you is holy, **you also be holy in all your conduct,** because it is written, "Be holy, for I am holy." And if you call on the Father, who without partiality judges according to each one's work, **conduct yourselves throughout the time of your stay here in fear.**
>
> —1 PETER 1:15-17 [EMPHASIS MINE]

> Therefore, since all these things will be dissolved, **what manner of persons ought you to be in holy conduct and godliness.**
>
> —2 PETER 3:11 [EMPHASIS MINE]

Those two books contain a lot of instructions and warnings about keeping yourself holy and pure before a holy and pure God. Every Christian should read and meditate on them often, as well as throughout the rest of the New Testament epistles. First Thessalonians 4:3-7 is also one of my favorite passages in this regard:

> For this is the will of God, your sanctification: that you should abstain from sexual immorality; that each of you should know how to possess his own vessel in sanctification and honor, not in passion of lust, like the Gentiles who do not know God; that no one should take advantage of and defraud his brother in this matter, because the Lord is the avenger of all such, as we also forewarned you and testified. For God did not call us to uncleanness, but in holiness.
>
> —1 THESSALONIANS 4:3-8

That passage pretty well sums it up, don't you think? What Paul told the Corinthians is the same thing he told all of his congregations, as we see here from this admonition to the Thessalonians.

I'd also like to point out that when Paul was giving instructions to the Corinthians about how to deal with the sexual sins in their church (see 1 Corinthians 5:2) they were told to *remove the sinful man from their fellowship*. Wow! What a politically incorrect position to take in our day!

In the perverted times in which we live now, many ignorant Christians as well as unbelievers stumble over themselves to try and convince us that because God is Love, we must "love" such people too! Unfortunately for them and those they deceive, their concept of "love " is a warped, twisted, erroneous lie. Their idea of "love" is allowing people to go on with their sinful lifestyles, and not "judge them" or "condemn them." I've had ignorant people try to sell me those lies, and it will never work with me because I know what the Bible says, and the Bible doesn't change just because people do. Those who think this way are "deceived and deceiving others," exactly as it says in 2 Timothy 3:13. According to 1 Timothy 4:1, they have given heed to "deceiving spirits and doctrines of devils."

True Christian love tells people the truth—plain and simple. It doesn't hide it or apologize for it; and it shows the courage to cut off fellowship with the guilty and unrepentant when a situation warrants it, because again, that's exactly what the Bible tells us to do. In the area of sexual sins, people need to be told the real truth. If the Bible warns the sexually impure about the consequences for continued sin in these areas, a truly loving Christian will tell that to those who need to hear, whether they like it or not. And, they'll not hesitate to remove such people from the fellowship until true repentance is forthcoming.

Inventing New Terms and False Definitions

As an example, contrary to what the fools in the secular media or liberal Hollywood may say, there is no such thing as "gay marriage," "homosexual Christians," or "safe sex" outside of marriage. These are all terms drummed up by those who look for excuses to ignore the clear warnings in the Bible about such sinful practices and lifestyles. Should we condemn such people? Absolutely not! But should we judge their sinful practices, separate ourselves from the unrepentant, and take the necessary steps to tell them the consequences for such sins? Absolutely, yes! That's our job as children of God, charged with the responsibility to tell people the truth.

We don't condemn them (even if they say we do). We love them enough to tell them the truth, with an attitude of humility and self-awareness. We are no better than they are—God loves everyone equally, and sin is sin no matter what kind you care to discuss. When we tell people the consequences for these sinful practices, we're not saying we're any better than they are because we're not. Everybody has issues in their life that the devil exploits in order to lead us into sin. What we should be saying is, "we love you enough to tell you what will happen to you if you don't change, and we're here to help you make those changes no matter what." That's all. That's true biblical love.

There are a number of people I know who have fallen prey to these end-time lies that try and condone and legitimize sins like this. I don't condemn them—I pray for their deliverance almost every day. They need it! Marriage and sexual activity is defined by the Creator, not by a group of unrepentant, unregenerate, rebellious sinners, or by a bunch of politicians who change their colors like chameleons every time there's an election. There are plenty of Christian people who are *struggling against* the temptation to be homosexual, or the temptation to engage in premarital sex outside of marriage, and they may even fall into sexual sin in moments of weakness—but that is entirely different from those who have no intention of changing and would have us believe that being gay, or sleeping with someone who isn't your spouse, is perfectly okay with a holy and righteous God.

God is the One who invented and designed the human body, both male and female. He is the One who told us to be "fruitful and multiply" (see Genesis 1:28), but only within His clear, easy-to-understand guidelines. An objective look at the anatomy of a man's body and a woman's body should be all we need to see to understand God's intent here. Marriage, and the marriage act of intimacy, is between one man and one woman for life, or until death do us part, and "safe sex" isn't using a condom with multiple partners so somebody doesn't accidentally get pregnant. You want to practice "safe sex"? Avoid any and all sexual contact with anyone except your husband or wife, and if you're not yet married, wait until you are. Period.

Politicians, judges, movie stars, sports personalities, and gay "rights" activists can all say what they want about it, but their warped ideas don't change the Word of God, and the Word of God will be the criteria used someday at the judgment seat of Christ for Christians (see Romans 14:10, 2 Corinthians 5:10), or at the great white throne judgment for sinners (see Revelation 20:11-12). Homosexuality is not an "alternate lifestyle." It's a heinous sin of bodily perversion that God calls an abomination (see Leviticus 18:22, Romans 1:26-28). Two cities in the Old Testament were literally wiped off the face of the earth because of it, and the Bible says that this was recorded in the Bible specifically to warn future generations about what God thinks of this particular sin (see 1 Corinthians 10:6-11, Jude 1:7-8).

It is a lie to declare that we are "walking in love" when we tolerate sexual sin and sexual perversion in our own lives, and make no effort to warn others to repent and cease doing the same in theirs. That is what James calls being self-deceived (see James 1:22). Every believer is responsible for keeping their own body under control (see 1 Corinthians 9:26-27), and showing those around us the many warnings in the Bible about the consequences for such lifestyles. It's tragic that many so-called Christians accept and "affirm" anybody *just as they are,* and then with great fervor and passion try to apologize for those of us who still preach the "old fashioned" message of repentance, sexual purity, and holiness.

Make no mistake about it my friend. The devil has worked very hard to minimize the terrible consequences of fleshly, carnal, sexual sin. Don't be deceived! Those who practice such things and make no effort to repent and live right are bound by their sins, and are on the road leading to eternal destruction.

Maintain Your Balance

The Word of God is truth. It doesn't just contain truth, it *is* truth (see John 17:17). However, according to John 8:44, there is an evil spirit called the father of lies, who is running loose on the earth and seeking to deceive and destroy. That's why the Bible talks about the importance of identifying the Spirit of truth from the spirit of error (see 1 John 4:6). So, to understand and separate truth from error, you must maintain your balance when you study God's Word. From front to back, the Bible is a book of balance. 2 Timothy 2:15 tells us the Christian must be able to *rightly divide the Word of Truth*. To understand and "rightly divide" the Word, you must take the time to dig, to make sure you're seeing the complete picture on any given subject found therein. Much error, confusion, and deception occurs when people fail to do this.

Much error has been taught on the subject of love and grace, and it has had a direct effect on how people react and respond to the carnal temptations to sin. You must not allow the backslidden masses to deceive you. Sin is sin, and God's definition for sin has never changed, even if people work to see those definitions changed.

Yes, God is love, and yes, Jesus died for everyone's sins. But even though the gift of salvation is free and for all (Jesus paid for our sins, not us), *it still must be received* (see Romans 5:15-18). And if you wish to receive it, you must be willing to change and forsake the old sins and sinful habits you were bound with before coming to Christ. And if we're really walking in true, biblical love, we'll tell that to every new babe in Christ, holding nothing back.

Jesus didn't mince words with those He spoke to, and neither should we. If somebody comes into our churches with an honest and open mindset, and wants to change when shown the importance of repentance and obedience to God from the Bible, then by all means, please stay and give us the chance and opportunity to help you. But if you're coming into our churches or Bible studies for the purpose of *enlightening us or changing us* to your unscriptural point of view, then we must remove such from the fellowship, and as Paul told the Corinthians, have nothing to do with you. A little leaven leavens the whole lump (see 1 Corinthians 5:1-7).

People can compromise the truth all they want, but they can't change it. The wages of sin is death, and people should hear that because it has never changed. Cultures change, societies change, people change, but the truth never changes. Go back and look at the sermons men like John the Baptist and Jesus delivered while here on Earth. The word "repent" is the major, central theme of their messages to the people. John's whole ministry was based upon the need for repentance (see Matthew 3:1-3). Jesus picked up the same message when He started His ministry. In fact, the very first word of His very first public sermon was the word "repent" (see Matthew 4:17)!

Learn to Move On!

If you've fallen in the area of carnal temptations, *repent*, receive your forgiveness, *and move on*, like what Jesus told the woman caught in adultery in John chapter 8. In my opinion, this is one of the most telling stories given in the Bible by the Holy Spirit, to help us deal with our own sins and shortcomings.

According to Old Testament Law, this woman should've been stoned to death, but how Jesus dealt with her and with her accusers shows us the way of the New Testament—the covenant for all time, for all men. He didn't condemn her for what she did. He didn't judge her and call her a whore. He didn't do anything like what the religious leaders were hoping to see take place. He showed mercy, compassion, sensitivity, and forgiveness. But, and this is a big "but"—He also refused to condone, excuse, or minimize what she had done. When all of her accusers had left for shame and religious hypocrisy, what was it He said to her, and what was it He told her to do? In verse 11 He told her, "*neither do I condemn you—go and sin no more*" (see John 8:11).

He didn't condemn the woman for who she was or for what she was doing when she was caught—He forgave her. But He did something else, too. He told her to *stop doing what she was doing*. In other words, He told her to move on in repentance and leave that old lifestyle behind once and for all. The Bible says that whoever confesses and *forsakes* their sins will receive God's mercy and forgiveness (see Proverbs 28:13). Occasionally falling prey to old habits or lusts is different than just going on with no intent to change or live a life pleasing to God. We're all a work in progress, and God knows that. Nobody is perfect, but all of us should be on the sanctification highway together. We should all be striving with all our heart to live pure, holy lives before a pure and holy God. To do otherwise is to court disaster (see Galatians 6:7-8).

Thanks be to God we've got the promise of 1 John 1:9. When (not if) believers trip up and momentarily yield to the flesh, we have an Advocate in Heaven who pleads our case before the court in Heaven, and obtains forgiveness for us. Not based upon what we've done, but upon what He's done!

People who are truly repentant don't play games with God's love, mercy, and forgiveness—they do their best, with God's help, to overcome the formers sins or lusts, and live sin-free lives consistently. It means you don't go back and dabble in that same old pattern of sexual sin that got you into trouble with God in the first place! You receive your forgiveness and move on, and do your best never to look back in shame or discouragement. God is not looking at your past, only at your future! You and I should do the same.

In my book, *Military Mentality*, chapter 5 talks about identifying more tactics of the enemy which he will try to use in his efforts to entice your flesh to sin. I encourage you to get and use that information as additional support to help you maintain victory over the carnal attacks of the enemy, so that you can maintain your ability to consistently advance under enemy fire.

CHAPTER 13

Mental Attacks:
Pressure on the Mind

*And do not be conformed to this world, but be transformed
by the renewing of your mind, that you may prove what is
that good and acceptable and perfect will of God.*
—ROMANS 12:2

You'll never be able to advance under fire if you don't learn
how to transform yourself by the renewing of your mind to the
Word of God. Remember, we are tripartite—human beings with
three distinct parts to our composition. We are spirits who possess
souls and live in physical bodies. On the subject of personal
control and influence while living here on Earth, the Bible makes
it very clear that the majority always rules—2 against 1.

After receiving Jesus as Lord and Savior, our spirit is born-
again, according to John 3:3. It's alive unto God and wants to serve
and obey Him. Our body is still dead-to-sin on the other hand,
and wants to continue to obey the lusts of the flesh and rebel
against God. That makes the soul the pivotal part of our being.
The soul will consist of our mind, will, and emotions, and is key to
determining our success or failure in managing our minds, and
keeping us in the place where we're pleasing to God, and "meet
for the Master's use" (see 2 Timothy 2:21).

If we renew our minds to God's Word, as it tells us to do in Romans 12:2, its 2 against 1—our born-again spirit coupled with our renewed mind will team up against the flesh and subdue it. If we fail to renew our minds to God's Word, then it's also 2 against 1—the sinful nature in our unregenerate flesh, coupled with the unrenewed mind, teams up against our born-again spirit to suppress it (see Romans 8:7). The soul is the hinge—swinging either to the side where God controls our lives, or to the side where the devil controls our lives. However, which way it swings is completely up to us—it's always a matter of choice and the most powerful weapon given to man: free will. That's why a renewed mind is so critical when attempting to live a life pleasing to God. God won't make you serve Him, and the devil can't force you to serve him. It's all up to you—that's why the "soul hinge" is so important to monitor and control.

Unseen Forces Are at Work on Earth

Make no mistake—you're being dominated by external forces that, comparatively speaking, are bigger and stronger than you—always! Either God is in control of your life, or the devil is in control of your life. *But their level of influence and control is based upon the daily decisions you make, not the decisions they make.* There is no such thing as an independently functioning human being, even if they think they are. For a person to think that they're in control of their life apart from the unseen forces that operate on planet Earth is nothing more than biblical ignorance and spiritual deception running amok.

We are born into a world at war—an unseen war for the souls of men. Humankind is the target for all that is done in the spirit world. We're the object of God's love and at the same time, the devil's hatred. That truth puts us right in the middle of this great global conflict. *We are the prize that everyone in the spirit world is fighting for!*

Depending upon what we do with our souls—the decisions and choices we make everyday—we empower either God or Satan in our lives. The power of choice is ours to use as we see fit, and God will honor our choices right up to the moment we breathe our last breath. God will love us always, but can only protect and provide for those who choose wisely according to His Word. The devil cannot touch us until we give him permission by making choices that open doors for the enemy to come in to steal, kill, and destroy. The free will of man is God's gift to each of us, and the devil *must* honor that no matter what. He can't come in and deceive people, keep them in sin, and wreak havoc in their lives just because he wants to. He must influence us to make a choice that legally gives him permission.

By His Spirit, God will always lead and suggest the right course of action that ensures our personal and spiritual well-being, and the devil will always work to tempt and pressure us with the wrong course of action that leads to suffering, heartache, and if possible, spiritual death. But in the end we do the choosing, so make sure you're not ignorant of the devil's devices. First Peter 5:8 tells us to be *sober and vigilant,* because the devil is always on the prowl, looking for someone to devour and destroy. In other words, keep your armor on and stay mentally alert!

Here are some of the major ways we have mental pressure brought to bear against us by the devil:

Stress

When I was growing up in the 1950s and 1960s, nobody talked about "stress." That term really came into its own sometime during the 1970s and 1980s, and has now become firmly entrenched in the psyche of millions of people worldwide. Even if the term itself is a relative newcomer to the social scene, it has managed to become the default buzzword for just about anything that brings uncomfortable pressure to bear in our lives. From the *American Heritage Dictionary,* here is how "stress" is defined as a noun:

a. A mentally or emotionally disruptive or upsetting condition occurring in response to adverse external influences and capable of affecting physical health, usually characterized by increased heart rate, a rise in blood pressure, muscular tension, irritability, and depression.

b. A stimulus or circumstance causing such a condition.

Does any of this sound familiar? Applying mental pressure against us is one of Satan's prime tools of destruction in our lives, and he's successfully sown it everywhere in these last days.

And let us not grow weary while doing good, for in due season we shall reap if we do not lose heart.

—GALATIANS 6:9

But as for you, brethren, do not grow weary in doing good.

—2 THESSALONIANS 3:13

The common denominator in these verses is the word "weary," or the subject of weariness. Stress leads to emotional and physical weariness. What does that word mean? *Merriam-Webster's Dictionary* gives the following definition for "weary" as an adjective:

1. *Exhausted in strength, endurance, vigor, or freshness;*

2. *Expressing or characteristic of weariness;*

3. *Having one's patience, tolerance, or pleasure exhausted.*

Synonyms for this word would be:

Beat, beaten, bleary, burned-out (or burnt-out), bushed, dead, done, done in, drained, exhausted, fatigued, jaded, limp, played out, pooped, prostrate, spent, tapped out, tired, tuckered (out), washed-out, wearied, wiped out, worn, worn-out, worn to a frazzle.

Would any of these words describe you? Don't be stressed out and become weary for God! Hang in there! When mental pressure and stress try to rob you of your vitality and joy, rebuke those thoughts in Jesus' name! Follow David's example, when his men were blaming him for all of the pain and heartache that took place at Ziklag.

> *Now it happened, when David and his men came to Ziklag, on the third day, that the Amalekites had invaded the South and Ziklag, attacked Ziklag and burned it with fire, and had taken captive the women and those who were there, from small to great; they did not kill anyone, but carried them away and went their way. So David and his men came to the city, and there it was, burned with fire; and their wives, their sons, and their daughters had been taken captive. Then David and the people who were with him lifted up their voices and wept, until they had no more power to weep. And David's two wives, Ahinoam the Jezreelitess, and Abigail the widow of Nabal the Carmelite, had been taken captive. Now David was greatly distressed, **for the people spoke of stoning him,** because the soul of all the people was grieved, every man for his sons and his daughters. **But David strengthened himself in the Lord his God.***
>
> —1 SAMUEL 30:1-6 [EMPHASIS MINE]

While David and his men were away, the enemy had come in and looted their town, burning it to the ground. Not only that, but they took away as prisoners all of their wives and children. You can imagine how distraught and upset everyone was at that moment. The Bible says they cried until they ran out of tears! But during this time of grieving, take special notice of verse 6. As distressed (stressed out) as David was over the loss of his two wives, he was even more stressed out by the fact that his own men spoke of stoning him because of what had happened.

What did David do in response? He did something you and I are going to have to do when we face the kind of stress and mental pressure he faced. We're going to have to strengthen ourselves in the Lord. The *King James* version uses the word "encourage," saying David encouraged himself in the Lord. Whichever word you use is fine with God—just do what David did! If you want to advance under fire and gain the victory when stress and pressure comes your way, you must follow David's example.

How do you encourage and strengthen yourself in the Lord? You take God's Word and you start meditating upon it, as it tells us to do in Joshua 1:8 and Psalms 1:2. (And when we talk about "meditation," we're not talking about sitting with our legs and fingers crossed in yoga class, listening to sitar music and sitting next to a bearded taxi driver from Calcutta named Raheeb). From a biblical perspective, meditation is the practice of talking to yourself in a low tone of voice, listening carefully to what you're saying. *Vine's* expository of Old Testament words says it involves the practice of sighing and musing to oneself—in other words, *muttering to yourself.*

Do you want to overcome the pressure and stress that comes against you mentally? Learn to meditate in God's Word, so you can strengthen and encourage yourself whenever you need to. The other important part of this truth lies in the fact that if you don't do it for yourself, it won't get done! It's great when we've got spiritually strong and faith-filled friends to surround us and help us in overcoming our mental battles. But that's not always going to be the case. What happens when they're not there and you're on your own? You had better know how to discipline yourself to do this with or without assistance from others! If you don't, the devil will turn you into mental mush.

The Bible has a lot to say about protecting your mind and keeping it stress free, especially in this tense and pressure-packed world in which we live. When the temptations to yield to stress threaten your mental health and well-being, let the Bible tell you what to do.

> *You will keep him in perfect peace, **whose mind is stayed on You.***
> —ISAIAH 26:3 [EMPHASIS MINE]

> *You will show me the path of life; **in Your presence** is fullness of joy; **at Your right hand** are pleasures forevermore.*
> —PSALM 16:11 [EMPHASIS MINE]

These are just two of dozens of verses that say the same thing. Because Christians fail to stay close to God, they become vulnerable to the mental attacks of the enemy, which are designed to create mental stress, instability, and double-mindedness. At that point, it's easy to become a mental wreck! (In my book *Be Strong, Stay Strong,* I list the seven spiritual priorities to be performed daily to counteract these mental attacks of the enemy.)

People who are able to stay consistent with their abilities to advance under fire for God have learned the discipline of mind renewal, according to the Word of God. Spending time with Jesus in prayer, praise, and worship, and meditating on both the greatness of God and the promises of God will produce a level of spiritual strength no mental test or trial can override or supplant.

Discouragement

Have you ever been full of excitement and anticipation over something you're using faith for with God, only to see failure and frustration instead? What happens when you see no growth, no progress, no fruit, or no results? I've been there many times, and I bet you have too. When we desire to accomplish meaningful things for Jesus in this life, it's easy to become discouraged when things don't work out the way we planned—especially when our actions or activities are based upon promises God gave us in His Word.

When the dream that you've been confessing for seems to fall apart, or is about to, the devil is going to try and hit you with the temptation of mental discouragement. To consistently advance under fire, you must learn how to resist this in Jesus' name. How do you do that? By doing what Hebrews chapter 12 tells us:

> *For consider Him who endured such hostility from sinners against Himself, lest you become weary and discouraged in your souls.*
>
> —HEBREWS 12:3

Notice that when we're tempted to become weary, discourage-ment comes along for the ride! In a state of mental fatigue, it's easy to be tempted to be discouraged as well. When that happens, we should do what Hebrews tells us to do: *consider Jesus.*

Stop and think about all that our Lord went through during His time on Earth. Stop and think about all the times He was tempted to be discouraged! *Jesus? Discouraged?* Yes, just like you and me, my friend. Remember, the Bible tells us that our Lord was tempted in *all points* like we, yet without sin (see Hebrews 4:15). If you've been tempted to become weary and discouraged, it's reassuring to know Jesus has already been where you are. He knows what you're going through because He was tempted in the same way.

People tend to forget these things when they're going through battles in the mind, but it's to our benefit to take the time to consider Jesus. He dealt with every kind of demonic temptation the devil could think of, yet was without sin! Praise God forever-more! That fact alone is, to me, an accomplishment so remarkable that words can't describe it. Truly, Jesus is the Lamb worthy to be praised, adored, and worship forever.

Thank God He came and saved the human race from their sins, but from start to finish with regards to His earthly life (espe-cially His last three and a half years in public ministry), it was a titanic struggle against the forces of darkness. If your life in Christ has been challenging in any sense of the word, understand that Jesus faced and overcame all the challenges we'll ever face—many times over! Yes, He had to overcome adversity, temptation, and persecution at every turn, because everything Jesus did was contested by the devil, every step of the way, every day. If you think you've been the object of intense mental attack from Satan, imagine how ferocious those attacks would have been against Jesus, once the devil realized Who Jesus was, and what He was on Earth to do?

Where did Jesus go when He needed to re-charge and re-group for the task at hand? Where did He go when tempted to become discouraged? He always went to His Heavenly Father in prayer. How many times throughout the four gospels do we see

Him doing this? The Bible records a number of times where He would go off to commune with God, in many cases all night long. You can be sure He was doing this a lot more than what is recorded in the Word of God. Here are some examples.

Before He selected His top leadership team, the Lord went off to pray all night, so that in the morning He could pick the right people with surety and confidence (see Luke 6:12-16). In another instance, just after feeding five thousand men from five loaves and two fish, He sent His disciples across the lake and dismissed the multitudes so He could climb a mountain to be alone with God in prayer (see Matthew 14:18-23). What was Jesus doing just before He was transfigured in front of Peter, James, and John? Praying. What was he doing as He was transfigured before their eyes? Praying (see Luke 9:28-29)! What preceded the giving of what we commonly call "The Lord's Prayer"? Times of prayer between God and Jesus (see Luke 11:1-5).

Jesus knew where to go and what to do when weariness and discouragement came against Him. Consider Him, *and do the same!*

Ungodly Thoughts

Mental attacks are always comprised of thoughts that the enemy is trying to plant. It is truthfully said that the greatest battles we will ever fight on Earth are the ones we fight in our minds. Every attack of the devil begins with a thought (or mental suggestion) that he wants you to accept as truth, or entertain until it becomes a stronghold (see 2 Corinthians 10:3-5). That's why the Bible is full of instructions on how we are to renew our minds, capture thoughts, and pull down strongholds.

The Bible tells us that we have (present tense) the mind of Christ (see 1 Corinthians 2:16). That means we have the God-given ability as a child of God to be the kind of godly, disciplined thinker that Jesus was while on Earth, and now in Heaven at God's right hand. We *can* think like Jesus. Not only is it possible, but *required.* How do we develop the mind of Christ, so we can success-fully manage our thought life? Look at what the Bible says.

> *For though we walk in the flesh, we do not war after the flesh: (for the weapons of our warfare are not carnal, but mighty through God to the pulling down of strong holds;) casting down imaginations, and every high thing that exalteth itself against the knowledge of God, and bringing into captivity every thought to the obedience of Christ.*
>
> —2 Corinthians 10:3-5 KJV

I'm using the *King James* version here because I love the way that translation words this truth. Notice verse 5 carefully. We're told to cast down imaginations (thoughts), and every high thing (thoughts) that exalt themselves against the knowledge of God (as recorded in the Word of God). Then, we're told to *bring into captivity every thought* to the obedience of Christ. Imaginations, high things, and thoughts—these are lies or half-truths the devil is trying to establish as a beachhead in your mind! That means we're to control our minds and only allow thoughts to remain if they line up with and agree with God and His Word.

How do you surround and take a thought captive? *By saying something to it!*

> *Therefore I say unto you, **Take no thought** for your life, what ye shall eat, or what ye shall drink; nor yet for your body, what ye shall put on. Is not the life more than meat, and the body than raiment? Behold the fowls of the air: for they sow not, neither do they reap, nor gather into barns; yet your heavenly Father feedeth them. Are ye not much better than they? Which of you **by taking thought** can add one cubit unto his stature? And **why take ye thought** for raiment? Consider the lilies of the field, how they grow; they toil not, neither do they spin: and yet I say unto you, that even Solomon in all his glory was not arrayed like one of these. Wherefore, if God so clothe the grass of the field, which today is, and tomorrow is cast into the oven, shall he not much more clothe you, O ye of little faith? **Therefore take no thought, saying,** What shall we eat? or, What shall we drink? or, Wherewithal shall we be*

clothed? (For after all these things do the Gentiles seek:) for your heavenly Father knoweth that ye have need of all these things. But seek ye first the kingdom of God, and his righteousness; and all these things shall be added unto you. Take therefore no thought for the morrow: for the morrow shall take thought for the things of itself. Sufficient unto the day is the evil thereof.

—MATTHEW 6:25-34 KJV [EMPHASIS MINE]

Again, I am using the *King James* version here because of its choice of words. When the devil tries to bombard your mind with thousands of ungodly thoughts, how do you take those thoughts captive? *By surrounding them and imprisoning them with the spoken Word of God.* This is a crucial truth that most Christians are ignorant of.

What did the passage in Matthew tell us to do? *Take no thought, saying.* . . . Did you catch that? *Saying!* How to you take the devil's thoughts? By repeating them out loud out your mouth! If you don't say or repeat whatever it is he's trying to plant in your mind, you won't be taking his thought. Instead, you counterattack by *saying* whatever verse or verses directly contradict the lies the devil is trying to plant in your mind. This is exactly what Jesus did when the devil came to tempt him, as recorded in Matthew chapter 4, and Luke chapter 4. Even when the devil tried using the Word of God as a part of his tactic to sow ungodly thoughts into the mind of Jesus, Jesus counterattacked by quoting scripture right back in the devil's face.

To advance under fire, you're going to have to take captive any and all ungodly thoughts that contradict the Word of God. To do that, you must replace the devil's thoughts with other thoughts that line up with the Bible. You're going to have to learn to say to the devil "It is written" or "It is also written" if he tries using the Bible against you. Then quote *out loud* the promise or promises that successfully incarcerate those demonic thoughts, which prevent them from becoming strongholds.

Don't Let Footholds Become Strongholds

When the devil tries to come at you with his lying thoughts, he's trying to gain a mental foothold in your mind. Don't let it happen! This is always his desired first step against you. If you don't take his thoughts by saying them out loud, he won't be able to create a foothold. Follow the instructions in Philippians chapter 4.

> *Be anxious for nothing, but in everything by prayer and supplication, with thanksgiving, let your requests be made known to God; and the peace of God, which surpasses all understanding, will guard your hearts and minds through Christ Jesus. Finally, brethren, whatever things are true, whatever things are noble, whatever things are just, whatever things are pure, whatever things are lovely, whatever things are of good report, if there is any virtue and if there is anything praiseworthy—meditate on these things.*
>
> —PHILIPPIANS 4:6-8

The Word of God tells us exactly what to think on, so do what God says and the devil will never be able to create a foothold that eventually becomes a stronghold! Here is the devil's three-step plan against your mind:

1. Plant ungodly thoughts to sow fear and/or deception in your mind.

2. Get you to keep thinking on those thoughts to create a mental foothold.

3. Keep the mental pressure on until you start speaking and repeating his lies, thereby creating a stronghold from the foothold.

A stronghold is simply an "air castle" that you've allowed the devil to create in your mind. It's a scenario or false reality that's based upon lies and half-truths. It's a thought, or group of thoughts, that holds you in bondage and captivity to fear, and to the whims and will of the devil. Over the years, I've seen plenty of people (saved and unsaved alike) who live in total bondage to a lie Satan successfully planted in their minds years before—a foothold that became a stronghold.

Here's one prime example from the arena of divine health and healing. Many good Christian people have gone home to Heaven prematurely, because they quit fighting the fight of faith, or never tried to stand in faith for healing in the first place. Why? Because they were told that it might not be God's will for them to get healed. They were told that He might want them to suffer in sickness and disease in order to teach them some kind of spiritual "lesson."

May I say it straight up? *That is a lie from the pit of hell.* And anyone biblically ignorant enough to accept it as truth allows the devil to create a mental stronghold that prevents them from tapping into the power of God for healing. At that point, people like that are at the mercy of medical science, and as well-intentioned as doctors, nurses, and hospitals may be, they'll be the first to tell you they're only *practicing* medicine, and we're the ones they're practicing on! On the other hand, Jesus doesn't practice medicine in the hopes of getting it right. He just heals people completely, from top to bottom, because as our Lord, Savior, and Creator, He knows exactly what He's doing.

By the stripes of Jesus we were all (past tense) healed (see 1 Peter 2:24). If we were then, we are now! Everybody has a legal right to health and healing once they receive Jesus as Lord. But of course, like anything else in the Word of God, that victory must be enforced and appropriated by faith. That's where the devil will attack in our minds. Once you buy into the lie that it might not be God's will to heal you, you've lost and the devil has won! If that's you or someone you know, pray that you don't get hit with some sort of terminal sickness or disease, because if you do, you're in big trouble, my friend! Don't let this happen to you!

First John 5:4 says that *our faith* is the victory that overcomes the world (which includes the lies, tactics, and tools of the devil). We need to know that from God's viewpoint, our victory doesn't come when we get whatever it is we're using our faith for, such as healing when we're sick. It comes when we make the decision to use our faith to get that healing. It comes when you decide that no matter what, and no matter for how long, you're going to stay strong in faith, as it tells us in Ephesians 6:13.

Since 1980, in thousands of Miracle Crusades in the Philippines, and in prayer lines in countless church services worldwide, we've seen God do healing miracles upon those who choose to exercise simple faith in God and His promises for healing. We preach the Word to people, and before the devil has a chance to pollute their minds with lies and half-truths to sow doubt and confusion, they just accept what God says and get healed as a result.

A person can't change the past, but they have control over the future. If you've already allowed the enemy to create footholds leading to strongholds, start today to reverse the confession of your mouth, and *only* repeat out loud what God says about you and your situation. In addition, surround yourself with others who know how to speak the Language of Faith, and separate yourself from those who don't. By doing that, you'll successfully develop the ability to consistently advance under fire, no matter how much mental pressure is brought to bear against you.

One of the most helpful books I've read on the subject of renewing the mind is *Right and Wrong Thinking* by Rev. Kenneth E. Hagin. If you don't have that book, I'd recommend it you without hesitation. It has helped me, and I believe it could help you, too.

CHAPTER 14

Financial Attacks:
All It Takes Is Money!

*A feast is made for laughter, and wine makes merry;
but money answers everything.*
—ECCLESIASTES 10:19

This verse just about says it all! Money answers all things, and that truth applies to saint and sinner alike. Whether a person is saved or not, the more money you have, the more leverage you have in life, and it's no secret that the majority of financial funds on this planet are in the hands of ungodly and unsaved people. The enemy plans to do his best to keep it that way!

We're going to need money to do whatever we want to do for God in this life on Earth, and that's why as the god of this world (see 2 Corinthians 4:4), Satan will fight us in this area more than in any other. To advance under fire when all hell is arrayed against us, we're going to need huge sums of money to go into all the world and preach the gospel. Salvation is God's free gift to all of humankind, but the business of enforcing that victory on Earth isn't free at all—it requires, among many other things, large amounts of money to fund the work of ministry worldwide.

If you're old enough to understand these things, you're old enough to know its true. Everything on this Earth requires money to buy or acquire. A few people have a lot, and most people don't. That's why God makes this statement in the Bible:

> *A good man leaves an inheritance to his children's children, but the wealth of the sinner is stored up for the righteous.*
>
> —PROVERBS 13:22

God knows we need money both to live and do business for Him. The devil knows this too, that's why he works day and night to create what one preacher referred to as "financial satanic reservoirs." Those are people (saved or unsaved) who selfishly hoard money for themselves, and won't let go unless it's for their own personal benefit, or for causes that have nothing to do with the work of saving souls for Jesus.

Even though God promises us prosperity in many places throughout the Bible, we must never forget that the devil is standing in the way of those promises, ready to steal as much money and resources away from us as possible. He knows that the more money we have, the more we can give and use for the funding of the gospel. He also knows that we can't give what we don't have, so he does his best to divert, delay, or steal whatever amounts we need to fulfill God's perfect will for us in this life.

Ministry Costs Money!

Anybody who is a student of Charismatic and Pentecostal history knows about the renowned evangelist Oral Roberts, and the great evangelistic and healing ministry he was gifted with through the 1950s, 60s, and 70s. His tent meetings attracted tens of thousands of people, where thousands of people were saved with notable signs, wonders, and miracles consistently taking place as well. He was the visionary that conceived and then built Oral Roberts University in Tulsa, Oklahoma, which included the City of Faith. No one can objectively deny the fact that Oral Roberts was a man heavily anointed by God, who accomplished tremendous things for the Lord in his lifetime.

A friend of mine told me once that he heard Evelyn Roberts, Oral Roberts' wife, say that in all the years of ministry work for God, their available cash on hand was never more that what could sustain them for a week or two beyond today! In other words, if their support unexpectedly stopped or dried up, they would be broke within a matter of weeks! When you stop and think about all that Oral and Evelyn Roberts accomplished for God, that's a remarkable fact. For me at least, it's also a very encouraging thing never to be forgotten, especially when we're active in the business of winning souls in obedience to the Great Commission of Mark 16:15-18.

In our present time, I personally know of large, fruitful, anointed ministries that consistently struggle to keep their heads above water financially. In our own ministry, since I started in 1980, there has never been a time when we had *any* financial surplus or reserve—ever. Since then until now, we literally live and operate this ministry day-to-day by faith, trusting God to meet our needs, pay our bills, and keep us from going bankrupt. For all these years, we have done what we've done for God by staying one step ahead of the bill collectors, and three steps ahead of the devil!

When you live and operate like this, you will have ample opportunity to fear for your financial future (I know I have)! When the bills are piling up, and we're going through the latest recession or economic downturn, and the support has been drastically cut, the temptation and pressure to fear becomes great. But you know what? I found out years ago that worry does nothing but give the devil free ammunition against me, so why worry? Philippians says it this way:

> *Be anxious for nothing, but in everything by prayer and supplication, with thanksgiving, let your requests be made known to God; and the peace of God, which surpasses all understanding, will guard your hearts and minds through Christ Jesus.*
>
> —PHILIPPIANS 4:6-7

When the Bible says we should be "anxious for nothing," it means we should never worry—ever! "Nothing" includes your finances. Have you ever been tempted to worry about your financial situation? I have—many times! And each time that kind of temptation comes my way, I must remember what I'm telling you here—worry is a waste of time and energy. It only empowers the enemy to continue in his efforts to steal as much of my finances as possible. It's like handing him free ammunition and inviting him to continue shooting at you.

Here is what verse 6 is telling us: *worry about nothing and pray about everything.* When you're under financial pressure, don't worry about it, because your worry won't produce one dime's worth of relief. Instead, take your situation to God in prayer, and once you've talked with Him and applied your faith to the matter, relax and let God be God! Get God's guidance and do what His Word tells you to do. Use your faith, exercise your authority, command the angels to help, and bind up the devil. That's your part. Once you've done all you should do as a believer, stand your ground and with patience, praise God for the financial victory (see Ephesians 6:11-14 and Luke 8:15).

This is the procedure I've used since 1978 when I was first born-again, and since 1980 when I started out in full-time ministry. It works. It's worked for me, and it will for you too. *We do what we can do, and then God does what we can't do.* We can pray, exercise authority, praise the Lord, read and quote the appropriate verses out loud to ourselves (and to the devil if he's listening nearby), exhibit patience and then—watch God work! If you look at Jesus in ministry, you never see Him worried about financial supply. He just *knew* His heavenly Father would take care of his needs, and operated with that kind of spiritual assurance from start to finish in His earthly ministry.

Serve God, Not Money!

Christians who worry about money serve money, not God. They don't think of themselves in that way, but that is what they're doing, even if they don't realize it. As I said earlier, I've operated our ministry by faith since September, 1980, when I landed in the Philippines with $20 in my pocket and no airplane ticket back to the USA (I only had enough money to buy a one-way ticket, not round trip). In all the years from then until now, we've always had to trust God for the next meal, the next crusade budget, money for the next pile of bills due, etc. We've never had a surplus or a reserve to work with. I honestly don't know what its like to operate our ministry with a comfortable cash reserve in the bank, because we've never had it. We believe God for the funds to run this ministry on opposite sides of the world simultaneously, trusting the Lord to provide the income necessary to keep going day by day. If I find myself worrying about where the money is going to come from to pay the bills to run the ministry, I'm trying to serve God *and* mammon (money), and Jesus said we can't do both (see Matthew 6:24).

And when you really stop and think about it, it's a slap in God's face when we allow worry and fear to usurp our faith in God's ability to meet our needs financially. If God could create and maintain *the universe,* don't you think He can handle our finances—especially when He's the One, according to Mark 16:15-18, who told us to go into all world to preach? Whether it is for our needs just to live and take care of the affairs of life, or for our needs to represent Him and share the gospel, God promises to provide. That being said, there is no reason to worry about your money! This is what Jesus was talking about when He told the crowds to *consider* the lilies and the birds!

"Therefore I say to you, do not worry about your life, what you will eat or what you will drink; nor about your body, what you will put on. Is not life more than food and the body more than clothing? Look at the birds of the air, for they neither sow nor reap nor gather into barns; yet your heavenly Father feeds them. Are you not of more value than they? Which of you by worrying can add one cubit to his stature? So why do you worry about clothing? Consider the lilies of the field, how they grow: they neither toil nor spin; and yet I say to you that even Solomon in all his glory was not arrayed like one of these. Now if God so clothes the grass of the field, which today is, and tomorrow is thrown into the oven, will He not much more clothe you, O you of little faith? Therefore do not worry, saying, 'What shall we eat?' or 'What shall we drink?' or 'What shall we

wear?' For after all these things the Gentiles seek. For your heavenly Father knows that you need all these things. But seek first the kingdom of God and His righteousness, and all these things shall be added to you. Therefore do not worry about tomorrow, for tomorrow will worry about its own things. Sufficient for the day is its own trouble."

—MATTHEW 6:25-34

This teaching segment from Jesus pretty much says it all, don't you think? Notice He's asking us to consider the birds of the air, and the lilies of the field. In other words, He's asking us to take a step back from our financial crisis, and remind ourselves about who tells us He loves us, will never leave us, and always takes care of us. God! Jesus! The Holy Spirit! If God be for you, no one (and no situation) can be against you (see Romans 8:31).

Have you ever seen two birds sitting on a branch, chirping about the tough times they're living in? One bird hangs his head, turns to the other bird to lament the fact that the price of twigs has just gone up again, and the bank is threatening to foreclose on their new nest if they don't catch up on their mortgage payments. The other bird nods his head in sad affirmation, puts his wing around the other bird to let him know he understands— he's having a hard time feeding his family too—the worms just aren't as abundant as they used to be.

No! That's not the way it is. No matter what's going on, the birds just keep on singing, flying, and doing what God made them to do. They don't worry about *anything.* They just do what they were created to do—fly around, look beautiful while doing it, and sing! Why not take a cue from the birds? Relax! Spend more time singing, smiling, laughing, quoting scripture, praising and worshipping God, and sharing Jesus with others. *Quit worrying about the money!* It'll be there when you need it because you are far more valuable to God than the birds!

Are not two sparrows sold for a copper coin? And not one of them falls to the ground apart from your Father's will. But the very hairs of your head are all numbered. Do not fear therefore; you are of more value than many sparrows.

—MATTHEW 10:29-31

It's the same thing when considering the flowers of the field. They don't worry about their needs being met—they just grow and look beautiful, the way God intended. They don't try to be beautiful, they just are! In the same way, we should just let God be our Heavenly Father, let Jesus be the Shepherd of Psalm 23 in our lives, and let the angels assist us as they're commissioned to, according to Hebrews 1:14.

Jesus finishes this teaching in Matthew by sharing this truth: if God takes care of all other aspects of His creation, such as birds and flowers, *how much more* will He take care of us—the objects of His love and affection? How much more?! It's a rhetorical question. That means everyone should already know the answer before the question is posed. When the devil is putting financial pressure on you, and tempting you to collapse in fear for the lack of finances, meditate on what Habakkuk did when confronted with frightening circumstances.

Though the fig tree may not blossom, nor fruit be on the vines; though the labor of the olive may fail, and the fields yield no food; though the flock may be cut off from the fold, and there be no herd in the stalls—yet I will rejoice in the LORD, I will joy in the God of my salvation. The LORD God is my strength; He will make my feet like deer's feet, and He will make me walk on my high hills.

To the Chief Musician. With my stringed instruments.

—HABAKKUK 3:17-19

Notice the last sentence in this passage. This was a song they were singing, not just words they were saying. And when were they singing this song? *In the midst of total financial wipe-out!* This would be today's equivalent to people losing their shirts in a stock market crash, or going bankrupt in a failed business venture, or having everything they owned destroyed in some kind of natural disaster like an earthquake, tornado, flood or hurricane. That's verse 17, but notice the reaction in verse 18. The word "yet" means "even so."

Habakkuk is saying that in spite of what has just happened to him, he's going to choose to advance under the enemy fire that has cleaned him out from top to bottom. He's declaring that even though he has lost everything and has nothing left to his name, he *chooses* to rejoice in the Lord, and be joyful before the God of his salvation. We must choose to do the same, otherwise we'll never successfully rise above the financial pressures the devil brings to bear against us.

When you've been hit broadside by some unexpected financial meltdown, you can choose to sit in fear for your financial future, or you can stand up, put your spiritual armor back on, and re-engage the enemy with faith! *It's just a choice.* Verse 19 is what you say when you decide to get up and get back in the fight. It's your confession of faith in God's love for you, and in His ability to strengthen you and get you through the tough financial times.

So when you look at these verses with your spiritual eyes open, here's what we see:

1. Verse 17 is what the devil does (stealing, killing, destroying).

2. Verse 18 is what you do in response to what the devil does (choosing to praise God in faith, rather than worrying yourself to death).

3. Verse 19 is what God does for you in response to how you responded to what the devil did (responding to your confessions of faith to strengthen, empower, and deliver you financially).

As we move through this life in Christ Jesus, we're going to face many financial challenges along the way. Learn to trust God no matter what it looks like, or how bad it seems at the moment. Do what the Bible tells you to do, and you'll be advancing under "financial fire" every single time!

A great little mini-book that gives further insight into this issue of financial prosperity is called *How God Taught Me about Prosperity,* by Kenneth E. Hagin. I recommend it to you.

CHAPTER 15

Doctrinal Attacks: Heresy Creeping In!

But there were also false prophets among the people, even as there will be false teachers among you, who will secretly bring in destructive heresies, even denying the Lord who bought them, and bring on themselves swift destruction.And many will follow their destructive ways, because of whom the way of truth will be blasphemed. By covetousness they will exploit you with deceptive words; for a long time their judgment has not been idle, and their destruction does not slumber.

—2 PETER 2:1-3

If you read the New Testament carefully, you'll discover that every writer dealt with the problem of false doctrine creeping into the churches. *Every letter* in the New Testament deals with this issue to one degree or another, and if you're going to advance for Jesus under fire from the enemy, you must be able to identify false doctrine when you encounter it, and do what the Bible says to keep that poison out of your heart and life.

In our opening passage above, Peter is warning his disciples about false prophets and teachers *secretly* bringing destructive heresies into the fellowship. Jude says the heretics and false teachers were *creeping* into the churches (see Jude 3-13). The emphasis in the warning isn't just for the fact that what was being taught was heresy, but for the fact that many in the churches weren't recognizing it as such. To "creep in secretly" means that little bit by little bit, these false teachers were introducing lies and half-truths that would ultimately undermine the integrity of the gospel message.

One could easily write an entire book on this subject alone, because it's an end-time sign that Jesus said would be rampant in the days just before His return.

> *Now as He sat on the Mount of Olives, the disciples came to Him privately, saying, "Tell us, when will these things be? And what will be the sign of Your coming, and of the end of the age?" And Jesus answered and said to them:* **"Take heed that no one deceives you.** *For many will come in My name, saying, 'I am the Christ,'* **and will deceive many."**
>
> —MATTHEW 24:3-5 [EMPHASIS MINE]

When the disciples asked for signs to indicate our Lord's imminent return, the first thing Jesus mentions is *many deceivers deceiving many people.* Therefore, the first sign to look for that tells us that Jesus is "at the door" is this issue of false doctrine and heresy infiltrating the churches and Body of Christ.

> *But evil men and impostors will grow worse and worse, deceiving and being deceived. But you must continue in the things which you have learned and been assured of, knowing from whom you have learned them, and that from childhood you have known the Holy Scriptures, which are able to make you wise for salvation through faith which is in Christ Jesus.*
>
> —2 TIMOTHY 3:13-15

This was a problem for Paul, and every other New Testament leader. It was bad then, but it's gotten a lot worse in these last days, which is exactly what the Holy Spirit said would be happening— evil men and imposters *growing worse and worse.* This isn't going away my friend, so you better know what you believe, why you believe it, and where you find it in the Bible, so you know how to defend sound doctrine when (not if) necessary.

There are multitudes of people out there, who are agents of Satan disguised as angels of light (see 2 Corinthians 11:14). They are not only deceived, but busy deceiving others—as many as they can, exactly as described here in 2 Timothy chapter 3. At this point, it's crucial to remember that people who are deceived don't think they are—that's the reason why deception is so deadly, and the reason why it's so critical to stay spiritually alert. People by the droves are being led away from sound doctrine, because they are either biblically ignorant, too spiritually dense, or too weak to put up a scriptural defense.

The Pastoral Epistles Are Full of Warnings

As I said, all the books in the New Testament warn us about false teachers teaching false doctrine in the end times, but Paul's writings to his two sons-in-the-faith, Timothy and Titus, amplify the point. Go through those three letters, and look at how many times the importance of protecting sound doctrine comes up in Paul's instructions to these two leaders.

1 Timothy 1:3-7: . . . *Charge some that they teach no other* **doctrine**.

1 Timothy 1:8-11: . . . *Contrary to sound* **doctrine**.

1 Timothy 4:6-7: . . . *Nourished in the words of faith and of the good* **doctrine** *which you have carefully followed.*

1 Timothy 4:13: . . . *Give attention to reading, to exhortation, to* **doctrine**.

1 Timothy 4:16: *Take heed to yourself and to the* **doctrine**. *Continue in them.*

1 Timothy 5:17: . . . *Especially those who labor in the word and* **doctrine**.

1 Timothy 6:1: . . . *So that the name of God and His* **doctrine** *may not be blasphemed.*

1 Timothy6:3-5: *If anyone teaches otherwise and does not consent to wholesome words, even the words of our Lord Jesus Christ, and to the **doctrine** which accords with godliness.*

2 Timothy 3:10: *. . . You have carefully followed my **doctrine**.*

2 Timothy 3:16-17: *All scripture is given by inspiration of God, and is profitable for **doctrine**.*

2 Timothy 4:3-5: *For the time will come when they will not endure sound **doctrine**.*

Titus 1:9: *. . . Holding fast the faithful word as he has been taught, that he may be able, by sound **doctrine**, both to exhort and convict those who contradict.*

Titus 2:1: *. . . Speak the things which are proper for sound **doctrine**.*

Titus 2:6-8: *In all things showing yourself to be a pattern of good works; in **doctrine** showing integrity.*

Titus 2:10: *. . . That they may adorn the **doctrine** of God our Savior in all things.*

Titus 3:10-11 KJV: *A man that is an **heretick** after the first and second admonition reject.*

In reading these three letters, you don't need to be a rocket scientist to see the obvious. Protecting the truth with sound doctrine was one of Paul's major areas of admonition and instruction to his sons and daughters in the faith. If it was for him, then it should be even more so for us today.

In our own ministry in the Philippines, we've been attacked in this area on a number of occasions over the years. We've had some of our most loyal and trusted pastors turn from the truth to embrace a lie. To protect the truth and the integrity of our ministry, we had to cut off all fellowship with them as a result. We've had others try to convince us that it's perfectly alright with

God to be a practicing homosexual *and* a Christian *and* a minister of the gospel at the same time. When we found out they were hiding their own homosexuality, they were also cut off completely from our ministry and our churches.

Another heretic was trying to secretly introduce heresy and false doctrine into our organization over a two or three-year span of time, taking advantage of the trust we gave, and the access he had to our personnel and churches. When we finally found out the extent of his efforts to completely poison our staff, students, and pastors in the field, he was confronted and immediately removed. Among many other things, this poor soul was trying to convince us that doctrine wasn't important, and that all we should be talking about is the love of God. I guess the Apostle Paul didn't get his memo about doctrine not being important, and neither did Timothy, Titus, and anyone else who wrote those Holy Spirit-inspired letters that now make up the New Testament.

Doctrine is not just important; it's *extremely critical and crucial* in determining the eternal destinies of men. What you believe makes all the difference in the world between spiritual life or death, Heaven or Hell, and blessing or cursing in this life and the next. One of the quotes from the Pastoral Epistles above directly emphasizes this point:

*Take heed to yourself and to the doctrine. **Continue in them, for in doing this you will save both yourself and those who hear you.***
—1 TIMOTHY 4:16 [EMPHASIS MINE]

According to this passage, your salvation, and that of others who follow you, is directly determined by how well you continue in sound doctrine! It's not enough to start out with sound doctrine as the foundation for what you believe. You have to protect that platform for the rest of your life, because Satan will forever be looking for ways to chip away at the core beliefs that define who you are in Christ, and what you can do for Him in this life.

Recently, I received a great reminder about these things from Rev. Bob Yandian, who was one of my Bible school instructors years ago when I was a student at Rhema Bible Training College in Broken Arrow, OK. I would like to share it with you here, because it has a direct correlation to the things we must know in these last days regarding doctrinal attacks.

Truth and Love
by Bob Yandian

We often hear the phrase, *"speak the truth in love,"* but what exactly does that mean? It is a common belief that if you are going to speak the truth in love, it will require you to be *"mean and ugly."* On the other hand, many believe if you speak the truth in love, you must tolerate every viewpoint.

Recently I spoke at a church dedication that was being held in a location where a gay church formerly met. The pastor for whom I was dedicating the church invited the gay congregation to join his congregation for one last meeting in their former church home. Someone approached me about this upcoming meeting and said, "It's so wonderful that we're going to drop our doctrinal differences and lay them aside to come together in unity and love."

I just looked at him and said, *"You know, doctrine is very important. If it wasn't for doctrine, we couldn't get saved. If it wasn't for doctrine, we couldn't get filled with the Holy Spirit. We're not coming to drop the doctrines of God's Word, but we are coming in the love of God."*

It is important to realize you cannot dismiss the truth for love. Neither can you ignore truth for unity. Truth is above everything. It's not truth or love; it's truth and love together, not one or the other. We must realize the importance of God's Word. Jesus came because of truth and because of love. He came to Earth because He loved the world so much and was willing to lay down His life so the world could be saved. But He didn't lay down His differences and say, *"Anyone can come into the kingdom no matter what you believe, no matter what religion you are, and no matter if you believe in Me or not."*

The Word of God is not something you can go through and hand-select what you believe and what you don't believe. Many come out of denominations that did that. Some say, *"We don't believe in tongues."* Others say, *"We don't believe in healing."* You begin to find out that really, it's by knowing *all* the truth that the truth makes you free, which is why it's important to know the Word of God. All scripture is given by inspiration of God and is profitable (see 2 Timothy 3:16).

I trust in your life there's no particular part of the Bible that you don't like so you ignore it, put it on the shelf, and say, *"I'm not going to believe that."* We must believe every part of the Bible whether we understand it or not. Sometimes it is a step of faith to believe it because it's God's Word, but if we do that, He will give us the understanding and it will cause great growth to come into our life.

Wheat and Tares Growing Together

The parable about the wheat and tares is an end-time warning against false teachers, and the importance of remaining vigilant against them until Jesus comes back.

Another parable He put forth to them, saying: "The kingdom of heaven is like a man who sowed good seed in his field; but while men slept, his enemy came and sowed tares among the wheat and went his way. But when the grain had sprouted and produced a crop, then the tares also appeared. So the servants of the owner came and said to him, 'Sir, did you not sow good seed in your field? How then does it have tares?' He said to them, 'An enemy has done this.' The servants said to him, 'Do you want us then to go and gather them up?' But he said, 'No, lest while you gather up the tares you also uproot the wheat with them. Let both grow together until the harvest, and at the time of harvest I will say to the

*reapers, "First gather together the tares and bind them in bundles
to burn them, but gather the wheat into my barn.""*

—MATTHEW 13:24-30

According to this parable, who sowed the tares? An enemy. When
did he sow them? While the workers were sleeping. Where were
the tares growing? Alongside the wheat—side by side. For how
long are they allowed to grow side by side? Until the harvest. Do
they both go into the barn after being harvested? No, only the
wheat goes into the barn—the tares are bundled up and burned.

This parable is showing the alert reader what is going to be
taking place in these last days. The enemy is Satan, and the tares
represent the false teachers, false teachings, and heresies he is
actively sowing worldwide. Some of his "tares" are represented by
large, organized, and worldwide religions. Other "tares" would be
the myriad of false teachers sowing false doctrine into the Body of
Christ. And as long as we live on Earth, we're going to have to put
up with these tares, because until the end of this age they're going
to be here. When Jesus comes back, He's going to separate all the
adherents to false religion, all the false teachers and heretics that
have tried to infiltrate the church, and cast them into Hell. For
now though, our job is to recognize them, avoid them, and have
nothing to do with them.

According to 2 Timothy 3:14, we're supposed to *continue in the
things we heard and were assured of.* That simply means that you're to
protect the heritage of sound doctrine you were taught in the
beginning of your walk with Christ Jesus. To do that, you must
understand the following seven truths:

1) **Perilous times are here.** Second Timothy 3:1-5 plainly tells us
   that we're living in perilous times. The word "perilous" means
   dangerous. These are very dangerous times spiritually, and if
   the devil can't derail you through other tactics or tools (such
   as carnal attacks, mental attacks, financial attacks, and so
   forth), he will try this one to see how alert and spiritually
   awake you are!

The dangerous times are not only here, but they're getting more dangerous with each passing day. Stay spiritually alert and stay spiritually alive!

2) **False teachers and heretics are very charismatic.** Second Corinthians 11:14 tells us Satan himself transforms himself into an "angel of light," and his ministers do the same. They're very charismatic, very alluring, and very persuasive with their mannerisms and presentations. They're not standing up in a red suit, horns, and pitchfork, proclaiming themselves to be false teachers and heretics! On the contrary, they're very "slick" with how they bundle and package their lies—making themselves as spiritually appealing as possible to the unsuspecting.

Ephesians 4:14 tells us not to be swayed by "every wind of doctrine, by the trickery of men, in the cunning craftiness of deceitful plotting." Second Peter 2:18-19 talks about their "great swelling words of emptiness." Romans 16:17-18 tells us they use "smooth words and flattering speech" to deceive the hearts of the naïve or uneducated. That pretty well sums it up, don't you think? These false teachers and heretics have very magnetic personalities, enabling them to draw many away from the truth.

3) **False doctrines re-define terms.** Another common tactic used by the devil is to use the same words and terminology as those who teach the truth, but redefine what those terms mean. I recall one time reading about a person that had just been set free from the lies of Mormonism. In recounting the experience of being in this cult, this individual said the key to making the decision to come out revolved around the errant definitions they gave for critical topics like salvation, but that it took *several years* of fellowshipping with the Mormons to finally find out what they actually meant by what they said when talking about "salvation." I have had false teachers and heretics try to convince me they're just as "righteous" in God's eyes as those in the Body of Christ who believe the Bible's traditional stance on subjects like salvation, damnation, Heaven, Hell, judgment, etc. They will say things like: "I believe in the devil, *just not like you do.*" Or, "I believe in Hell,

just not like you do." What are they trying to do? Re-define the terms that describe the truth.

I've already made mention of another politically correct, yet spiritually deceptive heresy: homosexuality. Many in these last days (including so-called Christians and Christian ministers) are telling the world that homosexuality is an acceptable lifestyle in the eyes of God. Hence, we've got gay churches filled with people who cry, praise, prophesy, sing, and preach sermons from the Bible—all while living the twisted life of a homosexual.

We've had to deal with this one personally in our ministry. According to them, God is perfectly at peace with people who practice such perversions, even suggesting that they were "born this way," and that their homosexuality is "God's gift to them." (Yes, I've actually heard people make such claims). You see, in the circles of the deceived, terms must be redefined to lessen the natural repulsion "normal people" have to such practices. Thus, homosexuality must no longer be referred to as the abomination or perverted lifestyle that it is in the eyes of a holy God, but rather, as an "alternate lifestyle" and a "personal choice" between "committed adults." And of course, once you start down this road of re-defining terms, you're a very small step away from a complete breakdown in social, biblical morality.

That is why we now have the biblically ignorant stumbling over themselves to embrace the warped concept called "gay marriage." Guess what? As I said earlier, there is no such thing as "gay marriage"! The Creator, not the created, defines what marriage is and what it isn't—not some group, some political party, or unre-pentant sinner. Marriage is between one man and one woman—period. You don't like that? Tough. Truth cannot be altered or changed, and God's Word *is truth* (see John 17:17).

Universalism is another heresy that is very popular in today's society, because we've got multitudes of people out there who don't want to offend anyone at any time over anything. In essence, this is the false belief that everyone is going to Heaven, no matter who you are, what you believe or what kind of life you've lived. According to them, since Jesus died for all, all are saved and on their way to Heaven, even if they don't know it yet! It's a complete distortion of the truth about Jesus paying the price for all sins for all time, but because it offends no one (except God and those of us who rightly divide the Word of God), it's extremely popular. Once again, ask a Universalist if they believe in critical theology regarding Hell and the devil, and immediately they'll say they do—just not like we do!

Never forget this. When in doubt concerning what people mean with the terms they're using, *ask for definitions.* Many times, with a heresy like Universalism, people are purposely twisting the Word of God so they can continue living a sinful life with habits or practices they know to be wrong, but are unwilling to give up. And in many cases, the teachers of such heresies go to great lengths to hide their central, core beliefs, hoping that by carefully interjecting heresy little by little, they'll break down the will of the people to resist their teachings.

According to Luke 16:15, these people love to be "politically correct." They package their lies in beautifully gift-wrapped boxes filled with much love, caring, generosity, tenderness, understanding, *and deception!*

4) **The tactic is to sow the master lie.** When discussing the internal attacks against the Body of Christ in the areas of false doctrine and heresy, the devil knows he must use the scriptures because that is what Christianity is based on. That's why all the major false cults and heresies so popular today use the Bible to "support" their teachings. Just like when the devil tempted Jesus by using the Word of God (see Matthew 4:6-7), he will use the Word of God to attack the Word of God. He does this by getting people to believe one master lie that when accepted as truth, negates all the legitimate and accurate truths built upon it. At that point, it will be error begetting more error, with the deceived getting deeper and deeper into false doctrine and heresy. On the all-important subject of salvation by faith and faith alone as an example, the deceived victim will simply compound his errors because from the base lie will come misapplied and misunderstood applications of all other doctrines related to the subject of eternal salvation.

In this particular case, going beyond the infiltration of the Body of Christ, entire religions have been built around the idea of salvation by works, not faith, because the devil knows it doesn't matter what is taught or believed after his lies about salvation have been accepted as truth. Once you've accepted the false idea that you have to work for your salvation, the beauty and truth of salvation by faith in Christ's work on the cross is lost, and the poor soul will spend a lifetime trying to earn what the Bible says can only be received by faith!

Once you accept a foundational lie through a twisted and distorted understanding of key Bible topics or verses, all Bible study after that is then viewed through the foggy glasses of that inaccurate, foundational doctrinal lie.

5) **Many deceivers can show supernatural signs.** In Matthew 24:3-5, Jesus said there would be *many deceivers* deceiving *many people* just before His return to Earth. In Matthew 7:21-23, Jesus said many of these false teachings and false doctrines will be accompanied by bonafide signs, wonders, and miracles *in the name of Jesus!* So beware! We are never to follow after the signs, wonders, and mighty deeds just because they're manifestations of the supernatural. According to Mark 16:20, the *only* time we embrace the signs, wonders and mighty deeds are when they confirm the Word of God already delivered—rightly divided and passionately defended!

6) **Where do the false teachers come from?** When you gather together with fellow saints, enjoy the fellowship but *always keep your eyes and ears open, and your spirit "on alert."* Why? Because according to numerous passages in the New Testament, the heretics, false teachers, and false prophets don't just come from outside the church, but from the inside as well—from among us. When writing to the Ephesian church leadership, Paul specifically warned them about the two sources where false teachers come from.

Therefore take heed to yourselves and to all the flock, among which the Holy Spirit has made you overseers, to shepherd the

church of God which He purchased with His own blood. For I know this, that after my departure **savage wolves will come in among you,** *not sparing the flock.* **Also from among yourselves** *men will rise up, speaking perverse things, to draw away the disciples after themselves. Therefore watch, and remember that* **for three years I did not cease to warn everyone night and day with tears.**
—ACTS 20:28-31 [EMPHASIS MINE]

Notice in verse 29, there are "savage wolves" that "come in" among us. These are the ones who come in from outside the church. They would be people who are not born-again Christians, but who nonetheless possess and share a message of deception that can effectively draw away believers from the truth.

And then in verse 30, notice the word "also." That means these false teachers and heretics don't just come in from the outside; they also rise up from amongst us. That means these people are already attending our Bible studies and fellowshipping in our churches on Sunday. They have already been assimilated into the ranks of the brethren. Either they're recognized (erroneously) as true believers in Jesus Christ when they're not, or they *are* true believers in Jesus who have erred from the truth and departed from the faith (see 1 Timothy 4:1).

In my opinion, those from "among yourselves" are the ones who pose the greatest threat to the saints, because they've already gained a certain measure of acceptance within the church. Using different words to give the same warning, Jesus told His disciples to watch out for the "wolves in sheep's clothing." He said they are disguised as true believers, but inwardly they are "ravenous wolves" (see Matthew 7:15). The word "ravenous" accurately describes their passion for deception. According to *Merriam-Webster's,* a ravenous animal is *one who is very eager or greedy for food.* Synonyms listed were words like *insatiable, voracious, and rapacious.*

Are you getting the point? These aren't just harmless, somewhat confused, brethren who promote minor areas of doctrinal disagreement within the Body of Christ. These are people *disguised* as "sheep," but inwardly they have a driving, consuming desire to deceive and lead astray as many Christians as they can into major areas of deception and heresy.

And for those out there who think preachers like me spend far too much time on this subject in our messages and ministry, and that we're too "negative" and not "walking in love," let me remind you how the Apostle Paul felt regarding this matter. In Acts 20:31, it says Paul was warning the Ephesian Christians about these very things *day and night for three years*—that's how serious of a threat he thought this was, and that's how serious of a threat we must realize it is for us today in these last days.

Let me repeat that truth for emphasis. *Day and night for three years!* Let that truth sink in for a minute. If this great apostle thought it necessary to warn his spiritual children with that kind of frequency, we would be foolish to do any less in this day and age.

Critical Bible subjects like God's love, God's grace, salvation by faith, eternal judgment, righteousness, purity, and holiness are all under attack from people hell-bent on redefining terms and doctrine. Churches are overflowing with deceived people being led further and further away from the truth by deceived heretics disguised as ministers of the gospel. Don't let yourself be a victim of this demonic deception. Don't become an end-time spiritual casualty of war!

Although the Apostle Paul's ministry was very broad and all-encompassing in outreach and influence, the essence of his ministry could be boiled down to just two main points of emphasis.

> *To them God willed to make known what are the riches of the glory of this mystery among the Gentiles: which is Christ in you, the hope of glory. Him we preach, **warning every man and teaching every man** in all wisdom, that we may present every man perfect in Christ Jesus.*
>
> —COLOSSIANS 1:27-28 [EMPHASIS MINE]

Notice that the preaching about Jesus included warnings as well as teachings. In our day, we've got no shortage of "teachers," who want to just talk about the "abundant life" Jesus came to provide (see John 10:10). Paul told the Corinthians there were thousands of teachers roaming around in his day doing that, just like there are today (see 1 Corinthians 4:15). There's nothing wrong with preaching and teaching about the abundant life in Christ, but to hear the "full gospel" (the term we Charismatics love to use to describe our doctrines and theology), there must not only be the teachings about all the good stuff we can have in Christ in this life, but also the warnings about the dangers in living and serving Jesus on this dead-to-sin planet, where Satan is still the god of this world who blinds the minds of as many as he can (see 2 Corinthians 4:4). *Warning and Teaching*—that is the real "full gospel."

Also notice the warning part came before the teaching part of Paul's ministry, because he knew how important it was. You don't issue warnings to people unless you know there's somebody or something out there that could inflict severe harm if you didn't pay attention, right?

7) **How do we deal with such?** When you're being attacked with false doctrine, recognize the type of enemy fire that is being directed at you, and remember this one simple truth:

> *Your glorying is not good. Do you not know that a little leaven leavens the whole lump? Therefore **purge out the old leaven**, that you may be a new lump, since you truly are unleavened. For indeed, Christ, our Passover, was sacrificed for us.*
>
> —1 Corinthians 5:6-7 [emphasis mine]

You can't allow false doctrines to remain influential in your life, and you can't allow those who teach them anymore access into your life. Once you realize what you're dealing with, you must get rid of the teachings and the teacher. If you think this sounds "harsh," I would only re-emphasize to you what is at stake here— your soul and your eternal destiny. The Bible tells us that if at all possible, we should live at peace with all men (see Romans 12:18), so of course, cutting off all contact with people should only be done as a last resort, or in recognition of the seriousness of the attack against us.

We are not to go around severing relationships with people (saved or unsaved) at the first indication of doctrinal disagreement.

If that were the case, we'd practically have no friends to fellowship with anywhere! Instead, we're to walk with spiritual sensitivity and discernment, and stay vigilant at every turn. We are to do our best to imitate God on Earth in this life, putting on *all* the armor He gives to us each and every day (see Ephesians 5 and 6). We're to maintain spiritual alertness at all times, and if necessary, defend the truth and cut off those who seek to alter it.

I heard one renowned Bible teacher say one time that *doctrine unites denominations, but vision unites churches.* His point was that there will always be differences in doctrine within the Body of Christ until Jesus comes, and I agree with that part of his teaching. However, he was also implying that because of that, we shouldn't get too "nit-picky" with regards to doctrine, since that will do more to divide us than unify us. I can't agree with that part at all. I've been at work in full-time ministry since 1980, and I can tell you from experience that a unified vision will come apart at the seams if our doctrines are not established, vigilantly protected, and passionately defended.

I don't agree that vision is all that's needed to unite our churches so that we can effectively advance under enemy fire. *We need both!* No matter how unified we may be in terms of vision (ministry assignments from God), we still must base our gospel message to the world on certain truths in the Bible that cannot be altered, adjusted, updated, edited, or changed just to suite the fancy of a backslidden, perverse, and sinful generation. The *methods* of reaching cultures, nationalities, and people groups can (and should) change and be flexible as times change. As an example, Paul said he was a Jew to the Jews, and a Gentile to the Gentiles, being all things to all men, hoping to win some to Christ (see 1 Corinthians 9:19-23). However, the *message* never changes! A careful and prayerful reading of Revelation chapters 2 and 3 amplifies that truth beyond debate. The seven churches discussed in those two chapters were commended for their achievements, but rebuked and corrected for their mistakes and sins. Jesus did not place undue emphasis on just the good—He also impartially dealt with the sins, mistakes, and failures of each church as well.

My point? Jesus wasn't changing to suit them—He was telling them to change to suit Him and His standards, or else!

> *Grace to you and peace from God the Father of our Lord Jesus Christ, who gave Himself for our sins, that He might deliver us from this present evil age, according to the will of our God and Father, to whom be glory forever and ever. Amen.*
>
> —GALATIANS 1:3-5

Jesus died for us, not so we could be free to embrace the evil that is rampant in the present age, but that we might be *delivered* from it!

Love people and assume the best of everyone until proven otherwise. The Bible is full of directions and instructions regarding this. However, a little leaven *still* leavens the whole lump, so beware!

CHAPTER 16

Relational Attacks: People Being Ugly

Then some rose up and bore false witness against Him,
saying, "We heard Him say, 'I will destroy this temple
made with hands, and within three days
I will build another made without hands.'"
But not even then did their testimony agree.
—MARK 14:57-59

One major tool the devil uses to stop us is *other people.* Many times people quit advancing under fire when the "fire" comes from other people, especially those they know. Whether they be saved or unsaved, people become the devil's best friend when they fail to walk in love the way the New Testament dictates. Jesus faced this in His earthly ministry, and we will too when operating in His name. Here in Mark's gospel, we read about the lies people were hurling at Jesus as He stood before the Sanhedrin, on trial for His life. Just like the people being used by the devil against Jesus back then, so it will be for us as the devil searches for ways to prevent us from advancing worldwide with the saving gospel of Jesus Christ.

If you're old enough to think for yourself and have friends, you're no doubt nodding your head in positive affirmation. As one minister once said: *Ministry would be wonderful if it just weren't for the people!* People are all around us every day of our lives, and there is nothing we can do to change that (as much as we might like to!). Ah yes—*people!* They could be immediate family, in-laws and other assorted relatives, co-workers on the job, fellow class-mates at school, or just unknown individuals we "rub elbows" with as we go about our business. And in this day of "social network-ing," many people are privy to our lives through electronic mediums made possible by the Internet. We have emails, chat rooms, blogs, texting, surfing the Web online, video conferenc-ing, and social networks like Facebook. And all of it provides the enemy with ample opportunity to find ways to cut us down as we endeavor to move forward for Jesus in this life.

Saved or unsaved, facts are facts—people are ugly to each other for all kinds of reasons, even if those "reasons" have nothing to do with evangelism and gospel outreach on their behalf. However, it gets a lot worse when you decide to make a difference for God in this world, and share the truth about salvation with the lost. Because it's been such a successful tactic in the past, the devil will definitely try to use other people to ratchet up the level of ugly, personal attacks against you and those you love or care about. In Matthew 10:24-25 and John 15:20, Jesus said the servant is never above his master. Using Himself as the example to teach this truth, He told the disciples to expect the same kinds of perse-cution that was brought to bear against Him. He said, *"If they perse-cuted Me, they'll persecute you."* "They" refers to the people we're trying to help, so get ready for it because it's proportional. The more you want to do for Jesus, the more you're going to rub people the wrong way, because working for Jesus demands your interaction with all the people He died for, and most of those people won't appreciate your efforts to help them!

And this is the condemnation, that the light has come into the world, and men loved darkness rather than light, because their deeds were evil. For everyone practicing evil hates the light and does not come to the light, lest his deeds should be exposed.

—JOHN 3:19-21

Jesus told Nicodemus (and us) that there would be a lot of people who didn't like His message (which is ours too) because they don't like having their dark, evil deeds exposed by the light of the gospel. It's certainly not pleasant for the senses to experience such persecution, when we're only trying to point people to Jesus and salvation. But it's inevitable and can't be avoided—if you intend to be a significant somebody for Jesus while living on Earth. There's an old saying I've never forgotten—a truth that has helped me stay steady in the face of intense persecution. *To avoid criticism, say nothing, do nothing, be nothing.*

Once again, we can brace ourselves for this kind of persecution out in the world as we encounter and confront sinners with the condition of their heart. But when the betrayals and attacks are coming from those close to us, it can be overwhelming if we allow it to be.

Friendly Fire!

It's hard enough dealing with the lies, half-truths, gossip, back-stabbing, betrayals, false rumors, and twisted statements about us when it's coming from the unsaved, or from strangers we don't know. It's even harder when the verbal or relational attacks are coming from other believers. It can be almost unbearable when those believers happen to be people whom we love, know, trust, confide in, and think of as close family or personal friends. Have you ever confided to another, sharing things very personal and private? I have, and I know how it feels when that trust is breached, and what was shared in confidence is divulged to others who don't know or shouldn't know. Solomon wrote about this.

> *A talebearer reveals secrets, but he who is of a faithful spirit conceals a matter.*
>
> —PROVERBS 11:13

Who is the talebearer revealing secrets? It could be your closest friend, or maybe your spouse, sibling, or family relative. It might be a classmate or a work associate—a person you've grown close to. It might even be a co-worker in ministry—someone you thought understood the challenges of serving Jesus in fulltime ministry. Doesn't it hurt when your trust and confidence is betrayed by those you love or are close to?

It did when it has happened to me!

How about when you need people and they're not there for you? The devil has all kinds of ways to use people to wound you, and this is another one of many. How about when you're about to stand trial for your life, and all your friends, staff members, subordinates, and loved ones desert you? Jesus wasn't the only one to experience this—Paul did too.

> *Be diligent to come to me quickly; for Demas has forsaken me, having loved this present world, and has departed for Thessalonica—Crescens for Galatia, Titus for Dalmatia. Only Luke is with me. Get Mark and bring him with you, for he is useful to me for ministry. . . . At my first defense no one stood with me, but all forsook me. May it not be charged against them.*
>
> —2 TIMOTHY 4:9-11,16

When Jesus told Ananias that He was going to show Paul what great things he would suffer for the name of Jesus, I'm not sure Paul understood all of what that meant (see Acts 9:16). It's obvious he found out about it soon enough along the way!

Notice verse 16—nobody stood with him in his hour of crisis and need. Nobody. Not one. All forsook him. That's pretty hard to take, don't you think? Would you be able to continue on for Jesus, advancing under this kind of enemy fire? Many out there wouldn't be able to. They'd get hurt, offended, indignant, vengeful, and jaded. What did Paul do? He forgave them and moved on. Could you do that? Can I? These are questions you have to ask yourself and be prepared to act upon, because if you haven't experienced this kind of attack yet, just wait! David experienced this kind of pain, and writes about it in Psalms.

All who hate me whisper together against me; against me they devise my hurt. "An evil disease," they say, "clings to him. And now that he lies down, he will rise up no more." Even my own familiar friend in whom I trusted, who ate my bread, has lifted up his heel against me.

—PSALM 41:7-9

Notice verse 9. David's own *familiar friend, in whom he trusted,* turned against him and was spreading lies and strife. The reference here to "eating his bread" refers to the fact that this person was a close friend who David felt comfortable sharing personal things with, things he wouldn't share with everybody. This person was trusted with information that David would never share with others. Personal issues. Personal struggles. Personal problems. He laments over this in other places as well:

For it is not an enemy who reproaches me; then I could bear it. Nor is it one who hates me who has exalted himself against me; then I could hide from him. But it was you, a man my equal, my companion and my acquaintance. We took sweet counsel together, and walked to the house of God in the throng.

—PSALM 55:12-14

Have you ever had this happen to you? I have, and as I said before, it hurts deeply. When we go forth to preach the gospel, we expect unsaved people to treat us with contempt. We're righteous people preaching a righteous message of repentance in an unrighteous world, and most of them aren't going to like it one bit. This is what Jesus said to Nicodemus (see John 3:19-20), and this is what Paul and David are saying here. If the backbiting, lying, and strife-peddling were coming from rank-and-file sinners, he could handle that because he knows what sinners are like before turning their hearts over to the Lord. It's when those who are close to us turn on us—that's much harder to contend with. When you open your heart to people and they violate your love, confidence, and trust, it can be extremely difficult to forgive them because they've wounded you in a very deep, intimate, and personal way.

There are many levels of intimacy the devil can try and breach this way. Jesus experienced this with those He poured His heart and life into for three and a half years of ministry teaching and travel. Paul experienced this with staff and spiritual sons and daughters in the faith he had bled and suffered with. And not only did David have to deal with staff and close friends betraying him, but his own son did it to him as well—Absalom.

> *Then Absalom sent for Ahithophel the Gilonite, David's counselor, from his city—from Giloh—while he offered sacrifices. And the conspiracy grew strong, for the people with Absalom continually increased in number.*
>
> —2 SAMUEL 15:12

When close friends and co-workers betray us it hurts deeply. When family members do it the hurt can be devastating. Absalom was David's son, and if you read the whole story about this insurrection, you'll find that he was not just plotting against his father for a few weeks or months, but for several years (see 2 Samuel 15)! Imagine how much this must have hurt David when he realized what was happening, and for how long it had been going on. His own son had turned against him, and had been conniving and plotting his overthrow for years.

We've had similar things come against our ministry, so I know by experience how hard this sort of attack can be to overcome. It's in times like these that we must remember that no matter who turns against us, Jesus never will! He's the friend that sticks *closer than a brother* (see Proverbs 18:24).

All through the Bible, whenever possible, we see the devil using those closest to us to try and destroy us. Job is another example of this.

> *Even young children despise me; I arise, and they speak against me. All my close friends abhor me,*
>
> —JOB 19:18-19

Who were the people abhorring Job? *All his close friends.* Not just friends, but *close* friends. And not just a few of his close friends either—*all of them!* How would that make you feel? How easy would it be to forgive such people if they did to you what they did to Job, or David, or Jesus, or anyone else God used throughout the Word of God? Job had every one of his close friends turn against him. David's own son tried to secretly steal the kingdom away from him. Jesus watched every one of his 12 closest disciples tuck tail and desert Him in His darkest hour (see Matthew 26:56). In fact, Peter's betrayal of Jesus took place in such close proximity that Jesus could actually hear his denials as they were taking place!

> *Then after about an hour had passed, another confidently affirmed, saying, "Surely this fellow also was with Him, for he is a Galilean." But Peter said, "Man, I do not know what you are saying!" Immediately, while he was still speaking, the rooster crowed. **And the Lord turned and looked at Peter.** Then Peter remembered the word of the Lord, how He had said to him, "Before the rooster crows, you will deny Me three times." So Peter went out and wept bitterly.*
>
> —LUKE 22:59-62 [EMPHASIS MINE]

Jesus heard Peter's betrayal as it was taking place. Peter was one of our Lord's closest friends on Earth. He was one of the "inner three," along with James and John. For three years, Jesus poured His life and energy into Peter, sharing with him, teaching him, and living with him. Imagine how hard it was for Jesus to stand there and listen as Peter denied even knowing Him, and according to Matthew's account, Peter was even *cursing* as he did it (see Matthew 26:74). On top of all the lies, false accusations, and vehement attacks coming against our Lord from the Jews as He stood there on trial for His life, imagine how hard it was for Him to listen to one of His three closest disciples curse and deny knowing Him—not just once, *but three times!*

Yes my friend, when the Bible says that Jesus was tempted in all points like we are, this is definitely one of those "points!" (see Hebrews 4:15). Remember that the next time Satan uses close friends or family to try and stop you from advancing for the kingdom of God.

But praise God; once again Jesus gave us the example to follow. Forgiveness was offered by God and Peter repented. When God sent one of His angels to inform the disciples of our Lord's resurrection and give them further instructions, he mentioned Peter by name. This was an obvious effort on God's part to let Peter know he was forgiven of his betrayal of Jesus, and that all was not lost.

> *But he said to them, "Do not be alarmed. You seek Jesus of Nazareth, who was crucified. He is risen! He is not here. See the place where they laid Him. But go, tell His disciples—and Peter— that He is going before you into Galilee; there you will see Him, as He said to you."*
>
> —MARK 16:6-7

God made sure Peter knew he was still on the team and hadn't been cut! He was forgiven and would still be used for the glory of God in ministry. That's just one of many examples throughout scripture, where we see the love of God and forgiveness of God in operation. And yes, we're commanded to do the same to those who betray us in this way, but it's still not an easy thing to do—the flesh will make sure of that! Unless you take the time to renew your mind to the Lord and His Word, forgiving people from the ugliness they've demonstrated towards you is practically impossible—especially when they are those people who are closest to your heart.

Don't Try to Run Someone Else's Race

Running in someone else's lane is another way the devil gets in to use people against us. The devil knows that for the most part, people are very poor listeners, and frequently recount the details of what we say or do inaccurately. Sometimes it's unintentional, while at other times it's on purpose. Either way, when this happens to you, or to those very close to your heart, it's very hard to resist the temptation to lash out in defense of the truth. When people misquote you or go around repeating what you never said, it becomes very easy to let your indignation and anger create what Hebrews calls "the root of bitterness" (see Hebrews 12:15).

Using Peter once again as our example here, we see that even though Peter was forgiven for his profanity-laced denial of Jesus before His crucifixion, he still found it necessary to comment on what God was using John to do in ministry after our Lord's resurrection. As Jesus shares His final comments and parting instructions to Peter about what he is supposed to do from that point on, Peter starts in with his rant about John.

> *Then Peter, turning around, saw the disciple whom Jesus loved following, who also had leaned on His breast at the supper, and said, "Lord, who is the one who betrays You?" Peter, seeing him, said to Jesus, "**But Lord, what about this man?**" Jesus said to him, "If I will that he remain till I come, what is that to you? You follow Me." Then this saying went out among the brethren that this disciple would not die. Yet Jesus did not say to him that he would not die, but, "If I will that he remain till I come, what is that to you?"*
>
> —JOHN 21:20-23 [EMPHASIS MINE]

The first thing to see here is that Peter is still having a hard time controlling his flesh in the areas of strife and carnal competition. Its only been a matter of days since he was totally forgiven of his own sins of denial against even knowing Jesus, but look at how he's getting into strife once again, this time over "this man" John. If you go back and read through the four gospels, looking at the conversations and interaction between Peter and John, you'll see that these two didn't always get along. And the fact that Peter chooses not to refer to John by name, calling him "this man," indicates these two were not the closest of friends on our Lord's ministry team! There was definitely some jockeying for position going on between these two, and probably some large doses of jealousy, pride, and competition mixed in, too.

So even though Peter had been forgiven for denying Jesus the night of His arrest, Peter was still trying to overstep the bounds of his authority by questioning Jesus about John's ministry assignment. What did Jesus do? *Rebuke Peter!* If I may paraphrase: Jesus told Peter to mind his own business. You and I should take a cue from that exchange—and mind our own business as well! Avoid strife! He that sows strife among the brethren commits the sin God hates *more than any other* (see Proverbs 6:16-19)!

According to 1 Corinthians 9:24-26, and in many other places throughout the New Testament, every Christian has a relationship with God and ministry for God that is compared to a runner running a race. Therefore, it's critical we stay in *our* lane, and not get off into someone else's. If you do, you'll find yourself in strife with your brothers and sisters, and that's playing right into the hands of the enemy. Stay in *your* lane and run *your* race—and resist the temptation to comment on how others are running theirs!

Yes, when it comes to doctrine, theology, and lifestyle for the brethren around us, we can and should make decisions about who we should or shouldn't fellowship with. But when it comes to personal preferences in how we view nonessential issues, or in how others are running their ministries, or in how we try to "take over" and do what others are assigned to do for God—those are areas we need to stay away from.

In Romans, the Holy Spirit had several things to say about this.

*Receive one who is weak in the faith, **but not to disputes over doubtful things**. For one believes he may eat all things, but he who is weak eats only vegetables. Let not him who eats despise him who does not eat, and let not him who does not eat judge him who eats; for God has received him. **Who are you to judge another's servant? To his own master he stands or falls.** Indeed, he will be made to stand, for God is able to make him stand.*

One person esteems one day above another; another esteems every day alike. Let each be fully convinced in his own mind. He who observes the day, observes it to the Lord; and he who does not observe the day, to the Lord he does not observe it. He who eats, eats to the Lord, for he gives God thanks; and he who does not eat, to the Lord he does not eat, and gives God thanks. For none of us lives to himself, and no one dies to himself. For if we live, we live to the Lord; and if we die, we die to the Lord. Therefore, whether we live or die, we are the Lord's. For to this end Christ died and rose and lived again, that He might be Lord of both the dead and the living. But why do you judge your brother? Or why do you show contempt for your brother? For we shall all stand before the judgment seat of Christ. For it is written:

"As I live, says the Lord, every knee shall bow to Me, and every tongue shall confess to God."

So then each of us shall give account of himself to God. Therefore let us not judge one another anymore, but rather resolve this, not to put a stumbling block or a cause to fall in our brother's way.

—ROMANS 14:1-13 [EMPHASIS MINE]

Notice verse 1 from this passage in Romans. Paul tells the Roman believers not to dispute over "doubtful things." What does that mean? It means there are always going to be areas of disagreement over things that are not that important to the Great Commission, and the business of winning souls for Jesus. Basically, Paul is telling the Romans to "major on the majors, and minor on the minors." Don't get caught up in the business of running around commenting upon, and criticizing how others are walking out their lives and ministries for God. In areas of nonessential disagreement, the Bible tells us to "let every man be fully persuaded in his own mind." That means there is room for disagreement over smaller issues of personal preference.

It's All about Balance!

But this same passage tells us to avoid the practice of judging another man's servant, which in this case refers to other Christians serving the same Jesus we serve! So you see, there must be a mature balance in how we run our race in our lane, versus how others run their race in lanes all around us. Some people misapply these verses, teaching us that it's wrong to "judge" others. But that position either ignorantly or conveniently over-looks many other verses that address the issue of judging. You always have to interpret scripture with scripture, and look at *all* the verses that address the topic in question. There are times when it's absolutely *vital* that we judge what's going on around us with what others teach or believe, and with the way they choose to live their lives. And then there are times when minor differences are to be overlooked and ignored (the doubtful things Paul talks about). As an example, Paul exhorted Timothy and Titus over and over about the importance of protecting sound doctrine and judging and staying away from those teaching heresy (see 1 Timothy 4:6 as one of many examples of this).

Bottom Line: we need to know when it's scriptural to get involved with what others are doing or not doing for the Lord, and when it isn't. When Peter started quizzing Jesus about what John's ministry was going to be all about, he was out of line—and Jesus told him so in no uncertain terms. You and I would be well to grasp the point Jesus was making to Peter! Don't get over into someone else's lane and try to run their race for them. That's a dangerous practice that will open the door to the devil, and hinder your ability to advance under fire for the Lord.

Repeating What Was Never Said

The second thing to see here, is that when Jesus and Peter had this verbal exchange, it was obviously within earshot of the other disciples, because false rumors starting flying immediately after-wards. Notice what Jesus said to Peter about John, and what the brethren were saying Jesus said to Peter about John. *It wasn't the same!* The recycled report was a twisted exaggeration, formulated in the minds of those who heard what they *thought* Jesus meant by what He said to Peter. And isn't this what people have been doing on a daily basis to each other ever since Adam and Eve? What people were saying about John never having to die wasn't even close to what was actually said, or close to what Jesus meant by what He said.

This kind of thing goes on all the time, much to the joy and glee of the devil. Another preacher once made this statement about Christians receiving guidance from God through the gifts of the Holy Spirit: *God gives a word, and Christians make sentences out of it.* That was a very astute observation that unfortunately is all too true. His comment was made to accurately describe the devil-inspired activity of embellishing upon what people actually say—adding our own slant to what was spoken, based upon the many areas of spiritual immaturity and lack of sanctification within us that cloud the truth. Without taking time to renew our minds to the Word of God, people will have many "filters" that truth is processed through before they finally settle upon *their version* of the truth, and the devil takes full advantage of that fact.

The point here for us is this: when people start twisting *your words,* or inaccurately describing *your actions,* it's a very short step to picking up an offense which the devil will use to try and bring you down and halt your forward progress with God. Don't let that happen. This is one of the many ways we're going to have to advance under fire in this world for Jesus.

When People Assume the Worst

In addition, when talking about relational attacks against you—have you noticed that when people have the choice between believing the best or worst about someone, more often than not they *assume* the worst is true, not the best? Instead of being "innocent until proven guilty," it's "guilty until proven innocent." That's because when people fail to renew their minds with the Word of God, its extremely easy to just go the way of the flesh, which *always* wants to believe the worst about any person or situation under discussion! And because the vast majority of people (including most Christians) you'll ever deal with in this life do *not* have minds renewed to God's Word, don't be surprised when they, by default, assume the worst concerning you. And that's on top of the lying, backbiting, backstabbing, betrayals, and abuse one must put up with as elite soldiers in the army of the Lord! Its one of the devil's prime tactics to discourage us from maintaining our position on God's front lines, so beware!

Everyone has issues, including you! Jesus is the only person to live His entire life free from sin. The only one. Aside from Jesus, everybody sins and needs God's mercy and forgiveness daily. That's why the Lord's mercy is new *every morning* (see Lamentations 3:22-23). The Word of God doesn't say God's mercy is new every once in a while, but daily—every morning. Why? Because we *need it every morning!* If we remember this, we won't be so eager to assume the worst about somebody, but instead, look for the best in every situation until proven otherwise. We'll practice the "golden rule" found in Matthew's gospel.

> *Therefore, whatever you want men to do to you, do also to them, for this is the Law and the Prophets.*
>
> —MATTHEW 7:12

If people don't remember this truth, its very easy to let the flesh take us to the place where we're consistently believing the worst about people, not the best. The flesh *loves* to do this, and the devil knows it, so he tries to keep us in the arena of carnality, because he knows how we'll deal with others when they fall or stumble before the Lord.

How to Handle Relational Attacks

Letting the love of God dominate in your life is the biblically-mandated way to insulate yourself from this kind of demonic attack. Among many things listed as love's characteristics in 1 Corinthians chapter 13, there is one particular attribute that has a direct bearing on our topic under discussion, which are relational attacks that seek to halt our forward progress in Christ.

*Love bears up under anything and everything that comes, **is ever
ready to believe the best of every person,** its hopes are fadeless under
all circumstances, and it endures everything [without weakening].*
—1 CORINTHIANS 13:7 AMP [EMPHASIS MINE]

The Amplified Bible's translation for verse 7 in the great love chapter
of First Corinthians is my favorite. When God's love dominates
your thoughts, words, and actions, you are *always inclined to believe
the best of every person, not the worst!* Getting to this place requires
much prayer, Bible study and meditation before God, but it's well
worth the effort. The flesh wants to do the opposite by nature—to
always believe the worst of someone, not the best. And the reason
this can be so challenging is because it takes no effort at all to go
the way of the flesh! The flesh, along with everything else in this
sin-cursed world, flows in a negative direction by default. You
don't have to try and be negative because your dead-to-sin flesh
already wants to go in that direction from the start. To assume the
best of people takes great effort and commitment, because you're
swimming against the current, so to speak.

But when you do take the time to renew your mind and allow
your born-again spirit to be in control, God's love will enable you
to overlook the lies and verbal persecution coming against you, so
you can avoid picking up an offense that empowers the devil
against you. This keeps you on the front lines for God—always
"meet for the Master's use" (see 2 Timothy 2:21 KJV). By assum-
ing the best of even your persecutors, you deflect the hurtful
things they say and do that are designed by the devil to emotionally injure you to the point you give up and quit advancing for
God. This kind of "enemy fire" has been responsible for eliminat-
ing scores of Christians who otherwise, up to that point in time,
were doing great things for God.

I know of one young couple, who used to be on fire for God,
and were pastoring a small but vibrant church with much spiritual
potential. I spoke for them and their church on multiple occasions. They even led several of their leaders and elders to the
Philippines to assist us in our crusade work. But they made some
lifestyle and ministry changes that didn't sit well with members of

the church, and the long and short of it was that eventually, they got so hurt and burned out by all the back-stabbing, gossiping and rumor-spreading against them, they not only quit the ministry, but got divorced as well.

I've tried talking to both of them since this happened, but as of this writing, no positive changes can be seen in either of them. They've definitely allowed the root of bitterness to take over in their hearts and minds. It's tragic, and my heart bleeds over what happened, but it didn't have to turn out that way. Don't let it happen to you! Be like Jesus, and learn to handle these kinds of attacks the way He did.

Be At Peace with the Truth

Oftentimes I think about how Jesus must have felt when He had to contend with all of the lies, gossip, and false rumors spread about Him. For example, remember when He asked the disciples one day what people were saying about Him?

> *Now Jesus and His disciples went out to the towns of Caesarea Philippi; and on the road He asked His disciples, saying to them, "Who do men say that I am?" So they answered, "John the Baptist; but some say, Elijah; and others, one of the prophets." He said to them, "But who do you say that I am?" Peter answered and said to Him, "You are the Christ." Then He strictly warned them that they should tell no one about Him.*
>
> —MARK 8:27-30

Look at all the wrong answers here! Although we can appreciate the truthfulness in how Peter identified Jesus, notice how all the other opinions about Him were incorrect. Would this bother you if all of this error was directed your way? All things being equal, I know this type of activity is definitely bothersome to me—unless I renew my mind to God's Word, and remind myself to rest in the fact that God knows the truth, even if so many who talk about me don't. The fact is, this sort of "behind-your-back" conversation would bother anyone who isn't able to rest in the fact that God knows all things, and gets fooled by nobody. It would bother anyone who hasn't taken the time to insulate themselves with the love of God.

Even though what most people were saying about Jesus was wrong, He didn't allow Himself to become upset, defensive, or impatient with them. He just went about His business for God, knowing that God knew who He was, and what He was there to do. This is true spiritual "security." *Learn to be at peace with the truth.* God knows the truth about you, and you'll stand before His judgment seat someday, not any of your critics, detractors, or persecutors. Jesus knew this, so all the erroneous statements made about Him never caused Him to quit in discouragement or frustration.

And that's what you and I need to do, too. Be at peace with the truth, no matter who gets it or not! Don't allow any gossip, false statements, rumors, or outright lies to affect your ability to advance under fire. When you get this kind of persecution as a man or woman of God, don't come unglued and fall to pieces. Leave it with God—and let Him vindicate you in His time and in His way.

Many times over the years in ministry, I've been attacked in this way as the devil tried to use people to spread lies about me. And every time I'm tempted to become angry and defensive, God gently reminds me that they did the same things to Jesus when He was here.

In Satan's toolbox of relational attacks and tactics, we'll find lies, half-truths, erroneous assumptions, broken promises, insensitive comments, and ignorant opinions expressed about us. No matter what kind of relational mud people are slinging your way, remember the Word of God and follow God's instructions. Do what Jesus did—commit yourself to the Lord your God, for He is no respecter of persons, and always judges righteously (see 1 Peter 2:23).

CHAPTER 17

Physical Attacks:
Sickness and Disease

How God anointed Jesus of Nazareth with the Holy Spirit
and with power, who went about doing good and healing
all who were oppressed by the devil, for God was with Him.
—ACTS 10:38

Although there are many verses that address the subject of divine healing, for me, this one sums it up. God anointed Jesus with His Holy Spirit, for the express purpose of doing good and *healing all who were oppressed by the devil.* The clear implication here is that the "oppression from the devil" includes sickness and disease—mental as well as physical.

While Jesus was here, He not only brought the message of salvation, but He also brought the blessing of healing. And if you've ever been seriously ill, you know what a blessing healing can be! Matthew talks about the three-fold ministry of Jesus while on Earth:

And Jesus went about all Galilee, teaching in their synagogues,
preaching the gospel of the kingdom, and healing all kinds of sick-
ness and all kinds of disease among the people. Then His fame
went throughout all Syria; and they brought to Him all sick people
who were afflicted with various diseases and torments, and those

who were demon-possessed, epileptics, and paralytics; and He healed them.

—MATTHEW 4:23-24

Jesus was a preacher, a teacher, and a healer. We need to see Him as all of the above, not just the Lamb of God sent to take away the sin (nature), and sins (the individual acts of rebellion because of our sin nature) of the world. For three and a half years, Jesus performed in ministry as a Man of God, the Son of God, and the last prophet of the Old Testament. Before He went to the cross as our Sin Substitute, He had to fulfill all the Old Testament prophecies, and fulfill the Old Testament law by living His life without sin from beginning to end.

When Jesus cried out on the cross, "It is finished," He wasn't referring to the plan of salvation, because there were still three days and nights in Hades after His physical death on the cross, and He hadn't yet put His shed blood on the heavenly mercy seat to ratify the New Testament. What Jesus finished (or more accurately "fulfilled") on the cross was the Old Covenant, or what most of us refer to as the Old Testament. That's why at the moment of His death, as He spoke those words from the cross, the curtain in the Temple was torn asunder from top to bottom (not bottom to top), signifying that God (not man) had now made the way possible for a New Covenant, which is the one we now live under today—and forever. Jesus is now called the High Priest of a *better covenant based upon better promises* (see Hebrews 8:6).

Most Christians have an incomplete picture of who Jesus was while on Earth in ministry. Everywhere He went, He was fulfilling all three parts of His earthly calling. He was preaching and teaching the Word, and then confirming it with signs, wonders, and mighty deeds. He went around doing good—not only preaching the good news of the Kingdom, but also healing all who were oppressed by the devil through sickness and disease.

Now, if He did it then, He's doing it now, because the Bible says He is the same yesterday, *today*, and forever (see Hebrews 13:8). God wants the sick to be healed as much as He wants the lost to be saved, because the two of them are part of what it means to be saved, according to the Great Commission.

> *"And these signs will follow those who believe: In My name they will cast out demons; they will speak with new tongues; they will take up serpents; and if they drink anything deadly, it will by no means hurt them; they will lay hands on the sick, and they will recover."*
>
> —MARK 16:17-18

The word for salvation here in this passage is the Greek word *"sozo,"* which according to *Vine's Expository of New Testament Words,* means *to save, deliver, protect, heal, preserve, do well, and be made whole.* That means that when Jesus was up on that cross, He not only took our sins away as the spotless Lamb of God, but our sicknesses and diseases too. Several key passages in the Word of God illustrate this:

> *Who Himself bore our sins in His own body on the tree, that we, having died to sins, might live for righteousness—by whose stripes you were healed.*
>
> —1 PETER 2:24

Notice that when our Lord was "on the tree" (the cross), He bore our sins through His shed blood (see Hebrews 9:22), and with His battered, beaten, and whipped body, purchased our healing as well. If it was a done deal then, it's still a done deal now, and will be forevermore!

> *When evening had come, they brought to Him many who were demon-possessed. And He cast out the spirits with a word, and healed all who were sick, that it might be fulfilled which was spoken by Isaiah the prophet, saying: "He Himself took our infirmities and bore our sicknesses."*
>
> —MATTHEW 8:16-17

Notice that His earthly healing ministry was an Old Testament prophetic fulfillment, which told of our Savior taking away not just our sins, but our sicknesses and physical infirmities as well (see

Isaiah 53). Did Jesus fulfill this Old Testament prophecy? Yes, He did. He healed all who were oppressed by the devil, as He fulfilled His responsibilities as the last Old Testament prophet. And then up on the cross, by His stripes He took away all sickness and disease that any of us would ever face while living on Earth.

The reason I take the time to share all of this is because the devil has been tremendously successful at sowing the ridiculous lie that God—the same One who anointed Jesus to go about doing good and healing *all* who were being oppressed by the devil—is also the one putting sickness and disease on people to teach them lessons!

Good Christian people have been held captive by this lie all their lives, so that when attacked with sickness or terminal disease, they're basically left in bed and abandoned to die by preachers, family members, and friends. And when I use the word "abandoned," I'm not necessarily referring to being left alone physically in some room somewhere. With words of doubt, fear, and unbelief, the sick can be spiritually abandoned—even with dozens of people standing around their sickbed at the same time!

My friend, if you're ever going to be able to advance under fire for Jesus, you must settle this issue about God's ability *and* willingness to heal the sick—once and for all in your life.

The Truth Is Simple to Understand

Myriads of great books have been written on the subject of divine healing, so there's no need for me to try to add my two cents' worth. For our discussion here, relative to our ability to advance under the "fire" of sickness and disease, suffice to say that divine health and healing is a very important part of the Gospel message, and must never be compromised in any way, shape, fashion, or form. That being said, it amazes me that people continually allow the devil to confuse them on this issue. Here it is friends, from me to you, the truth about where *all* sickness and disease comes from, and who is the author of such. You won't have to go to someone's

Bible school or Bible college to learn this—it's as plain as the nose on your face in the Word of God. Ready? Let's begin.

Two Bookends of Time

The issue of sickness and disease on Earth is like the tale of two bookends. The bookend on the left is named *Before Satan Shows up on Earth,* and the bookend on the right is named *After Satan Is Removed from Earth.* All the pain, suffering, sickness, and disease on Earth can be found in between those two bookends, so what does that tell us about where all of this junk comes from, and who its author is?

Read Genesis chapters 1, 2, and 3 carefully. *Before* the devil showed up in the Garden of Eden, there was no sickness or disease—period. When it was just Adam, Eve, and God, there was no sickness, disease, suffering, or pain. None of that existed on planet Earth until Satan came along, successfully tempted Adam to sin, and usurped humankind's legal authority to operate on Earth, thereby becoming the god of this world (see 2 Corinthians 4:4). *After* he got his evil "foot in the door," that's when people started to suffer from sickness and disease.

Now, go read Revelation chapter 20. *After* he is removed from the Earth, there is no sickness or disease—period. *After* Ol' Split-Foot is thrown into the bottomless pit and removed from the Earth during the 1,000-year millennial reign of Christ, there will be no sickness, disease, suffering, or pain, *until* he is released for a short season to tempt the people born during the millennium. Once he's back on Earth at that time, we will see a return of all the temptations, lies, pain, suffering, sickness, and disease we see all around us now.

Now also read Revelation chapter 21, especially verse 4. When Satan has finally been thrown into the lake of fire, to be tormented day and night forever, all that's left on the Earth is happiness and joy in the presence of the Lord. All the "former things" are passed away forever, and those "former things" refer to death, sorrow, crying, and all manner of pain.

There you go!

God is in the business of making people well, and the devil is in the business of making people sick—period. God is good, and the devil is bad. End of lesson. People need to read their Bibles without their religious sunglasses on! A third grade child could understand this, until of course they become brainwashed later in life with religious lies, half-truths, and misapplications of scripture.

This whole issue of the origin of sickness and disease is too simple to miss, yet with the help of the devil, religious and deceived people have been "missing it" on the subject of divine healing for generations. Wherever the devil *is*, there is sickness and disease and all the suffering that goes with it. Wherever the devil *isn't*, there is peace, harmony, joy, gladness, happiness, and nothing to cause pain or sorrow, like sickness and disease. Can this be any simpler to understand?

I don't think so.

God has **never** been the author of sickness and disease, and never will be. Sickness and disease came with the devil, and will leave with the devil. The devil is the author of all sickness and disease, and when he goes all sickness and disease will go with him. Give yourself an "A" if you understand this third grade material, and give yourself and "A+" for not allowing all the religious foolishness out there to convince you that in some strange, unexplained way, God puts sickness and disease on people to "teach them something."

Listen, my friend! The Lord can teach us anything He wants, any way He wants, without having to use the works of the devil to do it. As obvious as this is from the Word of God, just sit back and watch! When preachers like me start preaching divine healing, and the exercising of our God-given authority over sin, death, sickness, and disease, look at all the deceived preachers and believers who line up to argue! They'll cross land and sea, just to get in your face and fight for their right to stay sick! They'll get mad at you if you dare suggest that God wasn't the one who "took" little Suzy with cancer, "blessed" Uncle Bob with a stroke, "loved" your father with a fatal heart attack, "gifted" the couple down the street with a severely handicapped newborn, or "sovereignly bestowed" the human race with AIDS or some other global epidemic.

There is a curse on this planet because of sin, and it has enabled the devil to steal, kill, and destroy almost at will since Adam until now, and sickness, disease, pain, misery, and suffering is part of the package deal he unleashes upon the human race. But praise God, 1 John 3:8 tells us Jesus came *to destroy the works of the devil* (i.e. nullify their power in our lives)—*not to use them on us to teach lessons!*

Jesus said to Philip that whoever saw Him was looking at God, His heavenly Father (see John 14:9). So then, where do we *ever* see Jesus putting sickness on someone to "teach them something"? Nowhere! Give yourself another "A" if, as clearly as the nose on your face, you can see that the devil is the author of sickness and disease on Earth!

As I said, it's not my assignment to write an entire book on the subject of divine healing and health. Hundreds of others have been told to do that by the Holy Spirit, and they've produced many books and study aids to help people understand the truth about God's desire to heal *all those oppressed with sickness from the devil.* Don't just take my word for it—go read after them and learn this truth beyond doubt for yourself.

Sick Christians Can't Go

The reason why I'm listing this as a prime area of attack should be obvious. As long as you're on Earth doing God's work and God's will, the devil will be looking to put as much sickness and disease on you, or your loved ones, as he can. His goal in this effort will always be to kill you, but if that can't be accomplished, his backup objective is to so thoroughly immobilize you with sickness and disease, that you can't fulfill your particular assignment from the Lord in connection to the Great Commission. When you get right down to it, this is the bottom line: *only healthy people can really fulfill Mark 16:15-18.* Ol' Split-Foot knows that we are spirits living in bodies, and our bodies need to be healthy to be used in fulfilling the Great Commission as commanded.

In my own life, I know this is the reason why I've been attacked with all forms of sickness and disease over the years since answering God's call on my life in 1978. And even though I've used faith in God to appropriate my healing time and time again, I know the devil will never stop looking for another opportunity to slow me down or kill me via sickness and disease. In fact, many times as I'm writing chapters like this one, or when preaching and teaching on this subject in some public forum, I'm standing in faith for my own healing concerning a particular attack of sickness or disease the devil is trying to put on me. He has tried many times to slow me down with symptoms and sicknesses designed to impede my advancement in Christ, but he has never been successful—and he never will be.

I believe this is the main reason why many great soldiers of Christ are hit with sickness and disease repeatedly. The devil wants to stop us from reaching the lost in this world, and one very effective way he can do that is by making our bodies weak and sickly—unable to go into the entire world in the name of Jesus.

Resist Sickness and Disease!

Here's another truth to consider. Because Jesus commands us to go into the entire world to preach the gospel, He's also commanding us to stay healthy, and resist in faith any and all sicknesses or diseases the devil tries to put on us. It doesn't matter how "on fire" you are for God. If your body is sick and some type of disease is at work in you physically, your ability to fulfill God's plan and purpose to obey the Great Commission will be affected to the proportionate degree of pain and debilitation in your life. *You're commanded by Jesus not to allow this to happen!*

For the most part, I've been operating my ministry in a body that's pain-free. In fact, since 1980, when I began fulltime missions ministry in the Philippines, I can literally count on one hand the number of times when I had to cancel a speaking or ministry engagement due to sickness in my body. But on the other hand, there have been plenty of times when I've been ministering somewhere, or traveling to a meeting, while alarming symptoms of sickness and disease have been in my body, and fear is dogging me every step of the way. In one particular case, I had alarming and painful symptoms 24/7, every day and every hour for 22 months straight before healing came. In spite of the symptoms and the fear I had to constantly deal with during that particular fight of faith, I traveled back and forth between North America and Southeast Asia repeatedly, fulfilled all my travel commitments for ministry, and saw God save and heal multitudes of people—while I myself was fighting a fight of faith for my own healing every minute of every day. The pain never left me during that time, but very few people knew what I was going through because I refused to allow that attack to hinder my forward progress in the gospel.

So having said all of that, I can say by experience that it's a lot easier to obey God when you do not have to constantly deal with pain in your body!

Advancing in Pain Is A Choice

I encourage you to make the same quality decision I made years ago, when I first began to serve Jesus in fulltime ministry. Way back then, I decided that no matter how I felt, if it was at all possible for me to keep going—I would. No matter what I was feeling or experiencing in my body, I purposed in my heart that I would keep going and deal with the attacks whenever they came against me, and they sure did! Yet through the symptoms, the thoughts of fear, and the pain I was feeling, I have endeavored to advance under enemy fire, no matter how miserable I felt in my body.

On more than one occasion in the Philippines over the years, I've been sicker than the sick people I was praying for in our Miracle Crusades! I just decided to preach salvation and healing anyway. Many times I've been used by God to lay hands on the sick and see hundreds of people knocked to the ground by the power of God flowing from me to them, while I could hardly stand up for the fever and dizziness I was dealing with in my own body! I'm sure there were times when people who saw me staggering around on stage thought I was under the influence of the power of God, when in truth, I was feeling so sick I was just trying to hold on long enough to get through the service without collapsing on the platform! My wife Ethel can tell you, because many times she was the one who helped carry me to my bed after the crusade finished and the crowds went home.

And then when I minister and itinerate in the USA, another element enters the mix that the devil tries to take advantage of—traveling, ministering, and being alone and away from family and loved ones. Since 1980, when I have traveled coast-to-coast to itinerate and raise funds in churches, most of those trips have been made alone—Ethel stayed at home to take care of the kids and tend to the office needs of the ministry.

If you travel like I do, perhaps you can relate to the added challenges of fighting against symptoms when you're all by yourself, and there is no one around to encourage you, help you, or pray with you. So many times I've been standing in faith for my own healing as I travel through airports, fly on airplanes, stay by myself in hotel after hotel, and preach in my host's pulpit for scheduled services. Most of the time, no one knew what I was battling against, or what kinds of symptoms I was dealing with. No one knew except the Lord God Almighty, and my wife Ethel back home. I just kept quiet and ministered to the people to the best of my ability. In times like that, it's enough that I know and God knows.

As mentioned earlier, and in giving all glory to God, I can say that in all these years of traveling in ministry, whether it be overseas or in the USA, I've had to cancel meetings less than a half-dozen times because of something related to sickness or disease.

I'd like to think that's a pretty good track record—one that pleases God, and one that I intend to uphold by the grace of God.

If we're commanded to go, we're commanded to stay healthy and learn to use our faith to fight off any physical attack from the devil. This truth is beyond debate. If we have to take medicine or receive medical treatment, so be it—but our faith must be the foundation we rest upon when we resist the devil. That also means we stay in the fight and continue to advance under fire, to the best of our ability, even when we're under attack in this area of sickness and disease.

We Are Commanded to Control Our Bodies

Here is something else to be aware of. Because we live in flesh and blood bodies that grow old and die, the Bible talks about another factor to address in our defense of good health. *Diet and exercise.*

We have a responsibility to stay healthy physically, and take care of the bodies we're presently "renting" from God while we live on this earth.

> *Or do you not know that your body is the temple of the Holy Spirit who is in you, whom you have from God, and you are not your own? For you were bought at a price; therefore glorify God in your body and in your spirit, which are God's.*
> —1 CORINTHIANS 6:19-20

This passage tells us our bodies belong to God, not to us, and the Lord expects us to *glorify* Him in our spirit *and* in our body! To do that, we've got the additional responsibility of monitoring our diet and levels of exercise. Without putting too fine a point on it— obese or grossly overweight Christians are not giving God glory with their body. Neither are Christians who may be thin and appear to be physically fit, but are so out of shape they can't jog from their garage door to the end of driveway without collapsing in a state of exhaustion. If I'm talking to you, please understand I'm not making fun of, or trying to embarrass you. I love all my brothers and sisters in the Lord, and I don't want to see anyone unable to advance under fire because of issues like these. I want to encourage and help people in every area where, for whatever reason, it's been a challenge to maintain control.

All I'll say is this: If your body isn't where you know it should be in terms of physical fitness, then understand that this is an area where the devil will continue to attack, until you prove to him it isn't a stronghold anymore that he can use against you. That may sound harsh, but it's the truth, and no matter how offended people may get when they're challenged in an area like this, understand the devil *hopes* you will get mad and offended, and *hopes* he can use that against you as well! He doesn't care what door you open to invite him in—he'll just say "thank you" as he enters into your life to continue his efforts to cripple your ability to be used by God.

When you step on the bathroom scale and the scale answers back and says: *"One at a time please!"* then you'll know you've got your work cut out for you! So, do what you have to do to change that!

Take a look at yourself today, and honestly analyze your level of physical fitness. I'm not pointing my finger at anyone, so don't get offended or defensive on me! If you're out of shape, start on the road to wellness by admitting that you have no one to blame for this except yourself. If someone eats 30 donuts a day for 30 years, they can't blame God, or the devil, when they fall over dead from a heart attack! God didn't command them to eat like that, and the devil couldn't force them to eat that way either. Do that over the course of a lifetime, and at some point the body will just give up and die. Food doesn't jump into our mouths against our will. We make personal choices about what we eat, how often we eat, and how much we eat.

Not too long ago, I saw a TV report about the obesity problem in America. The report said that *70 percent of all adult Americans* are grossly overweight and getting heavier by the year! They then went on to talk about how this is negatively affecting our nation's ability to cope. I forget how many billions of dollars in healthcare costs they said this epidemic requires, but it was a lot! That's right—

obesity is now classified as an official epidemic in the United States, so it's a problem that is affecting a whole lot of people!

This doesn't mean you have to live at the gym 24/7, and it doesn't mean you become so kitchen or calorie-conscious that you can't enjoy life, or the food God put here on Earth for us to enjoy. It simply means you exercise balance and self-control (it's called *temperance,* and is one of the nine fruits of the spirit, from Galatians 5:23), and live a life that pleases God and eliminates excess, and the addictive consumption of man-made junk foods.

One more thing to remember: if you're not happy with the way you are, and it has taken years of gradual neglect to bring you to this point of time in life, don't get impatient with your decision to make changes and see positive results—because God isn't! You don't need to set unrealistic goals, or time limits that only an Olympic athlete in training could accomplish! If it took time to bring you to this place of physical weakness and susceptibility, understand it will take some time to reverse the effects of it all. Just be committed to the goal, and don't let the undisciplined lifestyles of those around you drag you back into your old way of living.

Beat Your Body into Submission!

My birth date was November 22, 1951, so you can figure out how old I am right now, depending upon when you read this. And actually, I will let you in on a relatively little known truth here—I was born on Thanksgiving Day, because in November of 1951, Thanksgiving Day fell on the 22nd of the month. Years later, my mother told me that after she gave birth to me, that same day at dinner time, two nurses came into her room. One carried me, and the other carried her dinner, which because it was Thanksgiving Day, consisted of a drumstick of dark meat, mashed potatoes, gravy, and stuffing. They weren't sure whether my Mom liked white meat or dark meat, so they brought both! (One can accurately say therefore, that I'm the ultimate turkey—and the consummate expression of "white meat"!)

But as I've grown older, I've been much more preoccupied with the importance of keeping my body fit, and closing off all avenues in this area where the devil could gain a foothold. When I was younger, I wasn't as concerned about my level of physical fitness and the way I was feeding my body, simply because younger adults can "get away" with a certain level of laziness, simply because they're still young! However, in my life at least, God was able to pull me aside while I was still in my early to mid 40s, and talk to me about lifestyle changes I needed to make—if I intended to live a long, productive, and fruitful life in ministry for Him.

So from then until now I've tried to stay healthy for the Lord's sake, for my sake, and for the sake of my loved ones and ministry relationships. I want to be like Caleb, one of my Bible heroes, who was just as strong for war at the age of 85 as he was at the age of 40 (see Joshua 14:6-12)! But just like your body, mine has never wanted to cooperate (especially when I get within driving distance of an Amy Joy donut shop in Cleveland, Ohio—oh Lord, save me from those raised donuts with chocolate icing and sprinkles on top!). It's been a daily discipline that I've applied in my own life, and which you will have to apply in your life. I've had seasons in life where I've gotten lazy and put on too much weight, and had to go on a diet to get rid of it. But I did—more than once. I didn't just let myself go, as so many people do. I refuse to do that because I have my eyes on the horizon, and I know that doing all I can to stay physically fit is to my long-term advantage for the work I must do in the name of Jesus. I'm never going to be rewarded in Heaven for how much food I could consume in an hour, and neither will you!

Dietary Adjustments

Now, I'm not suggesting some kind of extreme lifestyle change. I'm not suggesting you cut out all red meat, eat carbs before protein or protein before carbs, or go join some Vegan Booster Club. Have you ever looked at the array of diet and health-related books that are out there? There are literally hundreds of them, and every author or movement sincerely believes that their program is *the* program to make weight loss and fitness happen.

Of course, what we supposedly know now isn't enough—there's a new diet or fad seemingly every year or so, which in many cases, is in direct contradiction to some of the other diets that were popular before. A person can get very confused very quickly if they try to follow everyone's ideas about obtaining and maintaining good health, because there is much debate, confusion, and incomplete knowledge out there on the subject. What "experts" say they "know" today may be proven to be completely wrong a few years from now. That has already happened time and again.

That being said however, there *are* excellent books and resource materials out there that are available to read and study. I have a number of books and cookbooks on diet in my library and kitchen at home, and I have read them and refer to them for inspiration and information often. It's not a sin to read somebody's take on how and what we should be eating, just be sure you keep God in the loop, and let Him guide you through the sea of information that's available in print and over the Internet. And if you find one particular plan or routine or diet that works for you, and God says go for it—by all means follow it! I know in my own life there are certain diets or disciplines that work for me, and there are others that don't. You just have to wade in and rely on God's assistance and guidance for help. But if you intend to stay healthy as you age and grow older, it's an effort worth making!

Let God's Word Guide You

Bottom line: follow the Bible and let the Holy Spirit show you what is best for you. He knows you . . . better than you do, and a lot better than some dietician or self-proclaimed expert who probably isn't even saved. Just ask the Lord for guidance in the areas where you know a lifestyle change is needed, and He'll work with you. He's the best trainer you could ever have! God made us, so He knows how our bodies function, and what type of "fuel" keeps it running at peak performance. He also knows when enough is enough!

Here's some simple and obvious (at least I think so) advice. You can go spend lots of time and money to find the perfect "diet" or "lifestyle plan," and if you do and it works for you, good for you! I'm not against anyone's ideas on how to stay healthy per se, but remember this: you'll go a long way toward health and wellness if you just major on eating things God made, rather than the things man makes, and limit your intake levels and frequency of consumption. To me, that's just common sense.

Going to extremes one way or the other isn't biblical, because God never intended for us to deny ourselves the pleasures of a good meal! However, you need to watch what you eat, and how often you eat, because many people's definition of a "good meal" is just wrong, and gives place to the enemy over time. You just can't overdo it or make bad food choices, because that's what your body will always demand if that's how you program it, and the devil knows this. Look at the portion sizes people allot for themselves, the number of times they stuff food into their mouths each day, and the kinds of foods they're eating, and you can often see where the problems lie.

That doesn't mean we should all become vegans, or criticize those of us who are. If you want to go that route, that's fine, but you can't push that off on others under the guise of it being "scriptural." There's something to be said for the positive effects of eating protein such as red meat, chicken, fish, etc. as long as it's done in moderation. Eating meat and fish is fine—Jesus did it and so have generations of people since Adam. But make sure you do it with wisdom, as guided by the Holy Spirit, not by some cookbook or diet guru!

Here's something to else to consider. When God sent His prophet out into the wilderness and was solely responsible for feeding him, he only fed him *twice a day* (see 1 Kings 17:1-6). The man of God, the prophet Elijah, was fed by the ravens sent by God in the morning and evening. *No birds showed up at lunchtime!* Do you think God knows when it's best for us to eat, and why? As our Creator, I think He does. This may be too simple for some people to accept, but according to God's own dietary plan for Elijah, eating three meals a day wasn't necessary, because if it was, God would've done it when He personally fed His man in the desert. If it comes down to what God does, or what some dietician says I should do, I'll go with God, thank you! Twice a day is enough food for anyone. If you don't believe me, check with God and his prophet Elijah.

"But Mike, studies will indicate—" Yes, I know there are multitudes of "studies" conducted on the subject of diet and exercise, but once again, remember you're dealing with people who, for the most part, aren't born-again and therefore, have no ability to tap into God's wisdom or knowledge on the subject. That's why a study that proclaims today's latest "findings" will have a good chance of being replaced by new findings a year or two from now, which in many cases, contradicts what the old findings insisted on as truth!

Pray over Your Meals

"Well Mike, how about all of the chemicals that pollute our water and food supplies?" No doubt those concerns are real, and we should do our best to minimize our exposure to all of the pesticides, insecticides, and other harmful chemicals used today to produce and process our food supply. However, in the world we live in, it's just not possible to totally eliminate all of this from your diet, unless you choose to move to Tibet, climb to the top of Mt. Everest, and enroll in the "John the Baptist School" for locust and wild honey consumption.

In the meantime, I believe God meant what He said about the power of praying over your food before you eat it (see 1 Timothy 4:3-5). Most of us just mumble our way through a prayer before we eat because that's what we've been taught to do, but there's a *reason why* God tells us to pray over our food and receive it with thanksgiving each time we sit down at the table. God knows what's on or in the food we're about to eat, and if we pray in faith, sincerely believing God will protect us from harm if necessary, I believe He will! If you do your best to eat with the goal in mind of being physically fit, and ready for service in the army of the Lord, God will protect you from things beyond your control. So relax and enjoy your next meal!

Don't Forget to Exercise!

The other side of the fitness coin is exercise, but once again, you don't have to kill yourself in the gym to protect your ability to advance under fire for God! As always, balance and common sense should rule and reign. We should be realistic with ourselves when it comes to exercise and setting physical fitness goals, especially as we grow older. You know, my mind remembers the things I could do when I was in my 20s or 30s, but at this stage of the game, if I try to do what I could do back then in terms of exercise and exertion, my body will remind me very quickly that it is *not* that young anymore!

God wants for us to take care of our bodies, and keep them in good shape, but it's not necessary to go overboard. As an example, in my life, bicycling and weightlifting are my two fitness hobbies of choice. I personally like to work out in the gym several times a week, and ride bicycles as a way to stay in shape. When I'm in the gym, I'm not trying to bench press the moon, or pop all the veins in my forehead trying to lift the building off its foundation. I work out in the gym a couple of times a week, and try to keep the weights I push or pull at levels that will keep me fit and in good shape. I don't need to compete in the next Mr. Universe contest to stay ready and useable for Jesus.

For my love of bicycling, a good bike ride at least once a week is always on my calendar, unless my ministry and travel schedule prevent it. (I'm talking about serious bicycling here—not riding around the neighborhood on a Huffy bike purchased on sale from Wal-Mart, fully equipped with a basket, bell, and pink handlebar streamers.) When bike riding, I don't try to kill myself by going too fast or too far. A normal bike ride for me is usually doing an average speed of about 15 miles per hour, for distances between 40 or 50 miles. I've done many longer rides (more than 100 miles in distance), and I've done shorter rides when time is a factor. I've also done rides where my average speed and level of exertion is greater than the average, but that is not my norm at this stage of my life, because I stopped trying to win the Tour de France years ago.

I know my age and I know my limits. You should do the same, and set realistic goals. At this stage of my life, I can't bench press 500 pounds, and don't want to try! I'm inviting injury if I try to lift weights like men who are half my age. And as far as bike riding goes, it's foolish for me to try and keep up with 20-year-old bicyclists, or ride like I did 30 years ago, because I can't. I can't keep up with guys (or even girls) half my age, and I see no point in trying to. I just say "good morning" to them as they glide on by! I'm just happy to be out there, enjoying the day and worshipping God on my bike!

In short, you should do the same—act your age and live within the boundaries of reality. As I said, our minds remember what we could do back when we were young and in our prime, but when we try to jump back in time with our levels of physical activity and exercise, our bodies will remind us we've come a long way since then! I've seen and even known 50- and 60-year-olds trying to be 20-year-olds again, and it doesn't work! People end up injuring themselves unnecessarily, and as far as the devil is concerned, that's just fine, because the injured Christian is just as useless to God as the out-of-shape Christian!

No one is getting younger, including you and me! That means we can either get active and proactive with our diet and level of exercise, or slowly regress until physically we're of no use to God and the Great Commission. Aging definitely sucks, but it is part of the curse, and until Jesus comes back there's nothing we can do about that. But we *can* do something about our lifestyle, to limit Satan's access into our lives with physical attacks as we grow older that cripple our abilities to advance and progress for God in life.

All God expects us to do is manage our bodies wisely in every area, including diet and exercise.

As far as I'm concerned, the older I get, the more important it becomes for me to keep up with a regular routine of exercise, and many medical studies prove that as we age, those who stay active and physically fit stay healthy longer, and those who don't—don't! Bottom line, it's important for me to stay in tip-top shape because I represent God as a missionary, and need to be in shape for His sake, my sake, and the sake of all those He wants me to go to in His name. The same applies to you!

Find the Balance!

The Lord isn't impressed if you look like the Michelin man and can bench press 300 demons stacked on top of one another, and neither is the devil. But on the other hand, you shouldn't be so weak and out of shape that you're huffing and puffing—while stuffing down your fifth Twinkie! In short, if God ever needs you to exert a fair amount of energy, physical strength, and stamina to get a job done for him (like doing missionary work in a place such as the Philippines), you need to be able to answer the call! No excuses! If that means doing some consistent home exercising or joining a weekly spin class or two, do it.

These are just a few ideas and tidbits of thought that you can take into your prayer closet to discuss with God. But if you're out of shape and you know it, you owe it to God, to yourself, and to your family to change—now! Not ten years from now. We need all hands on deck for the fights of faith ahead, and we need them to be as physically sharp as they can possibly be. On the battlefield, have you ever seen pudgy, overweight soldiers going to war with a rifle in one hand and a bag of Doritos in the other, and an ammo belt packed with Snicker's bars? How long would they last in battle engaging a tough and determined enemy? I rest my case.

Why Does the Devil Want Us Sick?

This is important to understand, so you can be prepared for the next physical attack against you or your family. There are basically four reasons why Satan, the author of all sickness and disease, wants you sick:

1) He hates God.

The devil knows how much God loves us. God *so loved the world* He sent Jesus to die in our place (see John 3:16). Because he can't hurt God directly, he tries to inflict as much pain as possible on us, because he knows it hurts God to see us suffer with sickness and disease.

2) He hates us.

Humankind is God's greatest creation because we're made in the image and likeness of God. No other created being can say the same. Therefore, the devil hates us as much as He hates God. So, because He can't hurt God the way he wants, he hurts us instead because thanks to Adam's treason, he has legal access to humankind all over the earth.

3) He enjoys our suffering.

The devil destroys people's lives because he enjoys it. That is his sick, twisted nature. It's a simple as that. The more we suffer, the happier he becomes, and sickness and disease makes us suffer in different ways and many degrees.

4) He wants to delay his demise.

He knows that health is a prerequisite for fulfilling the Great Commission. The fact is that sick people cannot go into all the world as fast or as effectively as healthy people, and that gives him more time to stay on Earth to steal, kill, and destroy. In Matthew 24:14, Jesus plainly says that the end won't come until the gospel has been preached all over the world. The end for Satan means the bottomless pit for 1,000 years, then after a short time, the lake of fire for eternity. The longer he stays here, the more souls he can deceive, and the greater the delay in God's sentence being passed upon him.

Do All You Can to Prepare for the Attack

So therefore, do all you can in this life to prepare for the *next* attack of sickness and disease, because it's coming! If you're currently enjoying divine health in your body, praise God for it, and then continue to shore up your defenses, anticipating the next enemy attack in this area. Attacks of sickness and disease are just like the weather. You might enjoy sunny weather for a couple of days or even a week or two, but you know storms are coming— it will be raining sooner or later.

If you're presently in between storms, thank God for it, but stay alert and vigilant. Like army soldiers training for war, run your drills! (For a detailed study on this subject, refer to my book, *Military Mentality.*) By doing this, you'll consistently advance under the fire of sickness and disease that seeks to rob you of your potential for God as an ambassador for Christ on Earth. No surprise attack can overwhelm you when you stay alert and at your post in this area of life.

Do all you can to stay ready physically. So much sickness and disease is our fault, not the devil's. Oh yes, he's out there ready to pounce on people whenever he can, but we don't need to be handing him boatloads of free guns and ammunition by making poor choices concerning diet and exercise. Don't do that! Be sharp! Be alert! Be fit! Recover your "edge," and you'll be able to advance under fire anytime, anywhere!

Social Attacks: Persecution

Remember the word that I said to you,
'A servant is not greater than his master.'
If they persecuted Me, they will also persecute you.
If they kept My word, they will keep yours also.
—JOHN 15:20

E ven before Jesus left to return to Heaven, He told us to expect persecution for the cause of Christ. The Great Commission is a mission—to go into all the world and preach the Good News about God's plan of salvation. When believers obey that mandate, they can expect to be persecuted—collectively as a group and individually as members of the Body of Christ.

When talking about the importance of knowing how to advance under fire in this life for Jesus, the issue of Christian persecution must be understood and embraced. Failure to do so will cause even the most "in-love-with-Jesus" Christian to fall away from effective service to the Lord in the business of winning souls. This has nothing to do with whether a believer is living right with God, or living "in sin." *Anyone* who dares to publicly pronounce their salvation experience and allegiance to Jesus *will* suffer persecution, whether their relationship with the Lord is solid and strong, or tenuous at best. (As far as the devil and the world are concerned, backslidden and lukewarm Christians are no different than "on fire" believers when it comes to evangelism—they are just as much a threat to the kingdom of darkness as are the fully committed and passionate saints, so they're going to be persecuted as well).

Do More—Expect More!

For years in my preaching and teaching, I've told people that persecution is always proportionate to the level of Christian activity in our lives. In other words, the more you do to win souls, represent Jesus, stand up for righteousness, and refuse to compromise Christian standards, morals, and beliefs, the more you're going to get shot at (whether that be figuratively or literally!). All Christians are hated by the devil, and have a target on their back just because they're born-again. But that target gets bigger to the proportionate degree we're involved in the business of fulfilling the Great Commission.

The more you do for Jesus, or intend to do for Jesus, will determine the proportionate degree of attention Satan gives to you. Understand that, so that when you go forth to make a difference for Jesus in your world of influence (no matter what that means or where that takes you), you won't be shocked or surprised when the persecution starts coming against you in significant and intense ways.

It's amazing to me how this truth gets lost on so many Christians in countries like the United States of America. The fact is this: the western world portion of the Body of Christ understands very little about the kinds of persecution Jesus was referring to when He warned us about it in the gospel of John. Go back and read about what Jesus faced when He was here in terms of persecution, and ask yourself if any of this is, or has been, going on in *your* life! On a daily basis, our Lord faced intense persecution from many different angles. He had the Romans to contend with, who were brutal in their treatment of anyone thought to be rebellious against the empire and Caesar's rule. Then Jesus had the Sanhedrin—those hard-hearted, hard-headed, Jewish leaders of His time, known as the Pharisees and

Sadducees. As if that wasn't enough to deal with, He had a group of disciples who on their best days were spiritually ignorant, naïve, clueless, and immature. And for the icing on the cake, He had Satan and all of Hell itself set against Him in dedicated ways you and I have never experienced.

People who read the four gospels many times fail to really appreciate the resistance Jesus faced daily. He was accused of being demon-possessed, a liar, a deceiver, a false prophet, an instigator against the Roman Empire, and many other false allegations as well. He was misquoted, lied about, gossiped about, and misunderstood everywhere He went—not just by the Jewish leaders or the people in general, but from his own staff (remember Judas betrayed him with a kiss, and he had traveled and lived with Jesus every day for more than three years)!

Jesus' claims about being the Messiah were ridiculed and rejected by the religious leaders and the nation of Israel as a whole. In His hour of need, when the time came for Him to be offered up as God's sacrificial lamb to take away our sins, His entire staff fled for their lives, and Peter, one of His three closest friends and ministry associates, denied (with vehement cursing) that he even knew Jesus. Ultimately, He was murdered for who He was, what He stood for, and for what He came to Earth to do.

And what did Jesus say about those who would follow Him? *"If they persecuted Me, and you follow Me, they will do the same things to you."*

If you are going to advance under the fire of Christian persecution, you need to mentally and emotionally prepare for it, if you haven't already done so. It's not easy to go through intense levels of persecution, but that's part of the package deal called salvation!

> *But Jesus said to him, "No one, having put his hand to the plow, and looking back, is fit for the kingdom of God."*
> —LUKE 9:62

From the beginning of their walk with God, new believers must be taught that being saved isn't just about all the "goodies" we now get from God because we're His children. To the best of our ability in the Philippines, this is what we do when given the chance to work with those who accept Jesus as Lord and Savior in our crusades. We don't just tell them about all the wonderful things that become available to them because they've received Jesus—we give them the whole, complete picture—the good as well as the not-so-good, as plainly described throughout the Word of God. That complete picture includes the joys of living for Jesus, *but also the work of evangelism and the fulfilling of the Great Commission of Mark 16:15-18.*

Notice in our Lord's statement from the gospel of Luke, He talks about putting one's hand to the plow. This signifies the fact that once saved, a child of God must be ready and willing to get involved in the challenging, difficult and (sometimes) dangerous business of going into a very spiritually dark world to confront people with eternal reality and the judgment to come (see Acts 24:25). That is what Jesus is talking about when He refers to His disciples putting their hands to the plow.

And what happens if they take their hands off the plow and begin to "look back"? *They disqualify themselves for entry into the kingdom of God!* I didn't say it—Jesus did! Those are sobering words my friend! What then, exactly, does it mean to "look back" and "take your hand off the plow"? It talks about a believer who wants to be used by God in the areas of outreach and evangelism, initially expressing the desire to "get in the game" by witnessing and sharing their faith in Jesus with the unsaved all around them. But when persecution arises as a result, with intense and unpleasant pressure being applied against them, they shrink back from their expressed passion and stated intentions to reach people in the name of Jesus. In addition, to avoid having such resistance experienced in the future, they actually start longing again for the things of this world, believing that as they "blend back in," they'll be able to revert back to the "comfortable" life they had before they stirred up the hornet's nest in the name of Jesus! The Lord specifically addressed this in the gospel of Mark:

> *And He said to them, "Do you not understand this parable? How then will you understand all the parables? The sower sows the word. And these are the ones by the wayside where the word is sown.*

When they hear, Satan comes immediately and takes away the word that was sown in their hearts. These likewise are the ones sown on stony ground who, when they hear the word, immediately receive it with gladness; and they have no root in themselves, and so endure only for a time. Afterward, when tribulation or persecution arises for the word's sake, immediately they stumble. Now these are the ones sown among thorns; they are the ones who hear the word, and the cares of this world, the deceitfulness of riches, and the desires for other things entering in choke the word, and it becomes unfruitful. But these are the ones sown on good ground, those who hear the word, accept it, and bear fruit: some thirtyfold, some sixty, and some a hundred."

—MARK 4:13-20

This passage is one of the most telling in all of the New Testament. Notice Jesus said here in verse 13, that if you understand this parable, *you will be able to understand all parables!* In short then, this parable is the *master* parable, by which all the other parables should be compared in order to be understood correctly. And for our discussion here in regards to social attacks that seek to deter our forward progress in Christ, notice the ones who "stumble" because of the tribulation and persecution arising for the Word's sake. May this never be said about you and me!

Old Testament Examples

This New Testament problem could be compared to what happened to the children of Israel, who, after being delivered by God from Egyptian bondage, began mumbling and complaining when things weren't working out the way they thought they should. When their way became difficult and their "comfort zone" was being eroded, they began to declare their desire to return back to the slavery and harsh treatment they endured for hundreds of years in Egypt—the very oppression they had just been set free from (see Numbers chapters 13 and 14, as an example of what I'm referring to here). Obviously, this did not sit well with God, any more than it sits well with Him today when believers cave in to the social pressures to "shut up, sit down, be quiet and conform!"

We "full gospel people" need to understand the "full gospel!" A realistic, daily understanding of what the full gospel entails will help us avoid the common misconceptions that are rampant in Pentecostal, Charismatic, and Word-of-Faith camps, groups, denominations, and organizations out there. Yes, when we accept Jesus we become children of God, and as such gain access to all of what the devil stole, and which Jesus came to recover (1 John 3:8 is an example of many verses stating this fact). That means we can (and should) enjoy the "good life," the "abundant life," the "overcoming life," the "triumphant life," and so on.

However, that does *not* mean God becomes our divine butler or errand boy when we get saved! To be sure, as believers in Christ Jesus, all of those exceedingly great and precious promises become available to us, but on the other side of that coin comes the responsibility to get in people's faces and let them know that there is a Heaven and there is a Hell, and if they don't get saved they're going to spend their eternity in Hell. That's just as much a part of the full gospel and salvation package as the other. The people who embrace this are the ones who are going to get the rewards someday in Heaven, because they'll have been the ones who truly made an impact in their areas of influence while living on Earth. It sure won't be the anemic, spineless, and gutless "believers" that don't have the courage to stand up in the midst of social persecution and spread and defend the truth of the gospel.

Paul Knew What to Expect

Even before Jesus commissioned and anointed Paul for the work of his ministry, He told Ananias what was in store for Paul once his ministry got started.

> *Then Ananias answered, "Lord, I have heard from many about this man, how much harm he has done to Your saints in Jerusalem. And here he has authority from the chief priests to bind*

all who call on Your name." But the Lord said to him, "Go, for he is a chosen vessel of Mine to bear My name before Gentiles, kings, and the children of Israel. For I will show him how many things he must suffer for My name's sake."

—ACTS 9:13-16

Verse 16 is not a verse many Christians want to stand in faith for, is it? They have no problem standing in faith for their money, their healing, their protection, their happiness, their marriage, and all the rest. Schedule a prosperity seminar, where the speakers will talk and teach about nothing other than the "Hundredfold Return," and people will line up to attend. They'll even pay ridiculous amounts of money just for the "privilege" of attending, and huge sums of money are spent at the product table, as believers buy up all the materials the speakers have to offer. You know, Jesus *did* teach the hundredfold return message, and I believe in that message with all my heart, but many preachers and teachers today don't repeat *the entire* message as Jesus taught it.

Then Peter began to say to Him, "See, we have left all and followed You." So Jesus answered and said, "Assuredly, I say to you, there is no one who has left house or brothers or sisters or father or mother or wife or children or lands, for My sake and the gospel's, who shall not receive a hundredfold now in this time—houses and brothers and sisters and mothers and children and lands, with persecutions—and in the age to come, eternal life. But many who are first will be last, and the last first."

—MARK 10:28-31

American believers—pay attention! Western free-world believers around the globe—pay attention! If you're going to preach the hundredfold return message accurately, you're going to have to teach about *the persecution* that comes with the fact you've left everything to follow Jesus. Very few do this, and as a result, their idea of what the "prosperity message" entails becomes warped, incomplete, misleading, and erroneous.

Should we stand in faith for financial prosperity? Absolutely! I have taught prosperity since the beginning of my ministry back in 1980, but *not* for the reasons many others do. Accurate preaching about prosperity must *always* include the teaching about proportionate persecution to the level of evangelism and outreach. Failing to do so gives the listeners a very distorted picture about the biblical reasons for why God's promises to bless His children financially.

In addition, one must always be careful to see the world from God's perspective, not from a human perspective. For Christians living in countries that are extremely blessed by God, prosperity is thought of and defined in very different ways that for others trying to serve Jesus in places less fortunate. For people in closed, persecuted nations of the world, prosperity means something totally different than for those in countries like the United States of America. For many Christians in countries like China and North Korea, just owning a bicycle and having the ability to ride it to their next secret Bible study *is* prosperity. For believers born in nations dominated by fanatical Islam, just being able to own a Bible and practice their faith openly, without having radical Muslims try to kill them *is* prosperity!

My point? In many cases, biblical prosperity *includes* biblical persecution—you can't separate one from the other. I further submit to you that a Christian (no matter where they live) who has more than enough in terms of resources, and lives a very comfortable life here on Earth, but who isn't experiencing any meaningful levels of persecution for the cause of Christ, isn't prosperous at all and has no clue or accurate perspective as to what true prosperity entails from God's point of view.

I've met multitudes in Christian circles who are actively praying, believing, and claiming their hundredfold return from God for their finances, but I've *never* heard any of them just as enthusiastically stand in faith for that same kind of return on the subject of persecution! Yet, Jesus put the two together in the same verse, so what's that say about the subjects of prosperity and persecution? Here are some other things Jesus said along these lines:

Blessed are you when men hate you, and when they exclude you, and revile you, and cast out your name as evil, for the Son of Man's sake. Rejoice in that day and leap for joy! For indeed your reward is great in heaven, for in like manner their fathers did to the prophets.

—LUKE 6:22-23

People love to rejoice and leap for joy when the Holy Spirit manifests Himself in church services, Bible studies, seminars, and conferences. We've got no shortage of people who can have Jericho marches all around the convention center, declaring their victories in Christ, and the blessings of the Lord manifested in their lives. But here in Luke's gospel, Jesus talks about running, jumping, dancing, and leaping for different reasons—*reasons very few want to think about.*

Should we run, jump, dance, shout, and swing from the lights when God moves in our midst to bless us and minister to us by His Spirit? Of course! Enjoy those times, and praise God for every single instance. But how about these *other* times? How about running, jumping, laughing, and shouting for joy when, according to Jesus, you're hated, excluded, maligned, made fun of, lied about, and ostracized for being Christian. Can you do it then too? This is how you advance under the fire of persecution. This is how you take the devil's persecution, and shove it right back down his throat. This is how you overcome when the pressure of persecution comes against you.

"Blessed are those who are persecuted for righteousness' sake, for theirs is the kingdom of heaven. Blessed are you when they revile and persecute you, and say all kinds of evil against you falsely for My sake. Rejoice and be exceedingly glad, for great is your reward in heaven, for so they persecuted the prophets who were before you."

—MATTHEW 5:10-12

Notice the word "blessed" in these teachings from Jesus. Christians love to talk about being "blessed," and about the "blessings" of being a child of God, and about all the future "blessings" awaiting us when we see Jesus face-to-face. All of that is true and wonderful, and should be meditated upon daily. Ephesians 1:3 tells us that God *has blessed us with every spiritual blessing* in Christ Jesus. Already! Past tense! If you're in Christ (saved), you've already been blessed in every way spiritually by God! But that doesn't mean we're excluded from the persecution that comes from being a righteous person in an unrighteous world with a message of salvation and repentance from sin!

Do you want great rewards someday when you get to Heaven? Then look at what Jesus said in verse 12. When you leap for joy *because* you're going through hell on Earth in terms of persecution (whatever that means to you in your world, or in your area of the world), Jesus said your reward in Heaven would be *great!* Who gets the great rewards in Heaven someday? The ones who had huge ministries, built lavish cathedrals, and enjoyed opulent lifestyles? No! It will be the ones who *rejoiced their way through the intense levels of persecution* they faced in this life for Jesus.

What that tells me is that there are going to be many surprised, shocked, and disappointed Christians on "Rewards Day" in Heaven. From where I sit, as I read my Bible, the greatest rewards are going to those who suffered the most for their faith, and who didn't quit, give up, or fall away because of it, even if they ultimately lost their lives as martyrs. Never mind Tommy Television, Randy Radio, Sister Stadium, Pastor Perm, Bishop BMW, Elder Opulent, Deacon Deceived, and all the others. The lion's share of rewards in Heaven aren't going to people like that, but to those who endured and prevailed against all manner of evil brought against them for their faith.

> *Beloved, do not think it strange concerning the fiery trial which is to try you, as though some strange thing happened to you; but rejoice to the extent that you partake of Christ's sufferings, that when His glory is revealed, you may also be glad with exceeding joy. If you are reproached for the name of Christ, blessed are you, for the Spirit of glory and of God rests upon you. On their part He is blasphemed, but on your part He is glorified. But let none of you suffer as a murderer, a thief, an evildoer, or as a busybody in other*

people's matters. Yet if anyone suffers as a Christian, let him not be ashamed, but let him glorify God in this matter.

—1 PETER 4:12-16

We've got no shortage of preachers today who can make us laugh until our sides split, help us to see who we are in Christ, teach us all about "increase" in our lives, and *never* talk about the things we're talking about in this chapter. Stadiums, convention centers, and churches fill up when such ministers come to town. Well, as long as the event brings people to a saving knowledge of Christ, I'm certainly not against it, even if the people delivering the "gospel" have unscriptural motives or selfish lifestyles (see Philippians 1:15-18). But, if anyone does genuinely get saved in their meetings, what kind of "new recruit" are we getting here? Thank God they're saved—that's what we're here to do—but are these new believers being taught or told that along with all the "good stuff" *from* Jesus, there are intense levels of persecution awaiting them if they ever want to do something meaningful *for* Jesus in their life?

Look at what Peter tells his readers here. If we are *reproached* for Christ, *we are blessed!* And don't be ashamed if you *suffer persecution* for being Christian—instead *give God the glory for it.*

Go back and see what Jesus was talking about when He told Ananias He would show Paul what great things he would suffer for the name of Jesus and the cause of Christ. Time and space in this book prevent us from doing so because of the overall subject matter here, but on your own, carefully read the Pauline epistles, and as I've said before, especially the book of 2 Corinthians, chapters 1, 4, 6, and 11. Look and see what Paul, his companions, and the early-day Christians went through for the faith. At the beginning of His ministry, Jesus *showed* Paul what he was in store for, and we need that same kind of teaching and reminder from Jesus today, because too many are falling away for fear of what might happen to them if they dare speak out in the name of Jesus.

Also realize that Peter's two books were specifically written to encourage Jewish believers to hang on and hold on to Christ in the face of withering levels of persecution. In fact, in *every* book of the New Testament, the subject of persecution is addressed, and we would be well to remember that.

Attacks Come Collectively As Well As Individually

All through history, Christians have been persecuted socially, culturally, and methodically. Read books such as *Foxe's Book of Martyrs*, *Tortured for Christ* by Richard Wurmbrand, and many others that reveal, narrate, and expose the horrific levels of persecution experienced by believers globally from the time of Christ until the present.

As a whole and as individuals, we've been targeted for attack by Satan and those who do his bidding. All over the world today, entire governments have made it their aim and goal in life to stamp out Christianity. False religions like Islam or Hinduism declare war on Christianity collectively, and upon believers individually. In countries like the USA, we see different types of attacks. More and more we see the attempts of a godless, secular, hedonistic society to remove all public displays of Christian faith and Christian influence, and to put political and judicial pressure on us to "accept" and "embrace" all manner of sin and perversion.

Everywhere we're being attacked, and this isn't going away, my friend, no matter how much intercessory prayer is brought to bear. As this author understands the power of prayer in the light of end-time prophecies and the return of Jesus, I believe our prayers *do* have a powerful impact on the Earth in these last days, but primarily as a power only to *delay* what God has said is going to happen. Jesus will return to a world full of deception, heresy, apostasy, hedonism, sin, darkness, confusion, perversion, and so forth, and nobody's prayers are going to change that. All we can do (and should do) is actively share our faith, pray for those who need Jesus, and prepare for our heavenly departure!

As the return of Jesus draws closer, the levels of persecution against us will increase, never decrease. Don't be alarmed by this, just understand it, suck it up, and go with the flow! God will guide you and show how to deal with whatever levels of persecution you're dealing with in your life now, or in the future. And remember what Jesus said, when these things *begin* to happen, look up and rejoice because your redemption draws near (see Luke 21:28)!

> *For what credit is it if, when you are beaten for your faults, you take it patiently? But when you do good and suffer, if you take it patiently, this is commendable before God. For to this you were called, because Christ also suffered for us, leaving us an example, that you should follow His steps: "Who committed no sin, nor was deceit found in His mouth"; who, when He was reviled, did not revile in return; when He suffered, He did not threaten, but committed Himself to Him who judges righteously.*
>
> —1 PETER 2:20-23

Remember what Jesus said, which we quoted at the beginning of this chapter. If you are suffering persecution for your faith, *this is commendable before Almighty God.* Keep your heart right, don't get bitter towards God, and don't question Him in anger about the reasons why you're being persecuted. All over of the world, millions of Christians are suffering persecution for their faith, not because they've committed sin or done something wrong, but just because they're Christians. You and I should be a part of this, to one degree or another, so get used to it and learn how to advance in spite of it.

Theological Attacks: Unanswered Questions

*Trust in the LORD with all your heart, and lean
not on your own understanding; in all your ways
acknowledge Him, and He shall direct your paths.*

—PROVERBS 3:5-6

Through the years I've been called upon many times to bring counsel and encouragement to people who were dealing with some kind of unexpected tragedy or accident in their lives, or the lives of those they loved. To recount the details surrounding these various experiences would require me to write a book much larger than the one you're now reading. Suffice it to say, I've seen a lot of good Christian people go through things that left them with many unanswered questions about why a loving God would allow whatever happened to happen.

If you're going to develop the discipline of advancing under fire in this life on Earth, you must accept the fact that there will be times in life when bad things happen to good people—with no immediate explanation as to the "why."

Religious Persecution Is Promised!

First, let me just say that in many places in the Bible, God plainly tells us that religious persecution is a *normal* part of life when we serve Him and work to fulfill the Great Commission. We talked about this in the last chapter, dealing with social attacks against us. There, we quoted our Lord Jesus several times with regards to religious persecution, but here is another one of His statements relative to the certainty of religious persecution coming our way:

> *"You have heard that it was said, 'You shall love your neighbor and hate your enemy.' But I say to you, love your enemies, bless those who curse you, do good to those who hate you, and pray for those who spitefully use you and persecute you, that you may be sons of your Father in heaven; for He makes His sun rise on the evil and on the good, and sends rain on the just and on the unjust."*
>
> —MATTHEW 5:43-45

Not just from Jesus Himself, but from Genesis to Revelation, what we read in the Bible leaves no room for doubt. Religious persecution is not a mystery—it's promised over and over again in the Word of God. The more you want to do to spread the truth, the more the enemy will use religion and religious zealots to stop you! Read the book of 1 Peter, and see what God has to say about believers being beaten, imprisoned, stoned, attacked, and so forth. And as we saw when quoting 1 Peter 4:12 in our chapter on social attacks, we should not be surprised when these things happen. On the contrary, we should be *expecting* them! Once again, I exhort you to also read Paul's own record of religious persecution which is found throughout his epistles, but especially in 2 Corinthians, chapters 1, 4, 6, and 11.

All New Testament writers warned their disciples about this, and did their best to prepare them for intense levels of persecution, because the message they were bringing was to a world that, for the most part, loved the darkness they were living in (see John 3:19-20), and didn't appreciate the exposure!

As we see from our Lord's own words to His disciples, religious persecution is promised for those who operate in His name, specifically saying that if they persecuted Him, they'll persecute those who follow Him (see John 15:20). Sure enough, history is red with the blood of untold multitudes of martyrs, who gave their lives in defense of the truth. In fact, I've been told by ministries who research these things, that there were more people martyred for their Christian faith in the 20th century, then in all the first 19 centuries combined!

So, when we're talking about unexpected tragedies in life, we're not referring to the kinds of religious persecution God tells us is acceptable to Him for us to go through (see 1 Peter 2:20). In this chapter, we talk about the attacks that take the form of accidents and tragedies in life that seemingly have no explanation we can grasp and cling to for strength, comfort, and reassurance. Many times for many people, these are the kinds of attacks that may directly confront and challenge their very foundation of theology regarding a loving, caring God. Although I have no hard data to back this up, I've heard that many atheists were at one time Christians, who, because of some unexplained tragedy, decided to reject the entire Christian notion of a supernatural being who declares Himself to be "love" (see 1 John 4:8). I would have no problem believing this to be true, if in fact it is!

Unexpected Tragedies Happen to Believers

Make no mistake, people who love God and serve Jesus with all their hearts can—and do—experience unexpected hardship and tragedy. It's a part of life that many struggle with because when it happens, they have no real, tangible way to explain (to themselves or to others) why it happened. It could be the accidental death of some innocent child. It could be some horrific natural disaster that kills thousands of innocent people. It could be the birth of a baby physically deformed, or with severe mental disabilities. It could be the premature death of Christians through sickness and disease—people who ought to have had many years of fruitful life and ministry ahead of them. It could be someone aggressively standing in faith for their healing, who dies and goes home to Heaven anyway. Whether it is on a personal and individual level, or something like a tornado or typhoon that leaves a wide path of death and destruction, these are situations that can shake our theological beliefs to the core.

The Philippines—Ground Zero for Calamity

I work for God in the Philippines. That is where both my apostolic assignment and authority are to be found. Since the time of my arrival in September, 1980, until now, I don't think I've ever seen a country get hit with more calamity, death, and destruction on a national scale as the Philippines. Whether it is natural disasters or man-made accidents, there's no country that I know of that even comes close to what these people go through, time and time again. *On a regular basis,* they are victimized by volcanic eruptions, massive flooding, super typhoons, and killer earthquakes.

On top of that, they have experienced horrific man-made accidents that have killed thousands as well. As an island nation of more than 7,100 islands, the prime mode of transportation for the masses is via boat. Therefore, maritime accidents are common. As an example, the sinking of the Titanic luxury liner in 1912 is probably the most well-known ship disaster in terms of notoriety and massive loss of life. But in fact, the worst maritime disaster in history took place in December, 1987, in—you guessed it—the Philippines. A passenger ferry, the MV Dona Paz, collided in the dark with an oil tanker while enroute to Manila from Tacloban City, Leyte. The ferry boat caught fire and sank within minutes, killing 4,341 with only 24 survivors. (By comparison, the sinking of the Titanic claimed 1,523 lives.)

And yet, for all this and more, I've never met or been around a people group that is as friendly, warm, and hospitable as the Filipino people. On a national and cultural level, I've never seen people so able to smile and persevere in the midst of disaster after disaster. It truly is amazing to see—time and again!

What about God's Promise for the "Abundant" Life?

Any event in a person's life that goes contrary to the exceedingly great and precious promises of God (see 2 Peter 1:4) will create an opportunity for the devil to sow anger and offense towards God.

> *The thief does not come except to steal, and to kill, and to destroy. I have come that they may have life, and that they may have it more abundantly.*
>
> —JOHN 10:10

Jesus Himself said that He came to give us an *abundant* life, so when our lives experience something that is anything *but* abundant, the devil tries to use that against us with the temptation to blame God for what we can't explain or rationalize—according to our preconceived ideas about what an abundant life should be like.

Never forget that the definition for an "abundant life" will vary widely, depending upon who you talk to, what they've experienced, and where they're from. As I've said in a previous chapter about social attacks, when American Christians talk about the abundant life, their concept of what that means is vastly different from, as an example, believers who risk life and limb just to meet and have a service, as they do in many Muslim and Communist countries worldwide. That being said, I'm of the opinion that when Jesus was talking about coming to provide us with the abundant life, His definition of abundance was far more tied to spiritual things, rather than carnal or worldly things. Passages like Luke 12:15 back that up.

> *And He said to them, "Take heed and beware of covetousness, for one's life does not consist in the abundance of the things he possesses."*
>
> —LUKE 12:15

If you go on and read the verses that follow verse 15 from Luke chapter 12, Jesus talks about a man who thought abundance had to do with getting more, having more, and hoarding more—and how shallow and selfish that was in the light of life's fragility and unpredictable nature. In Luke 12:20, God calls such a man a "fool."

Once there was a seven day stretch of time where, one right after another, I found myself trying to help people cope with the kinds of unexplainable tragedies that left me just shaking my head. First, I had to minister to a young couple who had just lost their 2-year-old son in a freak farm accident, followed by my counseling a pastoral couple having to deal with the death of their daughter-in-law from a drug overdose, and then on to a close relative dealing with his wife leaving him for another man. In each case, the affected people were committed Christians, doing their best to serve God and live right. Their questions were both justified from their end, and hard to answer from my end! Though not as dire as these examples that I've just shared, I, too, have faced many situations or developments in my life and ministry that left me with unanswered questions before Almighty God.

The chief question asked is usually about the "why" of this tragedy, accident, or development. Why has this happened? Why did this accident take place? Why did God allow this? Why wasn't the devil prevented from doing what he did? Other questions would be: What did I do wrong? How could I have prevented this tragedy from happening? These victims were innocent children—how could this have taken place if God is love? If God is all-powerful, why didn't He prevent this from happening, or, why didn't my faith prevent this from happening? Does faith really work? And many more questions as well.

Why Is This?

Why do things like this happen? Some denominations and their preachers will go to great lengths to tell us that God is the author of such terrible things, and as the sovereign Creator, has every right to arbitrarily pick and choose who gets blessed and who doesn't. But to believe that about God contradicts hundreds of passages in the Bible that say otherwise. One of the best examples of this is what Jesus said about Himself and God the Father. When Philip asked Jesus if He could show them the Father, this is what our Lord said in reply:

> *"If you had known Me, you would have known My Father also; and from now on you know Him and have seen Him." Philip said to Him, "Lord, show us the Father, and it is sufficient for us." Jesus said to him, "Have I been with you so long, and yet you have not known Me, Philip? He who has seen Me has seen the Father; so how can you say, 'Show us the Father'? Do you not believe that I am in the Father, and the Father in Me? The words that I speak to you I do not speak on My own authority; but the Father who dwells in Me does the works. Believe Me that I am in the Father and the Father in Me, or else believe Me for the sake of the works themselves."*

—JOHN 14:7-11

Notice the emphasis here on two things: The *words* of Jesus and the *works* of Jesus. Words and works. Jesus told us that if we were listening to Him, we were listening to God, His Father. If we were watching Him do the works of God, we were watching God Himself doing the works. Why? Is it because God and Jesus were the same person? No, but because Jesus was so connected to His Father God, so "in sync" with Him, so *one* with God, that Jesus was the mirrored reflection of everything God wanted to say and do concerning men on planet Earth. In essence, when the disciples saw or heard Jesus in action, they were seeing God in action.

Well, what was Jesus doing for his three and a half years of public ministry? Healing people. Helping people. Rescuing people. Encouraging people. Teaching people. Protecting people. Doing good to people. As we have already noted in previous chapters, not once do we see Jesus purposely harming or hurting anyone to "teach them a lesson," and all the other unscriptural things we hear from the pulpits of many churches. So what gives? Why do bad things continue to happen to good people? First, it's important to clear up a very common and popular misconception in this area.

Don't Assume the Worst

Contrary to what many believe, not everybody who gets hit with sickness or tragedy is guilty of some kind of sin that opened the door to the devil. That may be true for some, but certainly isn't true for all. First of all, to automatically assume a person is being attacked because they're living "in sin" or "disobedience," or "spiritual rebellion" is to violate the clear teachings of Scripture. In First Corinthians 13, the Word of God tells us to walk in love towards others, which among other things, instructs us to believe the best of people, not the worst. So to automatically assume somebody was attacked because they're living a life contrary to God's Word is to believe the worst about someone, not the best— exactly the opposite to what the scriptures tell us to do.

Since I got saved on September 21, 1978, I've seen many energetic and dedicated soul-winners cut down in the prime of life due to sickness, disease, accidents, or tragedy. Maybe you have, too. Pastors doing a great work for God suddenly fall down dead in the middle of the day from a heart attack. Successful ministers get hit with some fatal disease like cancer. Anointed men and women of God go through horrendous fights of faith for healing that last for years; with some receiving their healing, while others die and go home to Heaven.

I've witnessed good Christian people lose everything in natural or man-made disasters like fires, hurricanes, tornadoes, or some terrible family accident. On more than one occasion, I've seen well-known, successful, and heavily anointed ministers die in airplane crashes at the height of their ministry's growth— many times killing not only themselves, but many of their devoted staff and support personnel as well. I don't know why these things happen to good, godly people, but they do and there *are* reasons why—I just don't know what those reasons are, and neither do you.

What I *do* know is what the Bible says about God, about the devil, and about man in the middle. God loves us, the devil hates us, and men have been given the right to choose which one they will serve, with eternal rewards or eternal punishment waiting for us on the other side of physical death. My theology revolves around these simple truths, nothing more and nothing less. In our lives, our choices can either empower God to be good, or the devil to be bad—but neither can help or hurt without our permission!

Why doesn't God make everyone get saved if He so loves the world, as Jesus said in John 3:16? It's because we have the right and responsibility to choose—to accept or reject the work of Jesus on the cross. Why can't the devil just kill us all in the next five minutes? He'd love to because he hates us that much, so why doesn't he? Because he can't force us to open a door and invite him in—we have to make choices that give him permission. And because we can't see into a person's heart and private life like God, that leaves a lot of gray areas between the black and white! Until God sits me down in Heaven to personally explain the unexplainable of this life, I choose to trust Him, and leave those gray areas alone. I know He will fill in the blanks at a time and place of His choosing—either in this life or the next.

We Should Mind Our Own Business!

Bottom line: until otherwise *proven* by indisputable facts, make no assumptions about why people experience unexplained pain and tragedy. Many people who are doing their utmost to live a sin-free life of sanctification, holiness, and purity before God will find themselves dealing with the emotional trauma that comes from an unexplained accident, tragedy, sickness, or death. When people want to do something for God, they're going to get shot at by the enemy, and the ammunition he uses can take many forms, from natural disasters, to freak and unexplained accidents, to individual sickness and disease. As the "god of this world" (see 2 Corinthians 4:4), the devil has a number of tools, techniques, and tactics at his disposal to try and hurt, harm, or kill people—especially when he's trying to eliminate those who are serious about serving God and fulfilling the Great Commission.

That's all we need to know about why others are dealing with a tragedy or difficult challenge. And unless we're in a position that has given us uncommon or confidential knowledge that explains the unexplainable, our responsibility is to take the scriptural high road of believing the best of people until proven otherwise. That means we pray for their healing, recovery, or restoration and nothing else—period. Leave the rest up to God!

> *Who are you to judge another's servant? To his own master he stands or falls. Indeed, he will be made to stand, for God is able to make him stand.*
>
> —ROMANS 14:4

If there are private issues in people's lives that may have given the enemy opportunity against them, that's none of our business, unless God specifically chooses to tell us otherwise. Let God deal with them by His Spirit, because they'll answer to Him—not you or me. Stay out of it, unless God decides you need to know for some related reason. Until that happens, if ever, don't make assumptions you don't have all the facts to make! If there *are* sins involved, trust me, God will deal with that. Nobody gets away with anything, so leave those things with the Lord.

> *How God anointed Jesus of Nazareth with the Holy Spirit and with power, who went about doing good and healing all who were oppressed by the devil, for God was with Him.*
>
> —ACTS 10:38

Earlier, we examined this verse in the light of physical attacks that would seek to stop us from advancing under fire for God. Here we will look at this truth from this chapter's angle of theological attack—specifically, bad things happening to good people. To briefly restate the obvious—no matter how much we study and learn about God's desire that we exercise dominion and enjoy an abundant life on Earth, we will still encounter events, incidents, or happenings in life that we can't explain, don't understand, and can't give verses for. Things happen to people that run contrary to all we read and know about our Heavenly Father. When God tells us that He *is* love (see 1 John 4:8), it can be hard to explain away the unexplainable—to ourselves or to others around us who want to know.

If Jesus went around doing good and never doing bad, why then do bad things happen to good people, and more specifically, to good Christian people? Evil men prosper while Christians suffer. Ungodly and unsaved people get rich, hoard their wealth, and squander it on themselves, while Christians struggle to build churches, send missionaries, or otherwise do the work of the Great Commission. Imposter preachers steal from, and get rich, at the expense of innocent and well-meaning people. Lazy, lukewarm ministers live lives of ease and opulence, while sincere, dedicated, and hard-working ministers struggle to pay their bills and win souls. While evil people go on their merry way without a care or concern, good people suffer needless tragedies in life. You and I aren't the only ones who sometimes have questions with no answers. As far back as the Old Testament, King David struggled with these very issues. Read all of Psalm 73, especially verses like these:

> *Truly God is good to Israel, to such as are pure in heart. But as for me, my feet had almost stumbled; my steps had nearly slipped. For I was envious of the boastful, when I saw the prosperity of the wicked. For there are no pangs in their death, but their strength is firm. They are not in trouble as other men, nor are they plagued like other men.*
>
> *For all day long I have been plagued, and chastened every morning. If I had said, "I will speak thus," behold, I would have been untrue to the generation of Your children. **When I thought how to understand this, it was too painful for me**—until I went into the sanctuary of God; then I understood their end.*
>
> —PSALM 73:1-5,14-17 [EMPHASIS MINE]

If you're familiar with the life and ministry of King David, you know there were times in David's life when his own sins created gigantic opportunities for the devil to attack, and attack he did. But, there were other times—times that this Psalm addresses— when he honestly had no clue as to why so many evil people prospered while so many godly people suffered. It created a theological crisis in his mind, which according to verse 2, almost convinced him to turn away from God!

The Answers Are out There!

I don't have answers for every single tragedy or trauma that I've seen, experienced, or tried to help others manage and make sense of. Neither would any other honest minister for that matter. But I can point out the spiritual truths, as revealed in the Bible, that keep everything in proper perspective and helps us navigate through those tragedies and situations without falling away from God!

First of all, notice the overriding truth that got David through this theological crisis of Psalm 73, found in verses 16 and 17. He admits that trying to reconcile the goodness of God with the pain in life was "too painful" to dwell on—until he went into God's sanctuary (meaning into His presence). What he did is what you and I will have to do as well, when we face suffering and sorrow and don't know why. *When David got alone with God long enough to regain the heavenly perspective, then, and only then, did he understand their end!*

We live in parallel worlds on this Earth. We are spirits living in bodies. There is the spirit world, which is the parent, and then there is the physical world, which is the child. The laws of this world are always subordinate to the laws of the spirit world. And everything in this world is temporary and subject to change, while everything in the spirit world is set and unchanging.

We have God and His angels, who are good. We have Satan and his demons, who are bad. Even though Jesus took back the keys of Hell and death from the devil when He rose from the dead (see Revelation 1:18), Ol' Split-Foot didn't disappear. He's still here on Earth, and his objectives and intent for man hasn't changed one bit. He still hates us all, and intends to drag as many of us to Hell as possible, inflicting upon us as much suffering and sorrow beforehand in this life as possible.

Jesus may have taken back the authority given to Adam when He came, died, and rose from the dead, but because men still make choices with their words and with their lives that empower the enemy (even if they don't know they're doing it), all of humankind is still subject to the whims of this evil and renegade spirit named Satan. Therefore, as long as we're here and he's here, bad things will continue happening to good people. But before you get too depressed, remember this world's present-day reality will soon be coming to an end! Jesus is coming back and when He does, the author of all that is bad, evil, and sinful will be banished from Earth, first for the 1,000-year millennium, and then shortly after that, to the lake of fire forever. Adam's lease will be completed, and through Jesus, God will wipe every tear from every eye (see Revelation 21:1-5). So until that time comes, whenever you have to, get with God until, like David, you understand the end of all things temporary.

Like a flitting sparrow, like a flying swallow, so a curse without cause shall not alight.
—PROVERBS 26:2

Here is the truth to remember and never forget about unanswered questions that challenge our theology about a loving, caring God. *There is always a reason for why things happen the way they do, even if we don't always know what that reason may be.* As a child of God, be determined to advance under the fire of unexplained tragedies, premature deaths, or seeming inequities with finances or financial fortunes, and settle these things in your mind once and for all. Proverbs 26:2 tells us the curse that is "causeless" cannot come. That means for *every* unexplained problem, test, tragedy, or situation, there is a cause or a reason for why it happened the way it did—even if we go to our graves still wondering why! It's what 1 Corinthians 13:12 calls *"looking through a glass darkly."* God Himself says as much in this passage from Deuteronomy:

"The secret things belong to the LORD our God, but those things which are revealed belong to us and to our children forever, that we may do all the words of this law."
—DEUTERONOMY 29:29

Yes my friend, there are "secret things" in this life that God isn't going to explain to you or me, at least on this side of Heaven. Why? It doesn't matter why—just do what our opening verse of this chapter tells you to do: trust Him with all your heart and don't lean to your own understanding. Why? Because our understanding regarding unexplained tragedies, calamities, or difficulties is *always* incomplete. As I said before, we can't see a person's heart like God can, and we can't be in all places at once to see and know what goes on in private, but God can. That's what the Bible refers to when Paul writes to Timothy, to encourage him to stay steadfast in the midst of trials and tribulations.

> *Some men's sins are clearly evident, preceding them to judgment, but those of some men follow later. Likewise, the good works of some are clearly evident, and those that are otherwise cannot be hidden.*
>
> —1 TIMOTHY 5:24-25

According to what God has chosen to reveal to us in the Word of God, it's obvious that from His perspective, our trust in Him is what He's looking for above all else. That is, in fact, the life of true faith, and Hebrews 11:6 tells us that without faith, it's impossible to please God. He knows we're living in a cursed world, and that curse brings with it all measure of sin, evil, and suffering. Therefore, when we encounter or observe people's pain and suffering in this world, from our limited and incomplete perspective, it's enough for us to know God knows everything. We don't know all the details about the present set of circumstances we have to deal with, and we can't know the future about them either. But God can—and does—and He gives us enough information in His Word to come to the correct conclusions about unanswered questions we encounter and struggle to explain in this life. Those are the things "revealed" to us in His Word. They are for us, and for us to teach our children, so we have a clear and balanced understanding about our Heavenly Father. This is what God talks about in Ecclesiastes chapter 7:

I applied my heart to know, to search and seek out wisdom and the reason of things, to know the wickedness of folly, even of foolishness and madness.

—ECCLESIASTES 7:25

God wants us to apply our heart to know, to search, to seek out wisdom *and find the reason for things.* Notice especially the part where we're to know "the reason of things." This is the same as what Paul told Timothy, as a young minister, that he needed to "study to show himself approved" (see 2 Timothy 2:15). He expects us to read and carefully examine His Word, so we find "the reason" for things from a biblical perspective.

However, that doesn't automatically mean we become privy to all secret things! What it does mean is that in a general sense, we're never to forget the basic state of life on planet Earth, as we've heretofore mentioned. And therefore, even if we don't have all the answers for all of our questions about "why," we're at peace within because a diligent study of God's Word always gives us the complete, correct, and biblically balanced perception of Who He is, and the good He has done, is doing, and will do for us. And as we "study to show ourselves approved," we'll be better able to understand the reason for things (the differences between the work of the Trinity and the work of humankind's archenemy the devil), even if for now at least, all the details for every test, tragedy. and hardship aren't readily known. In short, He expects us to *trust* Him with our unanswered questions; knowing they will all be answered—if not now, then later on after we have stepped out of these mortal bodies and put on incorruption (see 1 Corinthians 15:53-54).

Simple Truths to Remember

Have you ever faced unanswered questions in your life—even after giving your heart and life to Jesus? If you've been saved for any appreciable length of time, I'm sure the answer would be "yes." In a nutshell, here are the "reasons for things" that God wants you to know and live by. They are the basic Bible truths which always transcend every test, trial, or tragedy in life. Remembering them will always enable you to advance under fire for the work of God, even if you experience things in your life that have challenged you theologically with the tenets of your Christian faith.

1. God made all things good, but thanks to Adam, (for now) we live in a fallen world that labors under the curse of sin (see Genesis 3:14-17).

2. There is a renegade spirit (Satan) who is God's enemy, roaming freely (for now) on the earth, whose sole purpose is to hurt, damage, destroy, and damn to hell every human being alive, saved, or unsaved—but especially the saved (see 1 Peter 5:8).

3. This evil spirit has authored and is in control of a world-wide system of deception that is designed to enable him to destroy humankind and keep them in bondage to sin, which results in death, which results in eternal judgment (see 2 Corinthians 4:3-4; James 2:14-16).

4. Therefore, bad things do happen to good people (saved or unsaved) in this world, just because they're in this world, and made in the image and likeness of God (see Proverbs 26:2).

5. Therefore, bad things do happen to born-again, faith-filled, on-fire-for-the-Lord Christians, just because they're committed to the fight for souls, according to the Great Commission (see Mark 16:15-18).

6. There is always a reason for why bad things happen to good people, but we won't always know what that reason is or was while living on Earth (see Ecclesiastes 7:25).

7. A terrible and eternal payday is coming for those who serve sin and the devil, even if in this life, they enjoy the "passing pleasures of sin." (see Hebrews 11:25).

8. If we hold fast to our Lord God and His standards of holiness and purity, resist the devil, and defend and spread the truth, we will reap eternal rewards (see Galatians 6:9; James 4:7).

9. All unanswered questions of this life will one day be answered by God in the next. God will not be mocked (see Galatians 6:7-8).

Your Life Isn't About You!

If you're going through difficulties and trials because of sin or disobedience, go to God, ask for His mercy and forgiveness and get things right with Him—then get back in the fight. If you've been attacked because of no other reason other than you're in love with God and want to win souls in the name of Jesus, don't get discouraged either! Trust Him, and leave all the unanswered questions with Him for now.

You see, your life isn't just about you and the tragedy or difficulty you're facing or trying to understand at this moment.

From God's viewpoint, our lives are about much more than what we can have, receive, or enjoy at any given time along life's way here on Earth. Read your Bible, and you will see our lives in Christ are never to be all about ourselves, but instead, about partnering with God to help others who don't know what we know about Jesus. The more we do this, the more spiritual satisfaction we're going to experience, because that's how we're wired by the hand of our Creator. We're co-workers with God, which in my opinion, is the greatest privilege ever given to humankind (see 2 Corinthians 6:1). With or without men's applause, approval, or acceptance, we work with God to fulfill His divine purpose—the Great Commission of Mark 16:15-18.

Stay steady and keep your eyes on God, no matter what. Through the good, the bad, and the ugly, learn to live life on an "even keel," not allowing triumphs or tragedies to move you away from the "center line" of biblical balance and perspective. If you are used by God to accomplish something that is spiritually mean-ingful for yourself or others, praise God for it and move on! Don't expect the world to stop turning for the next ten years while the grateful masses hold parades on your behalf, because they won't! On the other hand, if you are going through tragedies, tempta-tions, trials, and testings with lots of unanswered questions as to the "why" of it all, just decide to keep going for God anyway. Don't expect everyone out there to stop living their lives for the next ten years so they can sit and cry with you, because they won't!

Pain Leads to Purpose

As a co-worker with God, with or without understanding of all things, and with or without men's accolades and acknowledge-ment, and with or without men's encouragement and support, you *can* allow your pain to become a purpose! You *can* continue to do your best when you feel your worst. You *can* continue doing good even when feeling bad. You *can* decide to forge ahead, even if or when unanswered questions swirl all around you.

If ever there was an example of this, it would be Jesus Himself. Hebrews 4:15 reminds us that even Jesus, our great High Priest, was tempted in all points as we are—yet was without sin. That means He understands what you're going through when you wrestle with unanswered questions and unexplained tragedies of life. That doesn't mean He experienced every *type of attack* that we experience, but it does mean He faced every kind of temptation to quit and become disillusioned with God—just like you and me!

That's startling to many Christians, but if it's not true, how could He say He's been touched with the feeling of our infirmi-ties, because He was tempted just like us? Go back and read care-fully those four gospels, especially the parts that describe His passion and crucifixion. Didn't Jesus plead with God to take the cup of the cross away from Him three times while praying in the Garden of Gethsemane? Didn't Jesus cry out while up on the cross, directly questioning God—asking *why* He had been forsaken? Yes, Jesus had "why, God, why?" questions in His life, just like you and me.

Who, in the days of His flesh, when He had offered up prayers and supplications, with vehement cries and tears to Him who was able to save Him from death, and was heard because of His godly fear, though He was a Son, yet He learned obedience by the things which He suffered. And having been perfected, He became the author of eternal salvation to all who obey Him.

—HEBREWS 5:7-9

If you think our Lord's earthly, public ministry was just one big party of miracles, wedding feasts, and anointed Bible studies, you're sorely naïve my friend! After John the Baptist made the public proclamation about Jesus at the time of his Jordan River baptism, all hell broke loose against Him for the next three and a half years. From birth right up to His 30th birthday, Jesus had lived a quiet life, living what theologians like to refer to as the "silent years." All those years with His parents, with nothing unusual, profound, or earth-shaking going on.

Aside from the one instance of staying over in Jerusalem for 3 days at the age of 12, without the knowledge or permission from Joseph and Mary (see Luke 2:49), there's no mention in the Bible of anything else happening out of the ordinary while Jesus was growing up. As far as everyone knew, Jesus was just a normal Jewish boy, woodworking at home in Joseph's carpentry shop. But once John made his proclamation about the Lamb of God who takes away the sin of the world, and God the Father audibly spoke about Jesus from Heaven, and the Spirit of God came down upon Him in the form of a dove, the fight was on!

In every conceivable way, the devil threw everything he had at Jesus for the next three and a half years—unsuccessfully! Not one time did Jesus sin and fail God—praise His name forevermore! But nonetheless, there were times of vehement (intense) cries, tears, and pleadings with God His Father about His duties and ministry assignments. Obviously, there were moments of crisis even in the life and ministry of Jesus. Exactly what they were we don't know, and we don't need to know. We only need to know He passed every test and resisted every temptation because He chose to—and so can we!

Advance under fire! Be like Jesus, and other modern-day heroes of faith, who rose above terrible tragedies and unexplained sufferings to become great examples of perseverance and dedication to the cause of Christ. Read and study about men like John Harper, a widowed Baptist preacher who was on the Titanic the night that great ship sank, choosing to forsake his own six-year old daughter and niece in the lifeboat, so he could continue witnessing to the doomed passengers on that ship before he himself drowned in the frigid water.

Study the life and times of Horatio Spafford, who wrote the now-famous hymn "It Is Well with My Soul"—a hymn written under circumstances that would test and try the most fervent of Christian soldiers. One night in the middle of the Atlantic Ocean, alone in his cabin as his ship sailed to England, Spafford penned this hymn while sailing over the exact location where just days earlier, his wife and children had been involved in a terrible ship collision where all four of his daughters had drowned. In Chicago, Spafford had been a successful businessman as well as an anointed minister, who was planning to move his family to England to assist D.L. Moody with his revival going on there. This great church hymn was written amidst horrific family circumstances in 1873, and was put to music by P.P. Bliss in 1876. Since then, it has been sung in countless churches worldwide to inspire and strengthen so many, but very few know about Spafford's torn state of mind the night he penned that powerful hymn.

Men like these, along with countless others from Adam until now, experienced the kind of heartache, suffering, and tragedy that could shake their theology to its core, but they pushed on through the barriers of pain and unanswered questions. They rose above the moment, and by doing so, inspired hundreds of thousands of Christian soldiers to persevere no matter what (yours truly being one of them).

Have you ever heard of the organization called MADD? Founded by a mother whose daughter was killed by a drunk driver, Mothers Against Drunk Driving® (MADD) is the nation's largest nonprofit organization that works to protect families from drunk driving and underage drinking. In short, she decided to move beyond her own grief and questions about "why," and form an organization dedicated to doing good when people feel bad.

When tragedy strikes and our theology is put to the test, we can choose to allow God to create something good out of what the devil meant for bad. We don't have to become theological cripples if we don't want to be. History is stained with the blood of martyrs for the cause of Christ. As mentioned earlier, books like *Foxe's Book of Martyrs*, or *Tortured for Christ* by Richard Wurmbrand, help us to realize that when we face something in life that's tragic, either for ourselves or others we love, we have to have the discipline to look *beyond* this episode in our life, to see that our race in Christ still has a long way to go before we reach the finish line! Many more people will still need to know what you know about Jesus, so never let a set of unanswered questions delay or deter you from the task at hand—telling people about Jesus and winning souls.

Always See the Bigger Picture

When we are going through bad experiences that can't be immediately explained, we must remind ourselves of the bigger picture. Storms of tragedy come and go in our lives, for some more so than for others, but they come to all of us. Understanding that we have a responsibility before God to keep moving forward under this kind of fire from the enemy—no matter what—will enable us to keep our eyes on the *finish line*, not the pain of the moment. All of us get knocked down in this life, but when we fall, we can make the decision to fall *forward*, instead of falling *backward*. If we fall forward, we're still advancing under fire!

CHAPTER 20

Spiritual Retaliation

Do not rejoice over me, my enemy; when I fall, I will arise.
—MICAH 7:8

As long as Christians live on Earth, they will be attacked again and again by the enemy. This truth is not debatable—it's a fact of life. Every Christian needs to know this, and live in the light of this truth. And because we're all "works in progress" when it comes to the business of spiritual sanctification, we must not become discouraged when, along life's way, we stumble and fall before a holy and righteous God. Even the most passionate and dedicated among us will come up short in God's eyes, and let sin have its way from time to time. It happens to all of us, with some more so than with others, depending upon many factors that include personal decisions, levels of spiritual commitment, obedience to God's word, cultural conditions, geographical locations, and surrounding events or circumstances.

Just because we love God and want to serve Him does not create a cocoon of protection while we live here on Earth. This is the battlefield—this world and this life. So for as long as we're here, the devil will never stop looking for ways to steal, kill, or destroy in our lives. And because of that truth, understand that *everyone* in the Body of Christ will fail God many times in between the time of the new birth (when they received their salvation by accepting Jesus as Lord and Savior), and the time of earthly

255

departure (whether it be by physical death or by the rapture of the church, whichever event precedes the other).

To really excel at the ability to consistently advance under fire for Christ, all of us need to develop the attitude reflected from this passage here in Micah chapter 7. It's what I like to call "spiritual retaliation." It represents an attitude that every believer should develop and protect, but which most have never acquired or cultivated. It's the mindset that refuses to stay down for the count when the enemy has knocked us to the canvas, so-to-speak. It's an attitude that enables every Christian to not only get back up from the sins or failures committed before Almighty God, but to *go after the devil* with a renewed sense of righteous anger and indignation for what he did to you, or to those you love around you.

Take Advantage of God's Mercy

Too many believers wallow in self-pity, self-condemnation, and remorse for having stumbled into sin or failure, but that's not what they should be doing! The first thing to do after we've fallen short before God is to go to Him to ask for His forgiveness and mercy. First John 1:9 tells us to do this, and we should obey whenever necessary!

> *If we confess our sins, He is faithful and just to forgive us our sins and to cleanse us from all unrighteousness.*
>
> —1 JOHN 1:9

It's important to note here that this passage from 1 John is written specifically to saints, not sinners. John was writing to believers, and including himself when making this point. He said if *we* confess our sins God will forgive *us*. The words "we" and "us" clearly denote all Christians, including John. Also notice the word "if." That means all Christians have the choice, and the responsibility, to come to God in acknowledgement of their sins, and ask Him for forgiveness whenever necessary. If we come to Him to ask forgiveness for sin, He gladly responds and grants it, but we are the ones who have to make that choice (see James 4:8).

God is for us, not against us. If He invested the life of His own Son on the cross, making Him our sin substitute as the holy Lamb of God that takes away our sins, He's not going to just throw us overboard every time we fall through sin, disobedience, or failure. *No matter how terrible you may feel after failing God, move past your feelings and by faith, believe the scriptures and receive your forgiveness!* He loves you, and *wants* to forgive you, *so let Him!*

There are those who teach that all sins—past, present, and future—are automatically forgiven in the life of a believer, but that's not what the Bible teaches. Once a person becomes a child of God by receiving Jesus as Lord and personal Savior, God expects that person to come to Him whenever necessary, and ask for the forgiveness needed. In short, as a believer, *God won't forgive what you don't ask Him to forgive!* Why? Because He has given us the dominion on this earth (see Genesis 1:26-28), and a free will to decide to come to Him or not. Hebrews speaks of this.

> *Seeing then that we have a great High Priest who has passed through the heavens, Jesus the Son of God, let us hold fast our confession. For we do not have a High Priest who cannot sympathize with our weaknesses, but was in all points tempted as we are, yet without sin. Let us therefore come boldly to the throne of grace, that we may obtain mercy and find grace to help in time of need.*
> —HEBREWS 4:14-16

Notice again the words "we" and "us" in this passage. This isn't written to unbelievers, but to those who have already made Jesus Lord and Savior. Unbelievers don't have Jesus in Heaven, serving as their great High Priest, but those that are born-again do. Even so, please note that even though we now have the Son of God as our sympathetic High Priest at the right hand of God, we still have the responsibility to *choose* to come to God's throne and ask for God's mercy and grace to help us in our time of need. According to the context of Hebrews chapters 3 and 4, this "time of need" dealt with sins committed—in this case the sin of unbelief by the Israelites back in Old Testament times, which is one sin that is very much alive and well within the ranks of Christians everywhere today! Well, as far as God is concerned, the wages of sin is death, and one type of sin is just as heinous as another (see Romans 6:23).

In order to get up and keep advancing, the first thing you're going to need to do is get God's forgiveness, mercy, and grace in that particular time of need. That's first and foremost. (Listen: when the devil has just knocked you flat on your back, and it seems like all of hell is coming against you from every side, that is definitely your time of need!) You'll never be able to effectively retaliate against the enemy until all your sins and failures have been confessed, repented of, and washed away by the blood of Jesus. When that has taken place, you're now in position to get up and go after the devil to make him pay for what he's done to you or those you love.

And here's another sacred cow that must be kicked over here. When we talk about the importance of confessing our sins to God, don't put yourself under the false pressure of thinking you have to remember every little sin and one by one confess them to God. Frankly, that's impossible, and God knows it is. Rest in the fact that God knows us, and He knows our hearts (see Psalms 44:21, Acts 15:8, 1 John 3:20). Our Heavenly Father knows if we're doing our best, and sincerely trying to make mention of specific areas of sin or compromise that we know of. And if there are any unknown or overlooked trespasses, God will forgive us of those when we confess the ones we know of (see Matthew 9:2, Psalms 103:3).

I also believe the scriptures indicate that because we've been given the dominion here on Earth, we can literally stand in the gap for others, and have the Lord forgive them of their sins—just because we ask (see John 20:23; 1 John 5:14-16; James 5:15; 2 Chronicles 30:18-20)! As an example, only God knows how many people were praying for my salvation, during the times of my ignorant youth, when I was doing just about anything I could to kill myself with drugs, alcohol, and loose living in the "fast lane." In particular, I'm well persuaded that the prayers of my beloved mother kept me alive and out of Hell more than once. I shudder as I think back on all the times I should've been killed for doing stupid and reckless things, but God kept me and preserved me until such time as I grew a brain and, like the prodigal son, came to myself and got saved. It sure wasn't *my prayers* that protected me from the devil for all those years—that much I know for certain!

Move on from Repentance to Retaliation

So therefore, once you've come to God in repentance for your sins, and allowed our great High Priest to intercede for you as your Heavenly Advocate, let go of your past sins and *never* let them be used by the devil to bring reproach or self-condemnation upon you again. The devil is called the accuser of the brethren in Revelation 12:10, and he will surely try to accuse you and remind you of your past failures. But when he does, remember *there is no condemnation* for those in Christ Jesus, according to Romans 8:1.

After you've come to God's throne of grace to receive forgiveness and mercy, the devil will try to come along with more lies, trying to make you think you really weren't forgiven, or convince you that even if you have been forgiven, your sins have somehow disqualified you from any future work or service in the army of the Lord. Understand that and anticipate the counter-attack, because it will surely come. When it does, you just remind the liar that you've gone to God, confessed and repented of your sins and failures, and received His forgiveness. Not by your feelings, but by your faith. His mercies are new every morning, according to Lamentations 3:22-23, so take advantage of that by confessing your sins, mistakes and failures to God, and then move on!

We've already seen Paul doing this in his own life in Philippians 3:12-16, and you and I must do the same.

Go after the Devil and Make Him Pay

The second thing to do when it comes to spiritual retaliation is to get up, as Micah tells us to do, and re-engage with an attitude and with activities that inflict pain and suffering on the enemy of our souls. In other words, you're not just going to get up from your failures and weakly and meekly attempt to pick up your weapons and start trudging forward again, but instead, you're going to dedicate yourself to the business of tormenting the devil like never before. You're not just going to get back in the fight, but you're going to make him pay in great anguish for coming against you as he did.

If you faint in the day of adversity, your strength is small.
—PROVERBS 24:10

For a righteous man may fall seven times and rise again.
—PROVERBS 24:16

As I've said and as Proverbs tells us, adversity comes to us all in this life, because we're living on a cursed planet where an evil, merciless, renegade spirit roams to and fro, looking for people to damn and destroy. But that doesn't mean you and I have to faint in the day of adversity! Not at all, because the Word of God still says that *greater* is the Holy Spirit *in you* than the devil who is in the world. In fact, caving in during times of intense adversity indicates a very low level of spiritual knowledge and strength, and lets the devil know you're a spiritual pushover. This will embolden him to ratchet up the pressure against you, because he knows you don't have what it takes to force him to back off.

It doesn't matter how many times you've been knocked down by the enemy's lies, tactics, and maneuvers against you. Get back up, and make him pay for it! As it says in Proverbs, you may fall seven times, but you should keep getting back up. And when you do, get up with an attitude! Many Christians don't think much about the fact that they can torment the devil, but we certainly can! Just look at Jesus for our example, because in John 14:12-14, He said the works He did we would do also, and tormenting the devil was definitely one of the works He did while on Earth.

When he saw Jesus, he cried out, fell down before Him, and with a loud voice said, "What have I to do with You, Jesus, Son of the Most High God? I beg You, do not torment me!" For He had commanded the unclean spirit to come out of the man. For it had often seized him, and he was kept under guard, bound with chains and shackles; and he broke the bonds and was driven by the demon into the wilderness.

—LUKE 8:28-29

We already examined this story earlier, but when you read about this deliverance from all three accounts in Matthew, Mark, and Luke's gospels, you can see that every demon inside of that poor soul knew it was time to go—even though Legion was begging and pleading with Jesus not to torment them. (The number of demons possessing this man was equal to the number of soldiers in a Roman Legion, which was around 6,000. But the many demons inside the man's spirit had only one leader, who was the demon who spoke directly to Jesus. His name was also Legion.)

As said previously, up to that point in time the demons that possessed this man had been tormenting him at will because they knew their victim had no ability to fight back, but look at how the tables turned when Jesus showed up! In a matter of seconds, as soon as Jesus confronted the evil legion of spirits, it was no longer the demons tormenting the man, but Jesus tormenting the demons possessing the man! In Christ, as God's children, we've been given the exact same authority as Jesus had that day, which He used to expel those demons from the man and set him free. *This is how we retaliate.* We go out there, make ourselves available to God afresh, and purpose in our hearts to set as many people free from sin and deception as possible, tormenting the devil at every turn along the way.

Another example of Jesus operating in spiritual retaliation against the devil is found in Matthew's gospel, just after Herod had John the Baptist beheaded in prison.

So he sent and had John beheaded in prison. And his head was brought on a platter and given to the girl, and she brought it to her mother. Then his disciples came and took away the body and buried it, and went and told Jesus. When Jesus heard it, He departed from there by boat to a deserted place by Himself. But when the multitudes heard it, they followed Him on foot from the cities. And when Jesus went out He saw a great multitude; and He was moved with compassion for them, and healed their sick.

—MATTHEW 14:10-14

Many Christians forget that John the Baptist and Jesus were cousins. They were not just friends and key figures in God's plan of redemption, but members of the same immediate family. As such, there was a special bond of love between them that any of us would understand if we ourselves are part of a close-knit and loving family. So you can imagine how devastated Jesus must have been when news was brought to him about what happened to his cousin John—beheaded in prison at the whim of a wicked King, his jealous wife, and her temptress daughter.

If you were given similar news about one of your family members you loved and worked with in ministry, how would it make you feel? Of course you'd be grieving for the death of your close relative, but how about any desires for retribution? Would you be angry? Would you want punishment meted out to those responsible for this? Would you cry out for justice to be served to avenge the death of your loved one? If it were me, the answer would be a resounding "yes!"

Jesus was just as much human as you or I. Hebrews 4:15 tells us He was tempted in *all points like us,* yet without sin. If you had to deal with thoughts of anger and revenge for what somebody did to your beloved family member like what happened to John, you can be sure Jesus was dealing with the same thoughts as well.

What did he do? First, He withdrew to a private place to grieve the loss and death of John, as any of us would do. But then when He came out from that place of personal prayer and reflection, He saw all the people in need, waiting for Him to address them and alleviate their afflictions. Did He lash out in anger at the people, incredulously asking why they couldn't see what He was going through, and to just leave Him alone for a while? No. Most of us would probably do such a thing, angrily telling the people to give us some "space" to process the loss and deal with our emotional upheaval due to this terrible tragedy. But that's not what Jesus did. Even though He was emotionally stung by what had just happened to John, He was still able to be moved with compassion, and *healed their sick.*

Know What Realm to Retaliate In

That's how you retaliate when you've fallen, committed sin, or taken some kind of hit from the devil. You don't retaliate in the natural, you retaliate in the spirit realm, because your enemy is a spirit, and everything he does in this world is designed to affect our eternal destiny in the spirit world. The devil is the author of all sickness and disease, which is designed to destroy our lives and make life as painful as possible, with the hopes of using those sicknesses and diseases to cut our lives short and take us to Hell before we have the chance to receive Jesus and get saved. So, what better way for Jesus to torment the devil and retaliate against him for what he did to John?

In the midst of His own grieving process over the loss of John, Jesus went forth and retaliated against what the devil had done. He healed sick people. You and I should be doing the same thing when similar circumstances come against us in life. Don't just lay there feeling sorry for yourself and angry at the devil. As we've already pointed out in earlier chapters, *it's your responsibility to get up and get back in the fight.* Having and exercising an attitude of spiritual retaliation is one of the ways you do that.

Has the devil hurt you, or those you love? Have you failed God because of some slick temptation the devil brought against you? Has the enemy made it a point to rob from you and make you suffer as much as possible? Retaliate! Make him pay dearly for what he's tried to do against you. I've done this many times over the years, and I can tell you it's powerful and spiritually therapeutic.

After I've fallen, committed sin, or failed God, I've gotten back up and before all of Heaven and Hell, told the devil what he's in for now. Out loud, I declare that I'm forgiven and the recipient of God's mercy once again. I confess that if God be for me, nobody can be against me (see Romans 8:31-37). At that point, I then tell the pig devil how it's going to be. More worship to God. More praise to the Lord. More time spent in prayer. More Bible study. More outreach and more crusades. More financial giving! More availability for the cause of Christ. Less of the world's influence in my life, and a greater commitment to excellence in Christ. In short, I read the riot act to the devil. I tell Satan flat out to his disgusting, ugly face—I'm going to make you pay for what you've done or have tried to do. You're going to be sorry for having come against me or those I love!

The Weapons of Our Warfare Are Spiritual

Above all else, when you develop the scriptural attitude of retaliation, remember your enemy is a spirit, your weapons from God are spiritual, and the net result of your retaliation must be something in the spiritual realm. Because we live in this five-sense physical world, its natural for us to want to see the effects of our retaliation against Satan in the natural world, but understand the real damage against the enemy must be directed to the spiritual world where he resides, and from where he launches all attacks against us. That's why Paul reminded us in 2 Corinthians 10:3-5 that the weapons for our warfare are not carnal (physical or fleshly), because we're not dealing with a carnal foe. So no matter what we're doing in the natural to retaliate against the enemy, make sure it's an activity that brings torment, anguish, and hurt to the devil in the parent world of the spirit. This is what Jesus did when he went forth and healed all the sick people after receiving the news about John's beheading. Our fight isn't against humans, but evil spirits who are ranked and listed in Ephesians 6:10-12.

This is why so many turned on Jesus at the end of His earthly ministry. Many of the people thought the Messiah was going to come and deliver them from Roman rule. That was their idea of what Jesus should do for them if He was indeed their Messiah, but it was not God's plan of salvation at all. The Jews wanted the Lord to do something for them in this natural realm, when Jesus had actually come to do something for them in the spiritual realm instead. The Romans were only the problem in the natural, but Satan was the root of their problems in the spiritual. That's why after Jesus' resurrection in Acts 1:6, the disciples specifically asked Him if this was the time when He was going to restore the kingdom to Israel (and take it away from the Romans).

The plan of salvation was a plan that went after the devil in the spirit realm, not the physical realm. In fact, 1 Corinthians 2:6-8 tells us that if the devil knew what he was doing when he had Jesus crucified, he never would've done it! I believe this was the primary reason why Judas made the decision to become our Lord's betrayer, allowing the devil to enter in and possess him as he did (see John 13:21-30). When he realized that Jesus was not going to be this great military deliverer, and that Jesus Himself was prophesying about His own death, he began looking for a way out to save his own hide. We all know where that got him (see Matthew 27:5, Acts 1:18).

Whenever you contend with the devil in this life, take stock of what he tries to do against you, and then purpose in your heart, depending on the type of attack brought against you, to find ways to make him pay. Torment him spiritually in direct response for his attempts to ruin your life naturally.

Some Examples We Use In Our Ministry

We've had situations in the past where staff, or family of staff, are involved in accidents or get attacked physically with sickness or disease. Since we know the Bible tells us God is never the author of such things, we know these things are not just coincidental. We know where these things come from and who their author is—the devil. We consider these attacks to be direct attempts by the enemy to steal, kill, and destroy in our ministry. So how do we make him pay for coming against us like that?

First, we increase our time in worship and praise to God, doing so privately and corporately in public. We know the devil hates praise and worship, so we purposely increase it to simultaneously bless God and bring more torment to the enemy. In the devil's face, we lift our hands to God, and declare Him to be our protector, healer, and provider.

Second, we find the promises of God that the devil has challenged with his attacks, and we quote them out loud to God in prayer, so all will know that we know what promises were challenged before God by the enemy.

Third, we look for ways to retaliate in the natural through our outreach and ministry activities. We increase our crusade schedule, holding more crusades to win more souls. We may call for a time of extra prayer, with fasting sometimes included. We make every effort possible to increase our time of daily Bible study. We schedule additional staff meetings where we do nothing else except worship and praise God for His deliverance.

If money was involved in the attempted theft, we tally up all the expenses we had to incur to pay for the accidents, issues, or sicknesses, and multiply by seven. Then according to Proverbs 6:30-31, we take authority over the devil and demand he return to us that amount—seven times the amount of money we had to spend because of this attack. And when doing so, we specifically declare that the monetary figure we're quoting is money to be taken out from the world, not from the Body of Christ. We want this money to come right out of the back pocket of the devil, that is, money taken from the world system or from unsaved people not serving God. Since God is the owner of the Earth and we merely the stewards (see 1 Chronicles 29:11-13 as one of many scriptural proof texts for this), God has the right to take away from the world whatever we take authority over to get. This is scriptural, and its one of the ways Jesus Himself supported His ministry while on Earth.

> *Now it came to pass, afterward, that He went through every city and village, preaching and bringing the glad tidings of the kingdom of God. And the twelve were with Him, and certain women who had been healed of evil spirits and infirmities—Mary called Magdalene, out of whom had come seven demons, and*

Joanna the wife of Chuza, Herod's steward, and Susanna, and many others who provided for Him from their substance.
—LUKE 8:1-3

It takes a lot of money to travel in ministry and support twelve full-time staff members traveling with you. Just like any traveling preacher, Jesus needed field support for this from loyal and devoted disciples. Joanna, Susanna, and Mary Magdalene were three such individuals. They were supporting Jesus with their finances, but in Joanna's case, much of the support she was giving came through her husband Chuza, who according to verse 3, just happened to be King Herod's steward! Imagine that! King Herod, as evil a man as he was, was supporting the ministry of Jesus financially and didn't even know it. As Herod's steward, Chuza was in charge of the King's wealth, and was no doubt being paid for doing his duties. So Joanna was tapping into those finances through her husband's salary, which was directly paid for by the King himself, and it was quite possible that additional funds were being funneled out of the King's treasury because as Herod's steward, Chuza had that kind of access.

Herod certainly didn't know what was going on, but Joanna, Chuza, Jesus, and God sure did! This is just one example of how God takes the wealth of the world and gives it to His children to cover the costs of any attacks brought against them by Satan.

In addition, if the devil was using people in his attacks against us, I go after them in the spirit realm, and claim their souls for Jesus. Proverbs 19:7 tells us we can pursue people with our words, and this is one way I retaliate against the devil for using people to attack me or my ministry. I keep a record of everything that has ever been stolen from me since the beginning of my walk with God in 1978. Whenever possible, I list the names of those involved in the theft, attempted theft, or attack. Then in prayer, I pray for the salvation of every person, named or unnamed, who was involved in the attacks orchestrated by Satan against us.

I get my staff involved too whenever possible, because there is more power generated when two or more agree as touching anything they pray about (see Matthew 18:19). Anyone the enemy uses against us is marked in our prayer closets, and we specifically call them out in our prayers, believing God will lead workers across their paths to keep the Word of God coming at them until they get saved.

And until I find out they've received Jesus as Savior, I continue to make mention of them in my prayers to this day, and for the rest of my days on Earth! I may not know where they are now, but God sure does, and I'm standing in faith that every one of them gets saved for God's glory first, and then to mock and taunt the devil after that.

This may not be how God directs you in these matters, but this is how we do it, and this is how you can do it too! And on a purely carnal note, knowing we're giving God glory with simultaneously tormenting the devil *feels good!*

Make the Devil Pay!

As stated previously, because Satan is the god of this world, bad things don't just happen to bad people. They happen to good people too, whether they're saved or not. You know this to be true. It's reality for now on Earth, until Jesus returns to set up the 1,000-year millennial reign. Until then, bad things will continue to happen to good people, especially to Christians who love God and do their best to serve Him. Everybody is attacked by the devil because he hates all humankind, but it's how you respond to his attacks that determines your worth to God in this life's warfare for the souls of men.

The enemy fire we take as we advance to fulfill the Great Commission will continue right up to our last day on Earth in this life. So never forget this truth: to advance under fire, learn to attack and counterattack in the name of Jesus. *Make the devil pay!*

Be the lethal weapon in the hands of the Holy Spirit that God intended for you to be. Torment the devil at every turn, and keep advancing under fire for the glory of God. It's your purpose. It's your destiny.

Things We Can Do

We need to consistently do all we can to prepare for Satan's next attempt to stop us. Here are some basic ways to create a wall of defense around you that will provide the kind the protection you need as you advance under fire from the devil.

First and foremost, stay out of sin! Romans 6:23 tells us the wages of sin is *death,* so do your best daily, with God's help, to stay clear of any and all forms of sin. It will kill you if you let it.

Second, do your best to stay physically fit with proper diet and exercise.

Third, stay obedient to God. Do what he says and don't disobey. Disobedience is a sure-fire way to open a door for the enemy, and he will take full advantage of that opening if you provide it.

Fourth, keep your overall perspective, and don't allow the pressure and stress of this world's pace to rob you of your peace of mind. As it says in 1 Peter 5:7, cast *all your cares* upon God, because He cares for you. Not most of them—but *all* of them! (For a detailed study of this subject, refer to my book *Divine Peace).*

Fifth, be careful with your words! I wrote a book called *The Language of Faith,* because Christians need to know that faith is more than just the substance of things hoped for, and the evidence of things not seen (see Hebrews 11:1). It's a *language* that must be learned and used to connect—and stay connected—to the power of God we need in our lives and ministries.

Some years ago, when asked by an interviewer what I thought were the foundational keys to my success and longevity in the ministry, I heard these points come up and out from my spirit. When the article was published, they entitled it my "Keyes to Success."

1. Maintain humility, but remain tenacious.
2. Live your life on the offensive.

3. Understand the big picture in everything you do.

4. Refuse to quit.

5. Desire to please God; never mind pleasing men.

That's good advice. It's time to attack!

CHAPTER 21

The Peril of Not
Progressing

But, beloved, we are confident of better things concerning
you, yes, things that accompany salvation, though we speak
in this manner. For God is not unjust to forget your work
and labor of love which you have shown toward His name,
in that you have ministered to the saints, and do minister.
And we desire that each one of you show the same
diligence to the full assurance of hope until the end,
that you do not become sluggish, but imitate those
who through faith and patience inherit the promises.
*—*HEBREWS 6:9-12

If we don't advance under fire, we're going to become vulnerable to the kind of attack that ultimately destroys our relationship with God.

I've said this for years—if you're not advancing you're backsliding, because God is always moving forward! All of us need to know this, and live our lives accordingly. There is a very real peril in failing to advance under fire, and God wants us to know what it is. Our salvation is a precious gift from God, but don't think for one minute it can't be lost. People who teach that once we're saved we're always saved—no matter what we do or say after receiving Jesus as Lord and Savior—don't know what they're talking about. These verses here, as well as many others, clearly teach something different. I, for one, don't want to take any chances with my eternal state. I hope you don't either. Paul felt the same way:

> *But I discipline my body and bring it into subjection,* **lest, when** **I have preached to others, I myself should become disqualified.**
> —1 CORINTHIANS 9:27 [EMPHASIS MINE]

Its hard for us to imagine this great man of God disqualifying himself before the Lord, but if it can't happen why is he so concerned about having it happen to him? If the great Apostle Paul knew of the inherent dangers of falling away—for even an experienced, anointed, and effective minister like himself, you and I should sit up and take notice. If he knew it could happen to him, for sure it can happen to us! Here's what else he said which we'd be well to remember:

> *Therefore let him who thinks he stands take heed* **lest he fall.**
> —1 CORINTHIANS 10:12-13 [EMPHASIS MINE]

If it's not possible for believers to fall away, then why would Paul exhort the Corinthians (and us) to "take heed" to their spiritual condition—so that they won't fall? One of the best ways to stay sharp and stay strong is to dedicate ourselves to the task of progressing spiritually in the Lord.

Don't Allow Any Spiritual Drifting

As you read these passages from the book of Hebrews, you can see these Christians were in a dangerous place and didn't even know it. They were not progressing. They were not advancing. They were stagnating, and falling behind from where they needed to be in terms of growth and spiritual maturity. Don't be found in a similar position in your life, my friend!

This hope we have as an anchor of the soul, both sure and steadfast, and which enters the Presence behind the veil, where the forerunner has entered for us, even Jesus, having become High Priest forever according to the order of Melchizedek.

—HEBREWS 6:19-20

Spiritual regression is the same as a ship drifting away from the pier. It happens so slowly and with such imperceptivity that people on the boat wouldn't even notice unless they were on deck looking at the pier for themselves. If they were below decks, or busy with other things, they wouldn't know they're drifting. I know because I've been on thousands of boats in the Philippines. I know firsthand how difficult it is to perceive the drifting unless you can *see* the shoreline! And unless a Christian *sees and realizes* the danger in not advancing, they'll also fail to recognize the perilous state they are in as they slowly drift away.

That is why hope is referred to as an anchor. It keeps us from drifting away to such an extent that it becomes a situation so dangerous that we would actually consider rejecting Jesus and going back into the world! You know, born-again Christians don't wake up one day and say, "You know, I think I'm going to reject Jesus and return to the world today." No! Decisions like that are made over time, and if the devil has anything to use against all of us, it's time. That's why our opening passage for this chapter includes Hebrews 6:12, which talks about the importance of faith *and* patience. (For more on this, refer to my book *The Helmet of Hope.*)

God Expects Us to Grow, Not Shrink!

It's no coincidence this warning about spiritual drifting is found in the same chapter six of Hebrews where these warnings about falling away are to be found.

For though by this time you ought to be teachers, you need someone to teach you again the first principles of the oracles of God;

and you have come to need milk and not solid food. For everyone who partakes only of milk is unskilled in the word of righteousness, for he is a babe. But solid food belongs to those who are of full age, that is, **those who by reason of use have their senses exercised to discern both good and evil.**

Therefore, leaving the discussion of the elementary principles of Christ, let us go on to perfection, not laying again the foundation of repentance from dead works and of faith toward God, of the doctrine of baptisms, of laying on of hands, of resurrection of the dead, and of eternal judgment. And this we will do if God permits. For it is impossible for those who were once enlightened, and have tasted the heavenly gift, and have become partakers of the Holy Spirit, and have tasted the good word of God and the powers of the age to come, **if they fall away,** *to renew them again to repentance, since they crucify again for themselves the Son of God, and put Him to an open shame.*

—HEBREWS 5:12-6:6 [EMPHASIS MINE]

If we want to live with acute awareness of these things, the perils of not progressing spiritually, we would be wise to spend much time in the book of Hebrews. The protection of our salvation and the perils of not progressing spiritually is a thread that runs throughout the book. And remember—even though the book of Hebrews was originally written to Jews who had accepted Jesus as their Messiah, God is no respecter of persons, therefore this passage here is a warning to *all* believers—Jew or Gentile, whether they lived at that time, or from then until now.

The author of Hebrews (whom I believe is the Apostle Paul) reprimanded these Jewish Christians because they were not growing and they were not advancing like they should have been. Hebrews 6:1 talks about going on to perfection, not laying again the spiritual foundation every believer starts out with when they begin their walk with the Lord. Then, the Holy Spirit reviews the six basic principles of the doctrine of Christ, followed by stern warnings about what can happen if Christians fail to advance under the fire Satan is bringing against them. Failing to advance under fire can move us, ever so subtly, to a place where we could actually talk ourselves right out of Heaven! This same warning is repeated a few chapters later.

> *For if we sin willfully after we have received the knowledge of the truth, there no longer remains a sacrifice for sins, but a certain fearful expectation of judgment, and fiery indignation which will devour the adversaries.*
>
> —HEBREWS 10:26-27

> *But recall the former days in which, after you were illuminated, you endured a great struggle with sufferings: Therefore do not cast away your confidence, which has great reward. For you have need of endurance, so that after you have done the will of God, you may receive the promise.*
>
> —HEBREWS 10:32,35-36

Now granted, this issue of falling away and becoming disqualified, as described in these passages, is *not* something a new babe in Christ could do, because the conditions for this sort of falling away are clearly revealed here. And it's prudent to remember that if a believer is fearful that he or she has committed the "unpardonable sin" (see 1 John 5:16), it's safe to say they haven't! Why? Because this sin can only be committed by a person who is a seasoned believer, who has walked with God for an extended period of time, and has operated in and flowed in the power of God and gifts of the Holy Spirit. *This is not a new believer, or even a carnal Christian we're talking about here, as the Corinthians were (see 1 Corinthians 3:1-3).* It's an individual who, despite an extended and meaningful relationship with the Lord, knows full well what they're doing in renouncing Jesus—and makes the choice to actively and willfully walk away from the Lord anyway.

That being said, it's still something to watch for diligently, because as I've said, nobody who is genuinely saved starts out serving Jesus with the premeditated intent of one day falling away and returning to the muck and mire of their former life. Peter also addresses this in the letters he wrote.

For if, after they have escaped the pollutions of the world through the knowledge of the Lord and Savior Jesus Christ, they are again entangled in them and overcome, the latter end is worse for them than the beginning. For it would have been better for them not to have known the way of righteousness, than having known it, to turn from the holy commandment delivered to them. But it has happened to them according to the true proverb: "A dog returns to his own vomit," and, "a sow, having washed, to her wallowing in the mire."

—2 PETER 2:20-22

No matter how long it may take for the devil to whittle away a person's defenses, he'll stay on it because he knows believers *can* make a decision to "fall away" and lose their salvation, as every New Testament writer indicates. If it weren't possible for this to happen, why is the Bible full of warnings for us to read and heed? And why, once again, did Paul in his first letter to the Corinthians, declare his own awareness of the danger of becoming a disqualified preacher—if it weren't possible for him to become one?

Read carefully the epistles of 1 John, 2 John, and 3 John, and you'll see the Apostle John's warnings throughout. James talked about it in his book (see James 1:12-16 and 5:19-20 as examples), and as we've just noted, Peter gives the same warnings to those he wrote to as well. In truth, the books of 2 Peter and Jude are very similar in style and content. In reading the book of Jude, look at how he warns his readers, much like Peter did.

But I want to remind you, though you once knew this, that the Lord, having saved the people out of the land of Egypt, afterward destroyed those who did not believe. And the angels who did not keep their proper domain, but left their own abode, He has reserved in everlasting chains under darkness for the judgment of the great day. . . . Woe to them! For they have gone in the way of Cain, have run greedily in the error of Balaam for profit, and perished in the rebellion of Korah.

—JUDE 5-6,11

To emphasize the perils of not progressing, Jude uses three Old Testament examples: Cain, Balaam, and Korah. Go back and study the lives of these three, and you'll discover the common denominator with all of them was the fact that at one time, all three walked in right relationship with God, but later turned away. They all died lost and out of fellowship with the Lord.

How should we effectively take heed to all of these warnings? One of the most effective ways to consistently stay "lean, mean, and clean" before the Lord is to grow and progress in the things of God.

*As newborn babes, desire the pure milk of the word, **that you may grow thereby,** if indeed you have tasted that the Lord is gracious.*
—1 PETER 2:2-3 [EMPHASIS MINE]

*You therefore, beloved, since you know this beforehand, **beware lest you also fall from your own steadfastness,** being led away with the error of the wicked; but **grow in the grace and knowledge of our Lord and Savior Jesus Christ.***
—2 PETER 3:17-18 [EMPHASIS MINE]

*But also for this very reason, giving all diligence, add to your faith virtue, to virtue knowledge, to knowledge self-control, to self-control perseverance, to perseverance godliness, to godliness brotherly kindness, and to brotherly kindness love. For if these things are yours and abound, you will be neither barren nor unfruitful in the knowledge of our Lord Jesus Christ. For he who lacks these things is shortsighted, even to blindness, and has forgotten that he was cleansed from his old sins. **Therefore, brethren, be even more diligent to make your call and election sure, for if you do these things you will never stumble;** for so an entrance will be supplied to you abundantly into the everlasting kingdom of our Lord and Savior Jesus Christ.*
—2 PETER 1:5-11 [EMPHASIS MINE]

Peter told his disciples the same thing God tells all of us in His Word. *Grow!* Grow and gain knowledge regarding the parameters of your salvation! Don't stay babies in Christ, spiritually speaking. Desire more and more of God's Word, so you can grow, learn, mature, and make progress in Christ, and for Christ. This doesn't happen automatically or by accident. It happens when you and I decide to *make it happen!* It happens when we make the decision to put God and His Word first place in our lives, each and every day. *Most Christians never progress because they don't follow these instructions.*

The Word of God is quite clear. God expects us to grow, mature, and acquire more knowledge about how He works, and how things work (or don't work) for us and in us, on this spiritual battlefield called life on planet Earth. This is how we stay sharp for Jesus all the days of our lives.

On the other hand, there is great peril in not progressing in Jesus, and people *can* fall away and be lost if they don't take all of this seriously. In short, that means we must advance, or run the risk of losing all we've achieved and worked for in Christ (see 2 John 2:8), and here is this truth summed up in one simple declaration: *our spiritual progress is measured by how much we know of the Word of God, and how effectively we apply what we've learned.*

All of us start this process the same way—by developing a love for God's Word. We must *desire* it, like newborn babies in need of milk from their mother's breast. We must learn to love God's Word, and learn why it's so important to grow in knowledge and grace. We must come to the place where we live our lives in obedience to what God told His people thousands of years ago, long before Jesus even came to Earth.

> *This Book of the Law shall not depart from your mouth, but you shall meditate in it day and night, that you may observe to do according to all that is written in it. For **then** you will make your way prosperous, and then you will have good success.*
>
> —JOSHUA 1:8-9 [EMPHASIS MINE]

If you want to progress by applying what the Word of God teaches you, it all starts here—with a working application of God's Word through diligent study of the same. In this conversation with Joshua, God tells him (and us) what the formula is for prosperity and good success. It's no secret or deep spiritual mystery—it's right here for everybody to read and apply if it is to be obtained.

Now I have a question for you: do you want prosperity and good success in this life? I'm pretty sure that your answer to this question would be, *"Yes!"* I've never met anyone who loved poverty, misery, failure, and pain, and was praying for more of the same! No—any normal human being (Christians included) wants a good life, full of success and personal prosperity. That's just something that is inherent in everyone—because that was God's original plan for all of us. But Adam's treason opened the door to the enemy, and as a result, Satan has been able to operate on Earth to bring death, suffering, and misery to us all. The devil works very hard to make sure prosperity and good success is kept as far from you as possible, but isn't that what Jesus said He came to Earth to die and be raised from the dead for? Yes! He came to destroy the works of the devil and give you the opportunity to enjoy an "abundant life" (see 1 John 3:8 and John 10:10).

But here is the "asterisk" to the truth of what Jesus did to neutralize the devil and take back the authority that was origi-nally given to Adam: *you have a part to play to see these things become reality in your own life.* In a legal sense, redemption has been purchased for all humankind, but in a vital and living sense, *you* have to make the choices that *allow* God to manifest these things in your life. So the question becomes this—even though you want success and prosperity, are you willing to *do* what God told Joshua to do to get it?

How many Christians actually love and desire God's Word to the extent described by God to Joshua? How many meditate in God's Word day and night, so they can consistently follow God's Word to the letter, and thereby position themselves for prosperity and good success? The answer—not many!

In fact, the things God told Joshua to do were the very same things He said to David many years later (see Psalm 1:1-5), and they are the same things He tells us today. You know, scriptures call David "a man after God's own heart" (see Acts 13:22), and one reason why is found in reading the book of Psalms, especially Psalm 119. After reading a Psalm like that, how many modern-day believers have the kind of love, reverence, respect, and awe for God's Word as King David did? The sad truth is very, very few!

And that's why so few of us advance and progress in Christ as we live out our lives on Earth. It is amazing that when it comes to appropriating promises like these for prosperity and good success, so many believers will follow what the secular world tells them to do without hesitation, but completely ignore God's instructions in the Bible! If you fall in love with God's Word, and make it your daily priority to be a doer of His Word, spiritual progression will be automatic in your life. God guarantees it! In fact, the more you love God's Word, the more it will control your speech, and if you can control your tongue, you can control *everything else* about you (see James 3:2). That is definitely prosperity and good success!

> *Then he said to me, "Do not fear, Daniel, for from the first day that you set your heart to understand, and to humble yourself before your God, your words were heard; and I have come because of your words. But the prince of the kingdom of Persia withstood me twenty-one days; and behold, Michael, one of the chief princes, came to help me, for I had been left alone there with the kings of Persia."*
>
> —DANIEL 10:12-13

When Daniel was in the midst of his prolonged fast, as recorded in Daniel chapter 10, the Lord sent an angel to him with answers to his prayers. Now of course, we all know God answers prayer, but take special note of what the angel told Daniel here in verse 12, about *why* those prayers were being answered.

First, you have to *want* to understand the things of God, and the realities of this spiritual war raging on planet Earth for the souls of men. Daniel had a hunger to learn and to understand, and that's where it all begins. Many Christians have no desire to learn anything about any of this—they just want to have all the spiritual "goodies" in life without exerting any effort, and without any willingness to understand and accept their responsibilities to be an effective ambassador of Christ (see 2 Corinthians 5:20).

Second, if your heart is right when you pray, and you are sincere about pleasing God and serving Him in humility with all your heart, your prayers are heard and answered *immediately*. Isn't it nice to know God is never too busy to hear your prayers when sincerely prayed from the heart? Think about it with me for a moment. Millions of people pray to God simultaneously around the world every day, but in some way we'll never be able to understand, God has the ability to sort out each person's prayers and handle and answer them as if those were the only prayers being prayed on Earth! Amazing! Not only that, but at the same time, God is able to discern each person's heart as they pray, separating those with a right heart from all the others, and responding only to those who have positioned themselves for an answer, as described by the angel's explanation to Daniel. That's why he was told the very day he prayed, God heard and responded with the answer.

Now of course, for various reasons, God's immediate response isn't always *seen* immediately in our lives, but they will come and they do come! The second part of this scripture tells us that in Daniel's case, evil spirits had blocked the angel from reaching him with God's answer for twenty-one days, and only after receiving reinforcements from Michael was the spiritual blockade successfully overcome. That's why we're told to stand, and to keep on standing until we see the manifestations of what God immediately responded to when we prayed (see Mark 11:24 and Ephesians 6:11-14).

God Comes to Us Because of Our Words!

And *third,* notice carefully what is said next. Specifically, what did God respond to? According to the angel, He responded to the *words* Daniel was speaking, and sent the angel with answers *because* of the words Daniel was speaking! If I were you, I'd bookmark what the angel told Daniel, and never forget it: *Your words were heard, and I have come because of your words.*

Why are these statements from the angel so important to understand? Because if any of us are ever going to progress in our ability to advance under the fire of enemy attack, we must develop an ever-increasing awareness of the direct connection between what we say and what God does (or doesn't do) *because* of what we say. Would you like God to come into your life because of your words, as He did for Daniel that day? I would, and I'm sure you would too. (This truth is so important, I wrote a book about it, entitled *The Language of Faith.*)

God is no respecter of persons (see Acts 10:34 and many other verses throughout the Bible), so if He came into Daniel's life and answered his prayers because of what he was saying, He'll do the very same thing for you and me. And here's the best part of this truth—what we say is always a matter of personal choice! What comes out from our mouths is entirely under our control, because no one forces us to say anything—we say what we say because we decide to! So, if you decide to align your conversation with God's Word, you are simultaneously enabling God to be great for you, and cutting off the opportunities of the devil to successfully attack you. God won't make you do it, and the devil can't force you not to—we have free will and we make the final choice about what we say or don't say.

To put it another way—the more we desire God's Word, the more we will grow in grace and knowledge. When that happens, we acquire an awareness of the importance of verbal management. As a result, we make wise choices with our spoken words that enable God to work in our lives, as Daniel did in his. God is always wanting to get involved in our lives to give us what Jesus died and rose from the dead to provide, but it's not up to God now, it's up to us! The angel didn't tell Daniel that he was there because of something *God* had said, but because of something *Daniel* had said. Please let that sink in for a moment!

Don't forget what we spoke about earlier in this book. You can *decide* to move on from defeat, failure, and sin. You don't have to stay condemned by the devil, or by other people. Paul told the Philippians he had moved on from all of his mistakes, errors, and sins, and in like manner, we are to do the same. You don't move on from the attacks of the enemy because you *feel* like doing it—you move on and don't look back because you *decide* to do it, and correct decisions can be made no matter how you feel at the moment!

Indeed—there is great peril when we fail to progress and advance for the kingdom of God. But there are also great rewards when we do! Make sure you have done your due diligence to protect your salvation. Make sure you are never content being just a carnal Christian. Make sure you are controlling your tongue and speaking words of faith. Make sure you are always moving forward. Make sure you are advancing under fire!

ABOUT THE AUTHOR

Mike Keyes grew up in Ohio and was raised in the Roman Catholic church. In 1973, he graduated from college to become a successful advertising executive and graphic artist. On September 21, 1978, at age twentysix, he was born again and Spirit filled two days later. Immediately, the gifts of the Spirit began working in his life. Through his local church, he began to witness on the streets, in area prisons, and anywhere he could hand out tracts.

In September 1979, Reverend Keyes resigned his job to attend Rhema Bible Training Center in Tulsa, Oklahoma, graduating in May 1980. In September 1980, he traveled to the Philippines with a oneway plane ticket, arriving without knowledge of the language or customs and with no one there to meet him. When he got off that plane to begin his ministry, he had twenty dollars in his pocket, one footlocker containing his Bible, class notes, a few changes of clothing, and the promise of support totaling $250 from no one except his parents and one small church in Toledo, Ohio.

From those humble beginnings and through his faithfulness to the calling of God over the years, the Lord has used Reverend Keyes extensively to reach untold numbers of people in the Philippines and around the world. Always emphasizing outreach to the remote, overlooked, outoftheway villages and towns that no one else has gone to, it is conservatively estimated that since the beginning of his ministry's outreach in 1980, over 750,000 souls have been won to Christ in his nationwide crusades in the Philippines.

Mike Keyes Ministries International (MKMI) is an apostolic ministry that reaches the lost, teaches the Christians and trains the ministers. With a consistent crusade outreach, a church network of hundreds of churches, and the Rhema Bible Training Center, Reverend Keyes and his staff, pastors, graduates and students continue to fulfill the Great Commission wherever he is instructed to go by the Holy Spirit—throughout the Philippines and around the world.

Reverend Keyes is married to a native Filipina, Ethel, and has two children.

For additional information:

- About Reverend Keyes and the MKMI ministry
- About becoming involved in prayer or financial support
- About participating in our annual missions tour
- About obtaining more copies of this book or other books and CD teaching sets

Please contact us at:

- Web: www.mkmi.org
- Email: ekeyes@mkmi.org

OTHER BOOKS BY
MIKE KEYES

Divine Peace | ISBN: 978-1-939570-17-8
How can you live above fear and pressure and the frantic
pace of life in these perilous times? *Divine Peace* reveals the
principles of knowing and walking in God's peace every day and
how to stand strong in the midst of every circumstance with a
peace that passes all understanding.

OTHER BOOKS BY
MIKE KEYES SR

Be Strong! Stay Strong!
ISBN: 978-1-939570-00-0

God's perfect will is for every believer to be triumphant and victorious in life. *Be Strong! Stay Strong!* shares seven spiritual priorities and the importance of practicing them consistently, bringing any believer to the place of superior strength and victory over an attack of the enemy in these last days.

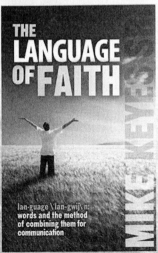

The Language of Faith
ISBN: 978-1-939570-02-4

Have you ever wondered how to communicate with God? In *The Language of Faith*, Mike Keyes, Sr. reveals the rules that govern the language of faith, how you can use those rules to speak faith, and as a result, see the windows of heaven open up on your behalf.

OTHER BOOKS BY
MIKE KEYES SR

Helmet of Hope
ISBN: 978-1-939570-01-7

When a new recruit joins the army, he is issued a helmet and it can mean the difference between life and death in battle. Every spiritual battle is won or lost in the mind - if you lose hope, you've lost your helmet and your head is unprotected. The Helmet of Hope was written to make you a skilled soldier fully prepared for every fight of the faith.

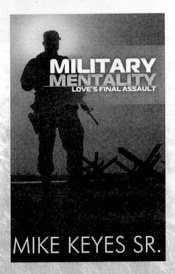

Military Mentality
ISBN: 978-1-936314-98-0

Military Mentality concerns the global war raging at this moment over the souls of humankind. The Body of Christ is at war. Our weapons are different than physical battle and our enemies are not flesh and blood. However, we can apply many crucial lessons learned in wartime to fight our fights of faith today.